AGE OF RESISTANCE

VILLAINS

AGE OF RESISTANCE

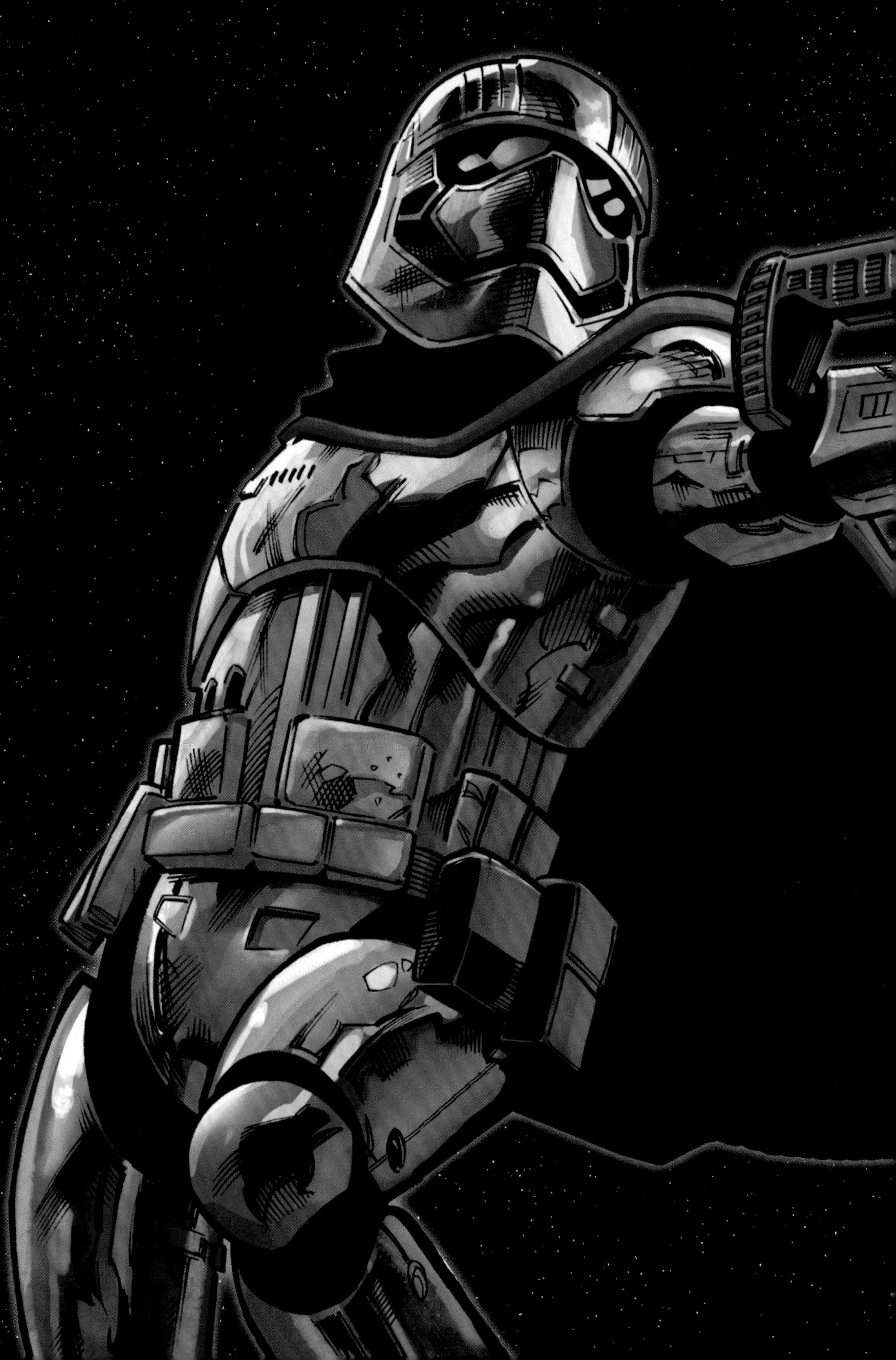

VILLAINS

Writer TOM TAYLOR
Penciler LEONARD KIRK
Inker CORY HAMSCHER
Color Artist GURU-eFX

Letterer VC'S TRAVIS LANHAM
Cover Art PHIL NOTO
Assistant Editor TOM GRONEMAN
Editor MARK PANICCIA

Editor in Chief C.B. CEBULSKI
Chief Creative Officer JOE QUESADA
President DAN BUCKLEY

For Lucasfilm:
Senior Editor ROBERT SIMPSON
Creative Director MICHAEL SIGLAIN
Lucasfilm Story Group PABLO HIDALGO, MATT MARTIN & EMILY SHKOUKANI
Lucasfilm Art Department PHIL SZOSTAK

Collection Editor JENNIFER GRÜNWALD
Assistant Editor CAITLIN O'CONNELL
Associate Managing Editor KATERI WOODY
Editor, Special Projects MARK D. BEAZLEY

VP Production & Special Projects JEFF YOUNGQUIST
SVP Print, Sales & Marketing DAVID GABRIEL
Director, Licensed Publishing SVEN LARSEN
Book Designer ADAM DEL RE

STAR WARS: AGE OF RESISTANCE — VILLAINS. Contains material originally published in magazine form as STAR WARS: AGE OF RESISTANCE — CAPTAIN PHASMA #1, STAR WARS: AGE OF RESISTANCE — GENERAL HUX #1, STAR WARS: AGE OF RESISTANCE — KYLO REN #1 and STAR WARS: AGE OF RESISTANCE — SUPREME LEADER SNOKE #1. First printing 2019. ISBN 978-1-302-91730-2. Published by MARVEL WORLDWIDE, INC., a subsidiary of MARVEL ENTERTAINMENT, LLC. OFFICE OF PUBLICATION: 135 West 50th Street, New York, NY 10020. **Printed in Canada.** DAN BUCKLEY, President, Marvel Entertainment; JOHN NEE, Publisher; JOE QUESADA, Chief Creative Officer; TOM BREVOORT, SVP of Publishing; DAVID BOGART, Associate Publisher & SVP of Talent Affairs; DAVID GABRIEL, SVP of Sales & Marketing, Publishing; JEFF YOUNGQUIST, VP of Production & Special Projects; DAN CARR, Executive Director of Publishing Technology; ALEX MORALES, Director of Publishing Operations; DAN EDINGTON, Managing Editor; SUSAN CRESPI, Production Manager; STAN LEE, Chairman Emeritus. For information regarding advertising in Marvel Comics or on Marvel.com, please contact Vit DeBellis, Custom Solutions & Integrated Advertising Manager, at vdebellis@marvel.com. For Marvel subscription inquiries, please call 888-511-5480. **Manufactured between 9/27/2019 and 10/29/2019 by SOLISCO PRINTERS, SCOTT, QC, CANADA.**

10 9 8 7 6 5 4 3 2 1

CAPTAIN PHASMA

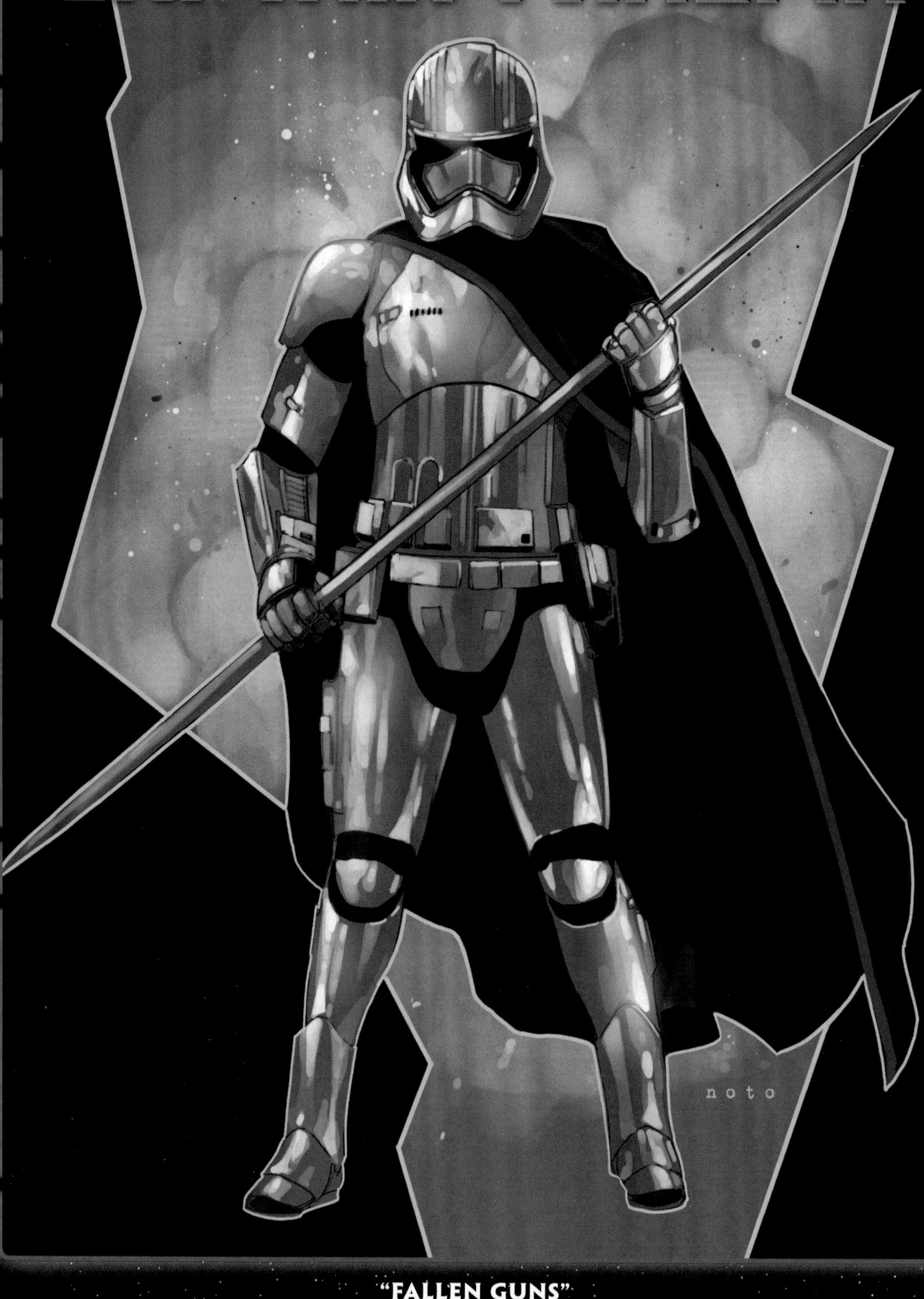
noto

"FALLEN GUNS"

The New Republic maintains peace and order after the fall of the Empire. But the evil First Order, modeled after the old regime, rises from its ashes. And with an untold number of powerful war machines and legions of dogmatic stormtroopers at its disposal, the First Order stands poised to seize control of the galaxy.

And one ruthless stormtrooper could be the weapon of war that leads the First Order to total victory

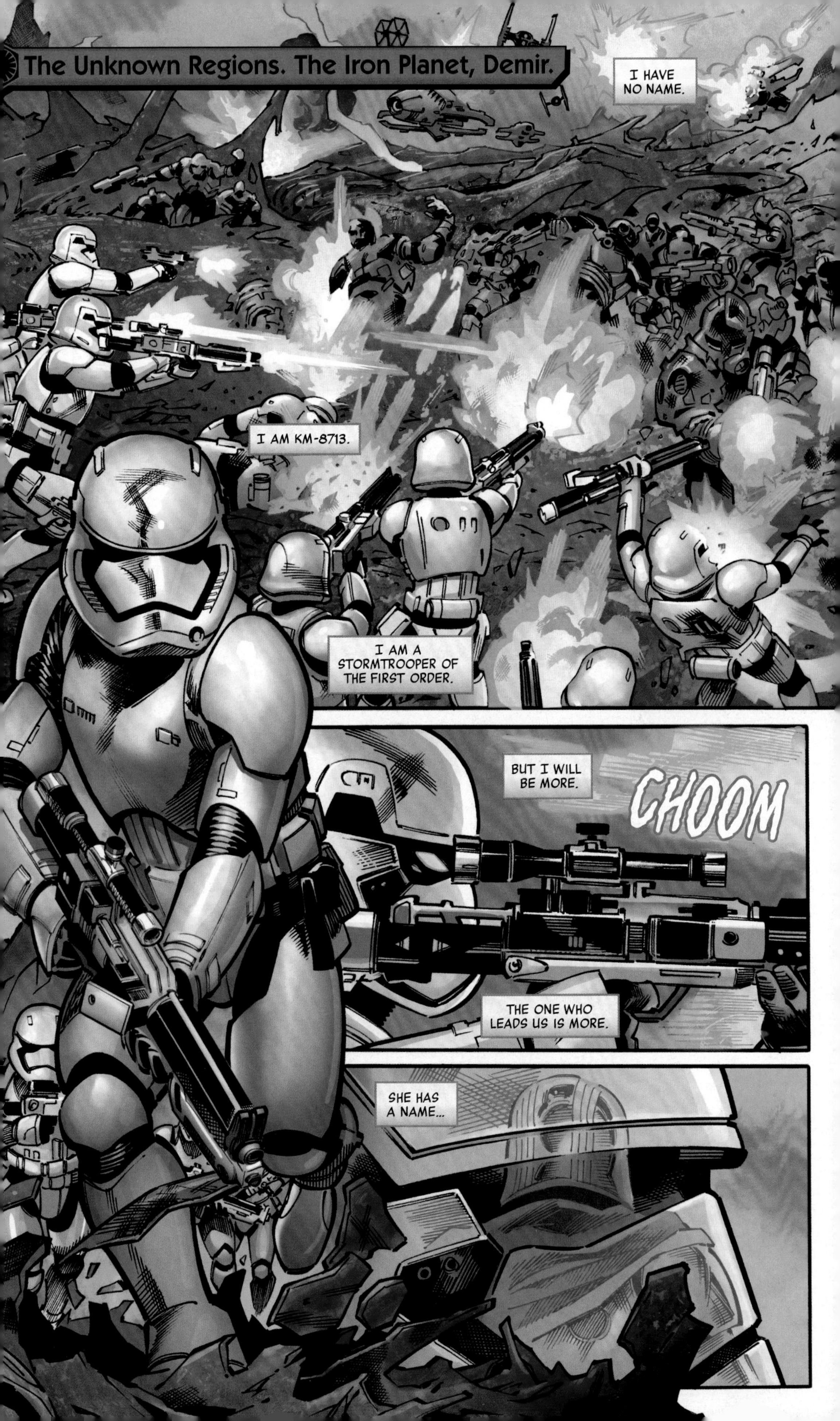
The Unknown Regions. The Iron Planet, Demir.
I HAVE NO NAME.
I AM KM-8713.
I AM A STORMTROOPER OF THE FIRST ORDER.
BUT I WILL BE MORE.
CHOOM
THE ONE WHO LEADS US IS MORE.
SHE HAS A NAME...

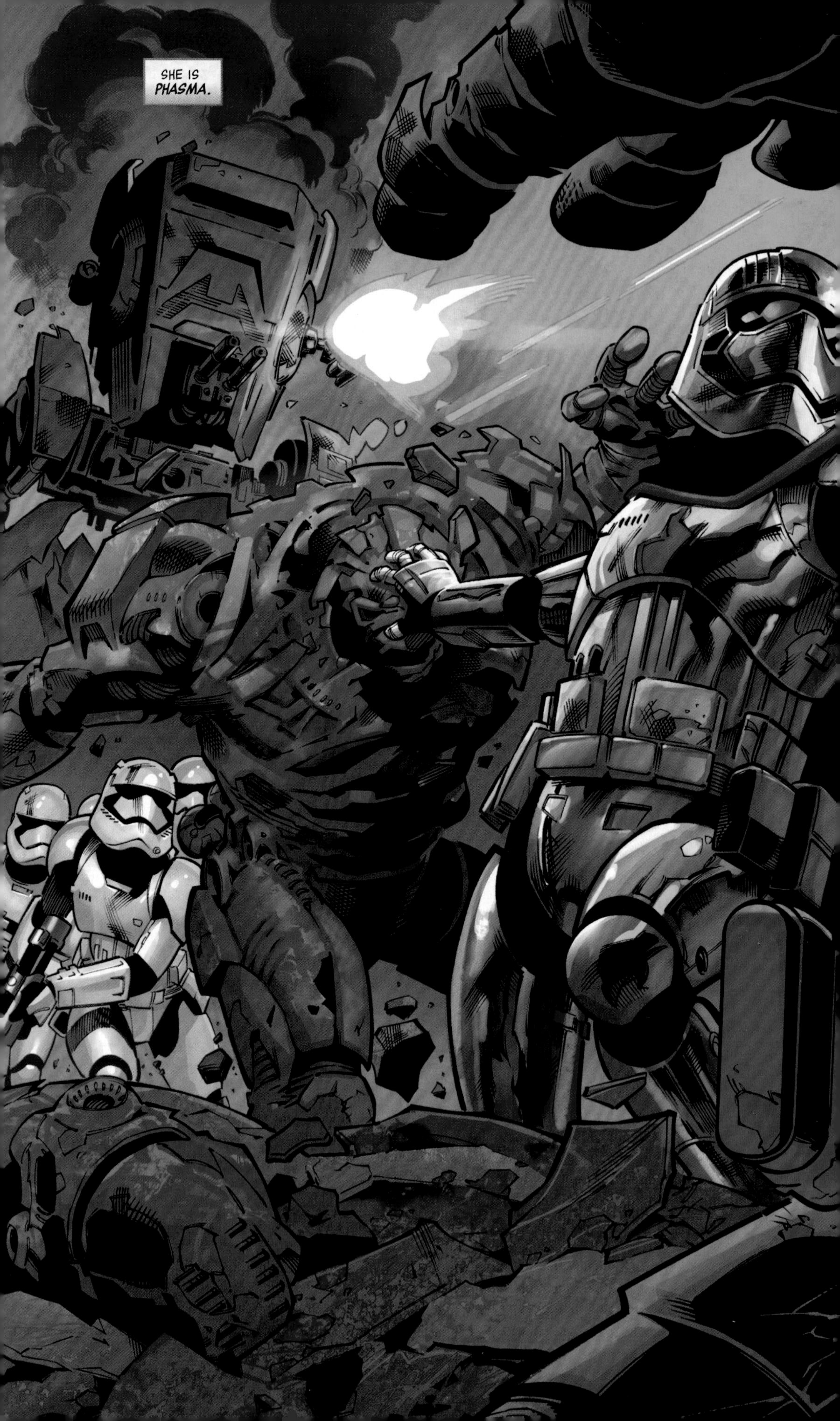
SHE IS PHASMA.

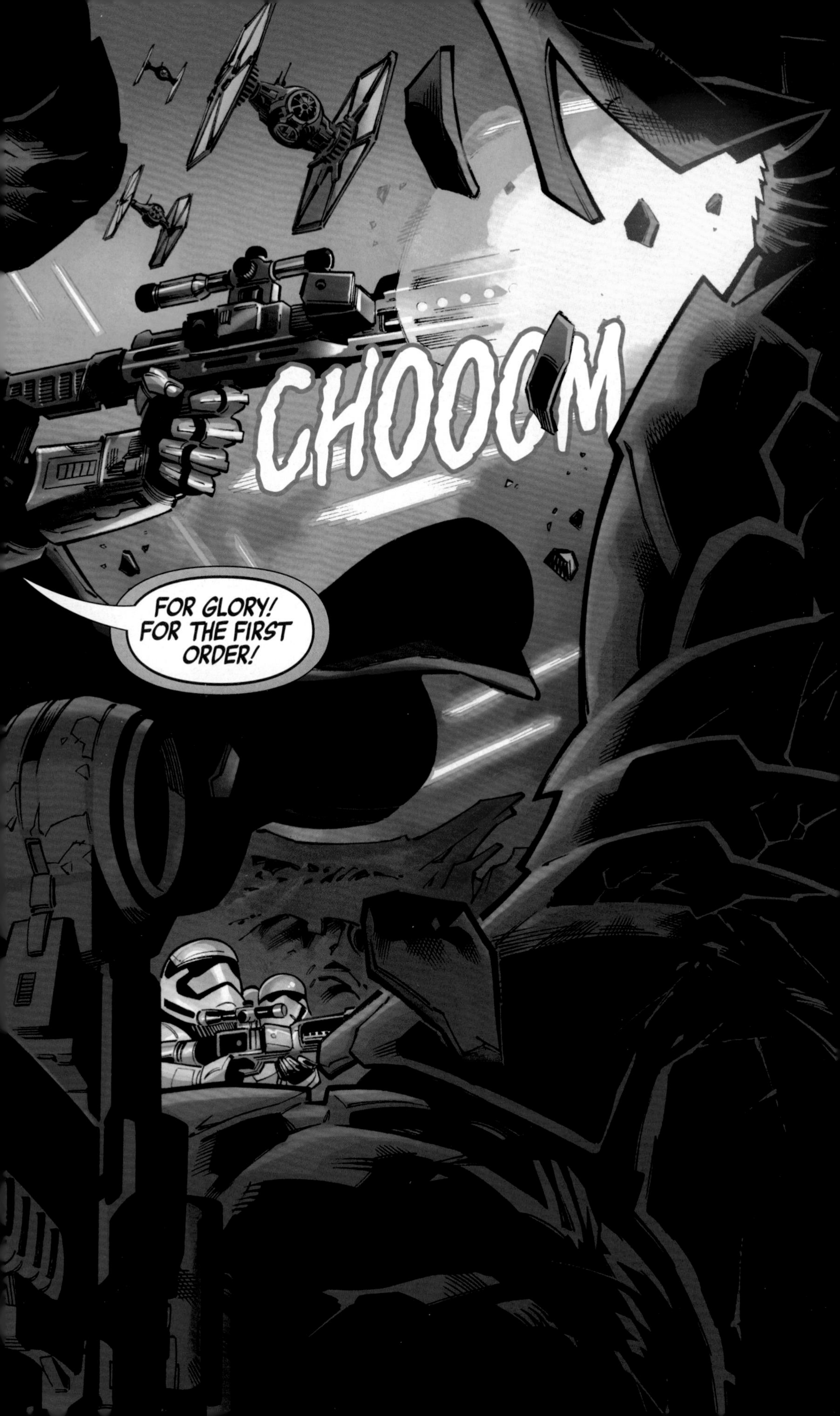
CHOOOM
FOR GLORY! FOR THE FIRST ORDER!

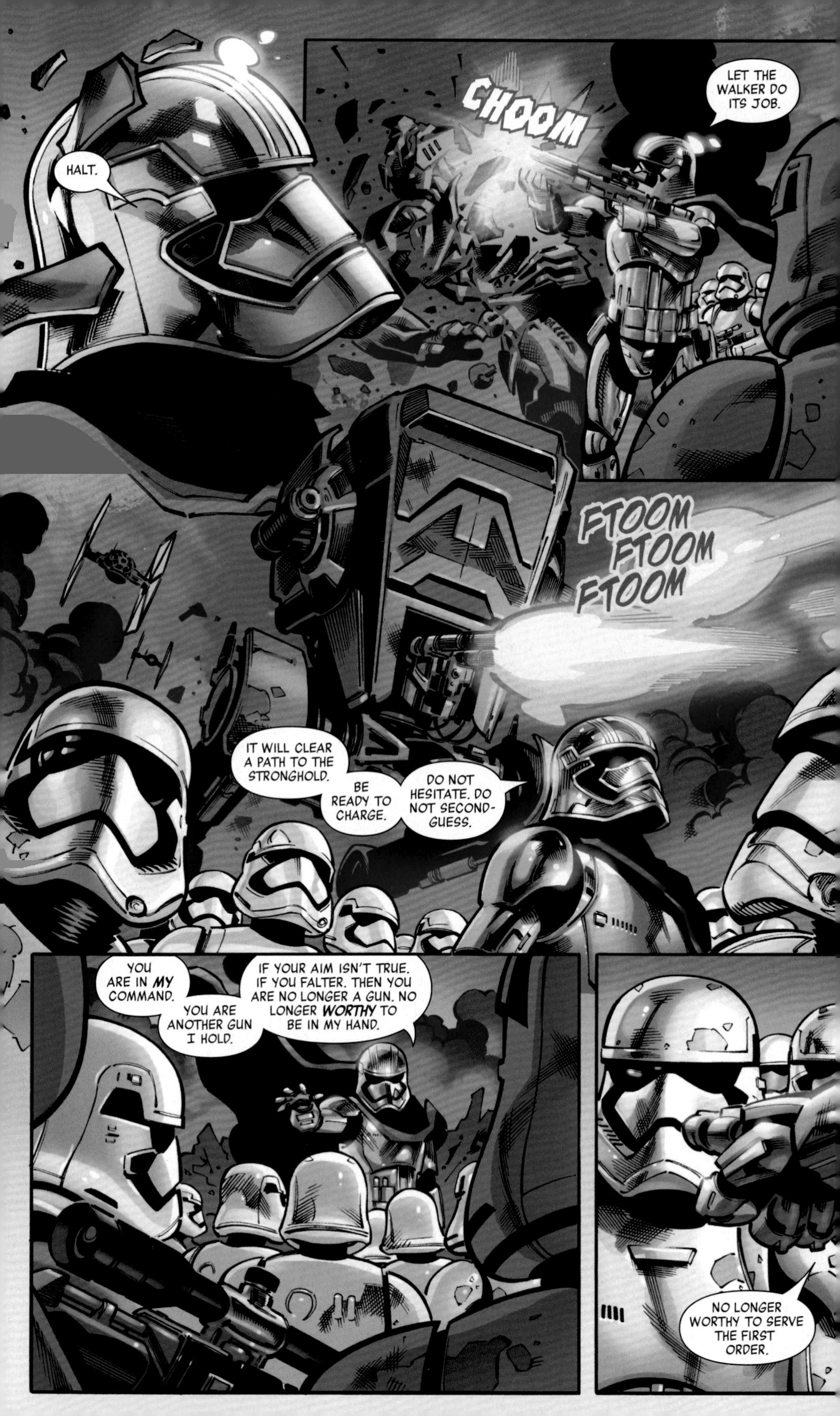
HALT.
CHOOM
LET THE WALKER DO ITS JOB.
FTOOM FTOOM FTOOM
IT WILL CLEAR A PATH TO THE STRONGHOLD.
BE READY TO CHARGE.
DO NOT HESITATE. DO NOT SECOND-GUESS.
YOU ARE IN MY COMMAND.
YOU ARE ANOTHER GUN I HOLD.
IF YOUR AIM ISN'T TRUE. IF YOU FALTER. THEN YOU ARE NO LONGER A GUN. NO LONGER WORTHY TO BE IN MY HAND.
NO LONGER WORTHY TO SERVE THE FIRST ORDER.

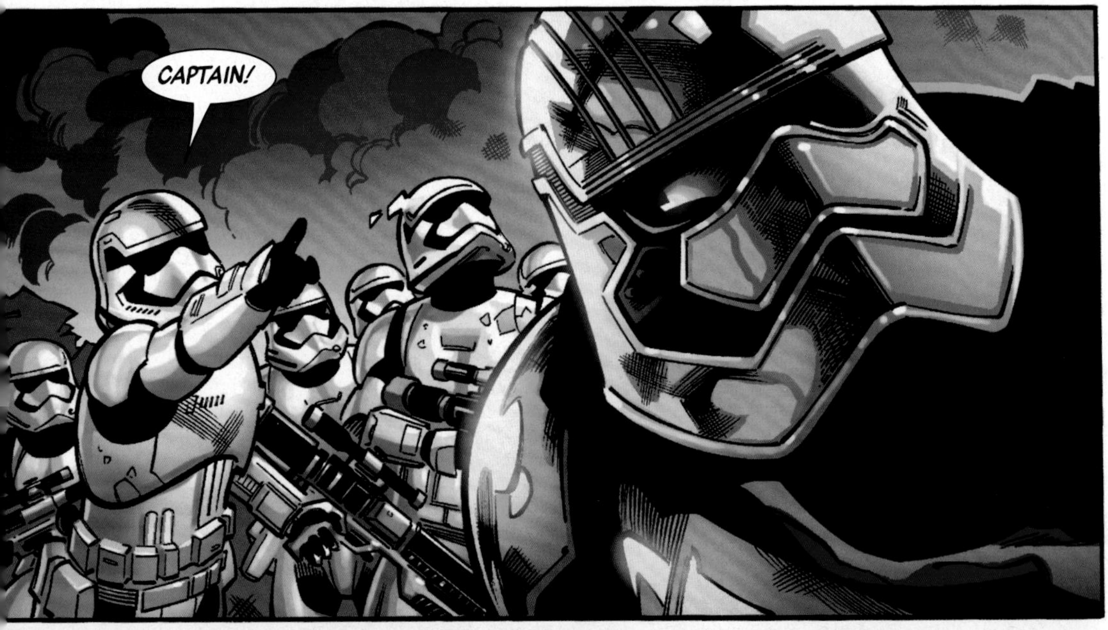
CAPTAIN!

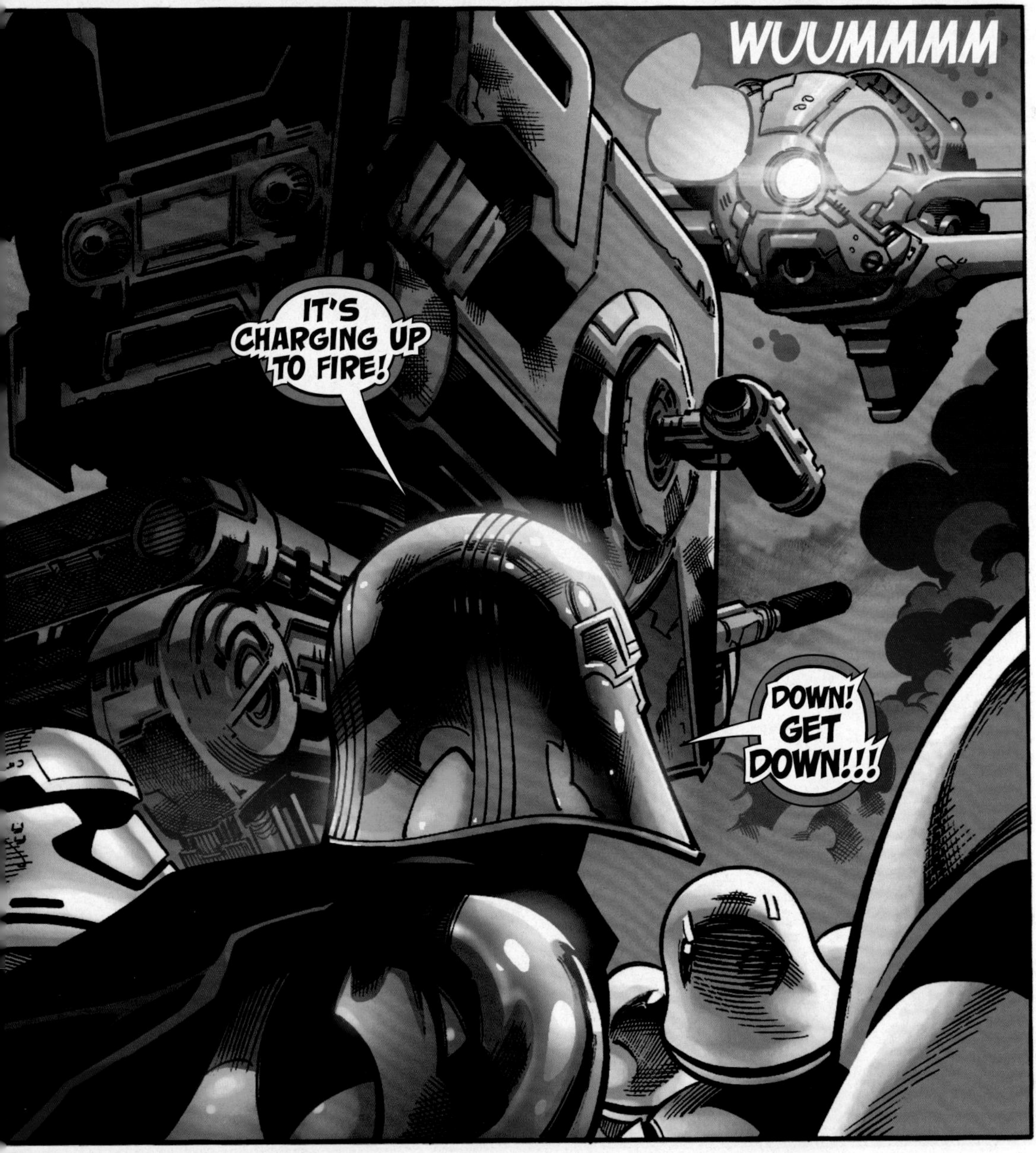
WUUMMMM
IT'S CHARGING UP TO FIRE!
DOWN! GET DOWN!!!

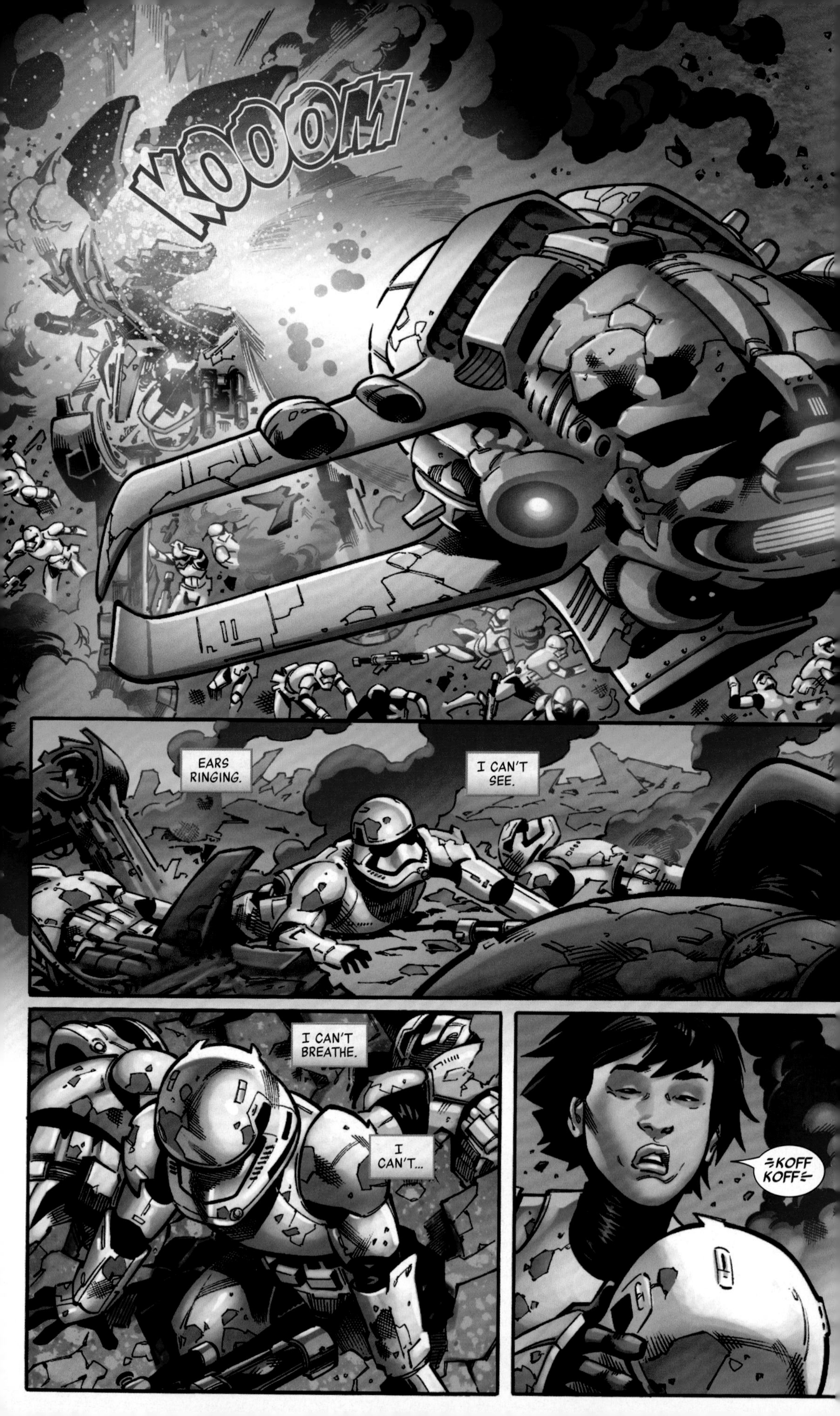
KOOOM
EARS RINGING.
I CAN'T SEE.
I CAN'T BREATHE.
I CAN'T...
KOFF KOFF

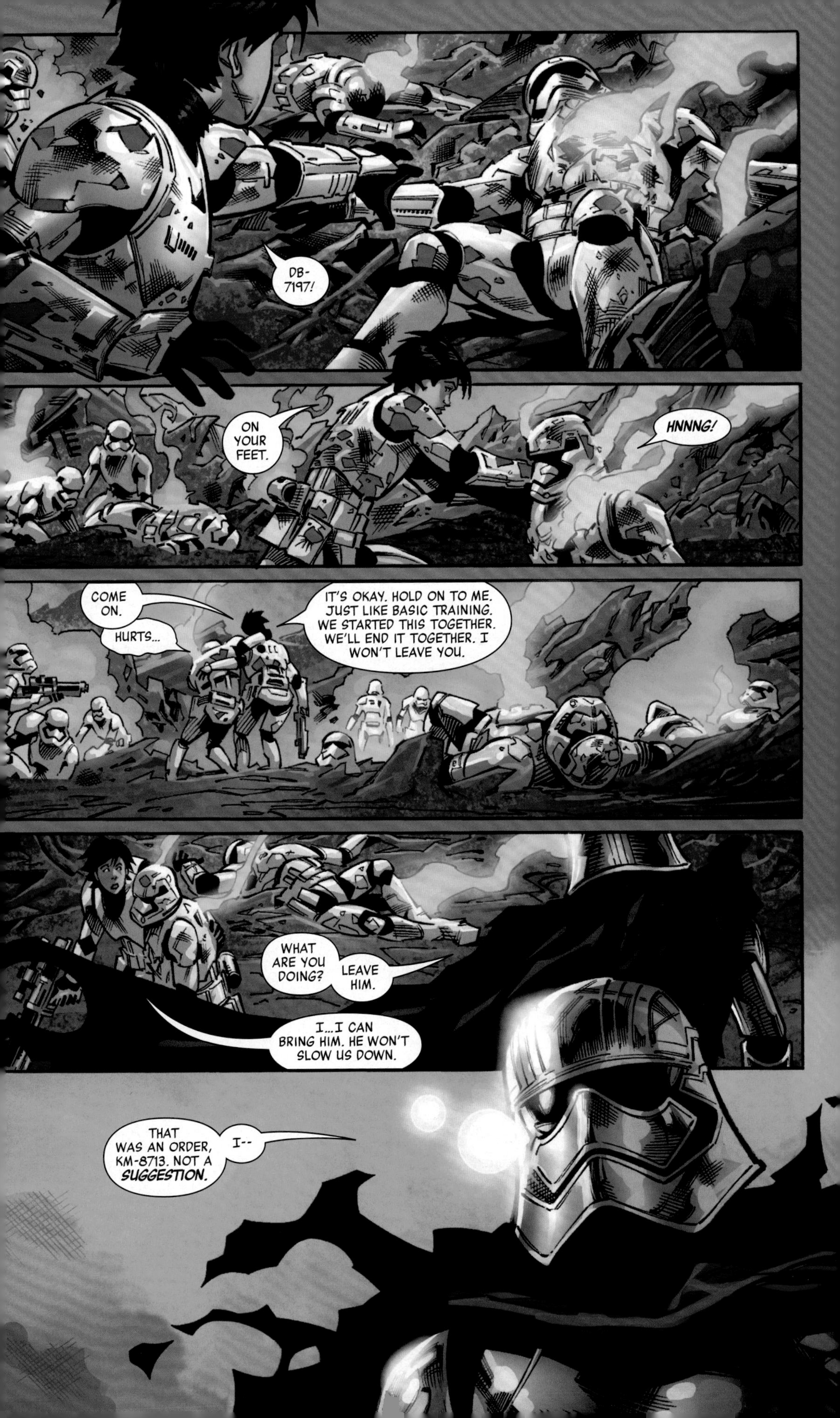
DB-7197!
ON YOUR FEET.
HNNNG!
COME ON.
HURTS...
IT'S OKAY. HOLD ON TO ME. JUST LIKE BASIC TRAINING. WE STARTED THIS TOGETHER. WE'LL END IT TOGETHER. I WON'T LEAVE YOU.
WHAT ARE YOU DOING?
LEAVE HIM.
I...I CAN BRING HIM. HE WON'T SLOW US DOWN.
THAT WAS AN ORDER, KM-8713. NOT A SUGGESTION.
I--

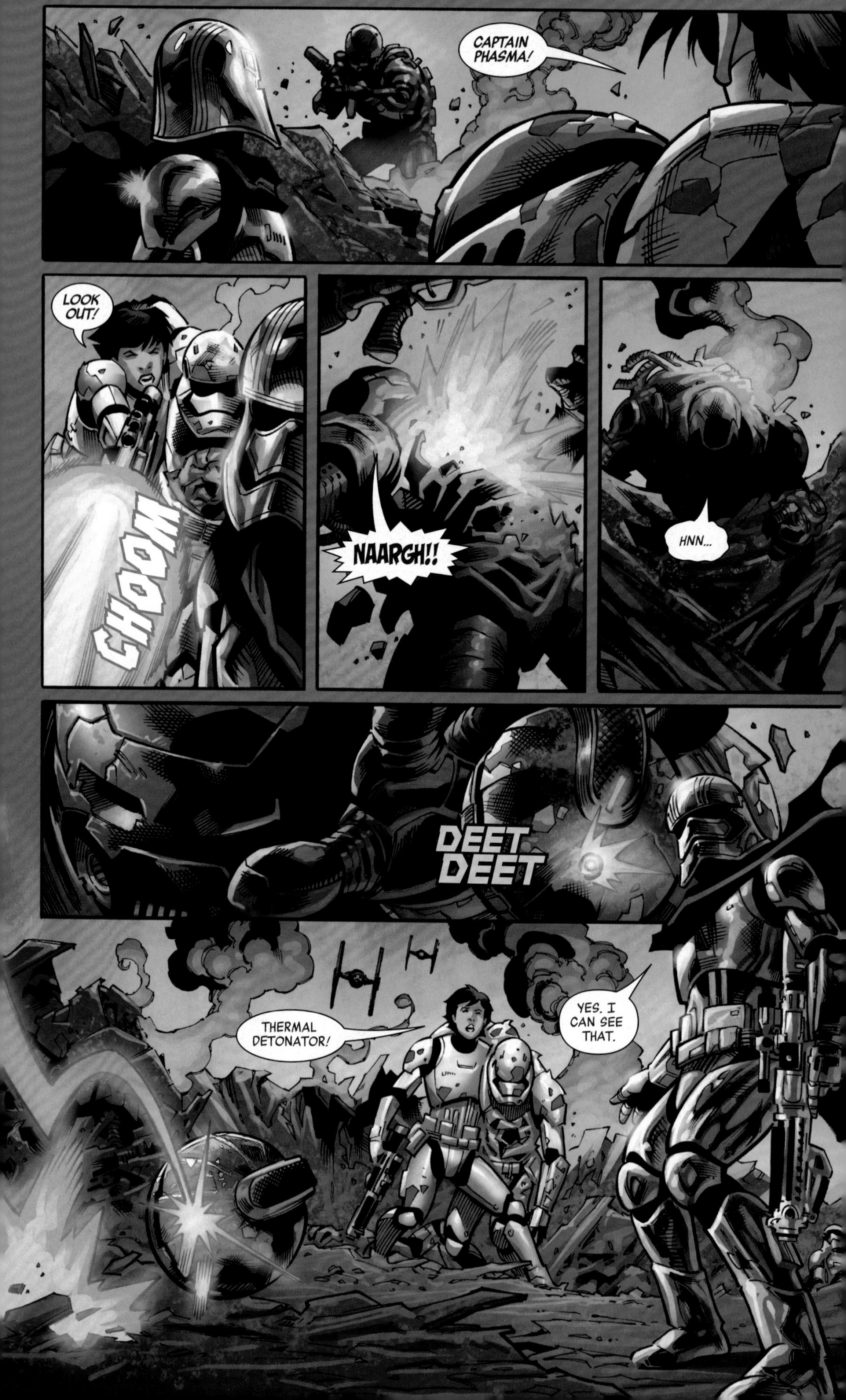
CAPTAIN PHASMA!
LOOK OUT!
CHOOM
NAARGH!!
HNN...
DEET DEET
THERMAL DETONATOR!
YES. I CAN SEE THAT.

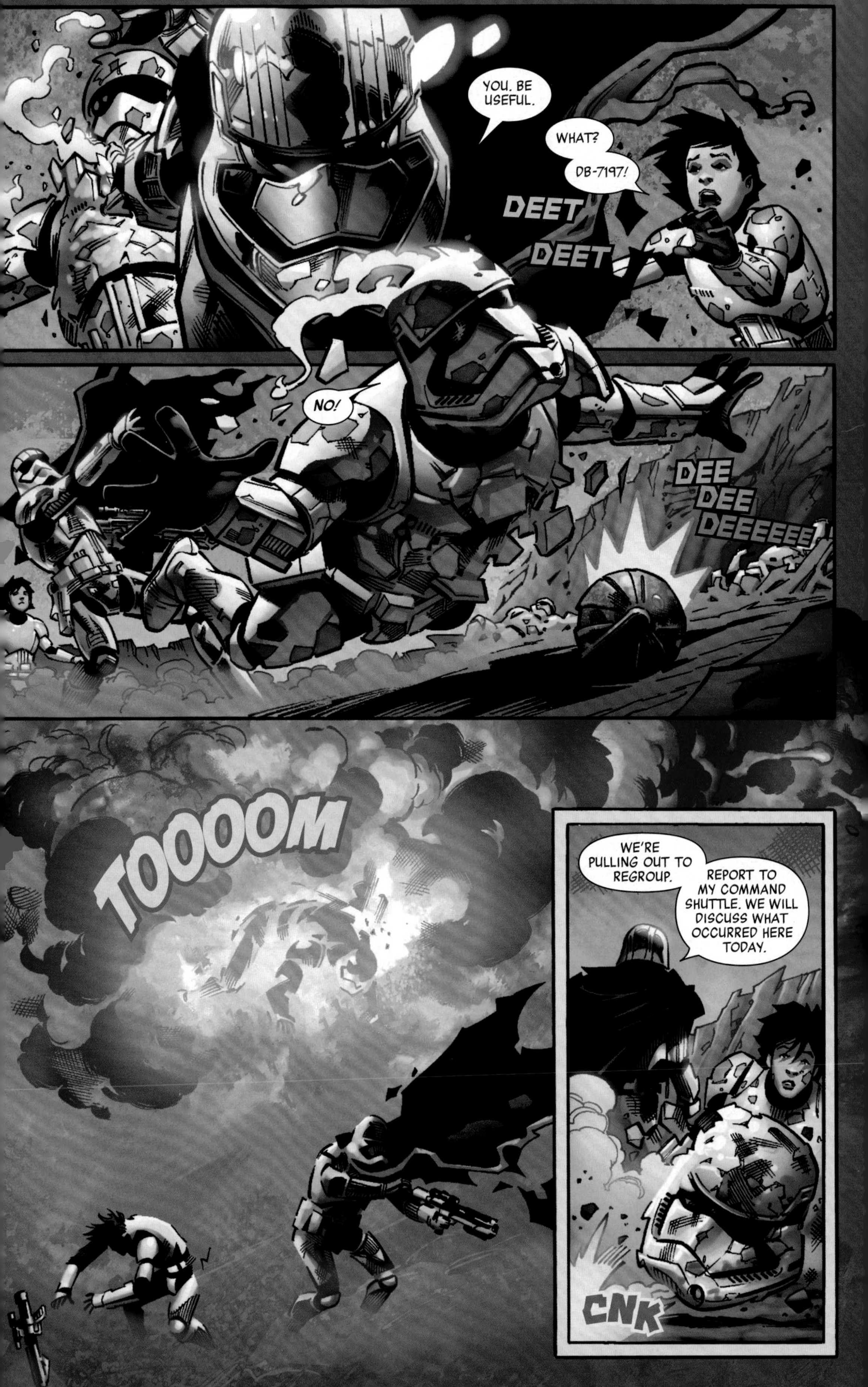
YOU. BE USEFUL.
WHAT?
DB-7197!
DEET
DEET
NO!
DEE
DEE
DEEEEEE
TOOOOM
WE'RE PULLING OUT TO REGROUP.
REPORT TO MY COMMAND SHUTTLE. WE WILL DISCUSS WHAT OCCURRED HERE TODAY.
CNK

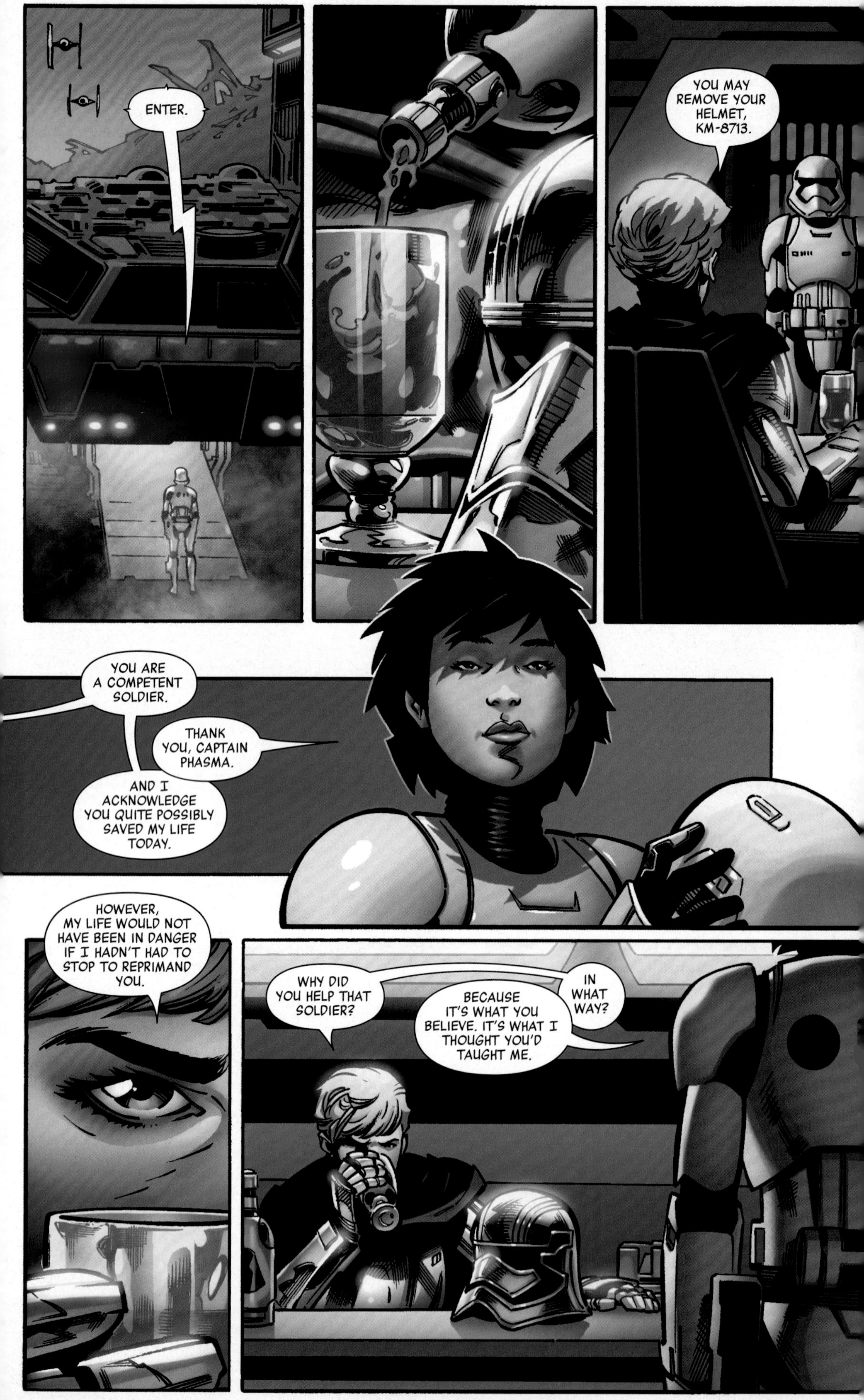
ENTER.
YOU MAY REMOVE YOUR HELMET, KM-8713.
YOU ARE A COMPETENT SOLDIER.
THANK YOU, CAPTAIN PHASMA.
AND I ACKNOWLEDGE YOU QUITE POSSIBLY SAVED MY LIFE TODAY.
HOWEVER, MY LIFE WOULD NOT HAVE BEEN IN DANGER IF I HADN'T HAD TO STOP TO REPRIMAND YOU.
IN WHAT WAY?
WHY DID YOU HELP THAT SOLDIER?
BECAUSE IT'S WHAT YOU BELIEVE. IT'S WHAT I THOUGHT YOU'D TAUGHT ME.

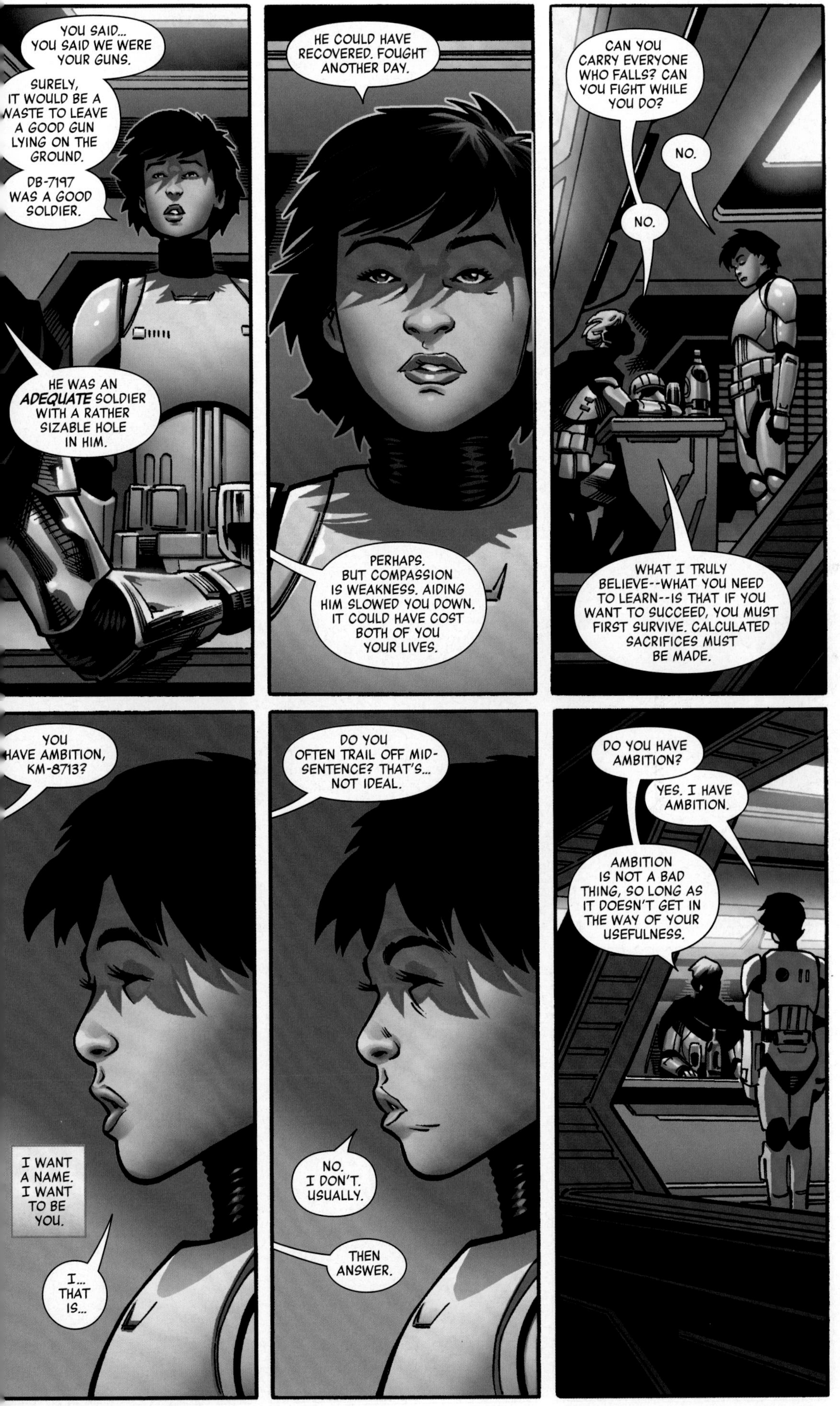
YOU SAID... YOU SAID WE WERE YOUR GUNS.
SURELY, IT WOULD BE A WASTE TO LEAVE A GOOD GUN LYING ON THE GROUND.
DB-7197 WAS A GOOD SOLDIER.
HE WAS AN ADEQUATE SOLDIER WITH A RATHER SIZABLE HOLE IN HIM.
HE COULD HAVE RECOVERED. FOUGHT ANOTHER DAY.
PERHAPS. BUT COMPASSION IS WEAKNESS. AIDING HIM SLOWED YOU DOWN. IT COULD HAVE COST BOTH OF YOU YOUR LIVES.
CAN YOU CARRY EVERYONE WHO FALLS? CAN YOU FIGHT WHILE YOU DO?
NO.
NO.
WHAT I TRULY BELIEVE--WHAT YOU NEED TO LEARN--IS THAT IF YOU WANT TO SUCCEED, YOU MUST FIRST SURVIVE. CALCULATED SACRIFICES MUST BE MADE.
YOU HAVE AMBITION, KM-8713?
I WANT A NAME. I WANT TO BE YOU.
I... THAT IS...
DO YOU OFTEN TRAIL OFF MID-SENTENCE? THAT'S... NOT IDEAL.
NO. I DON'T. USUALLY.
THEN ANSWER.
DO YOU HAVE AMBITION?
YES. I HAVE AMBITION.
AMBITION IS NOT A BAD THING, SO LONG AS IT DOESN'T GET IN THE WAY OF YOUR USEFULNESS.

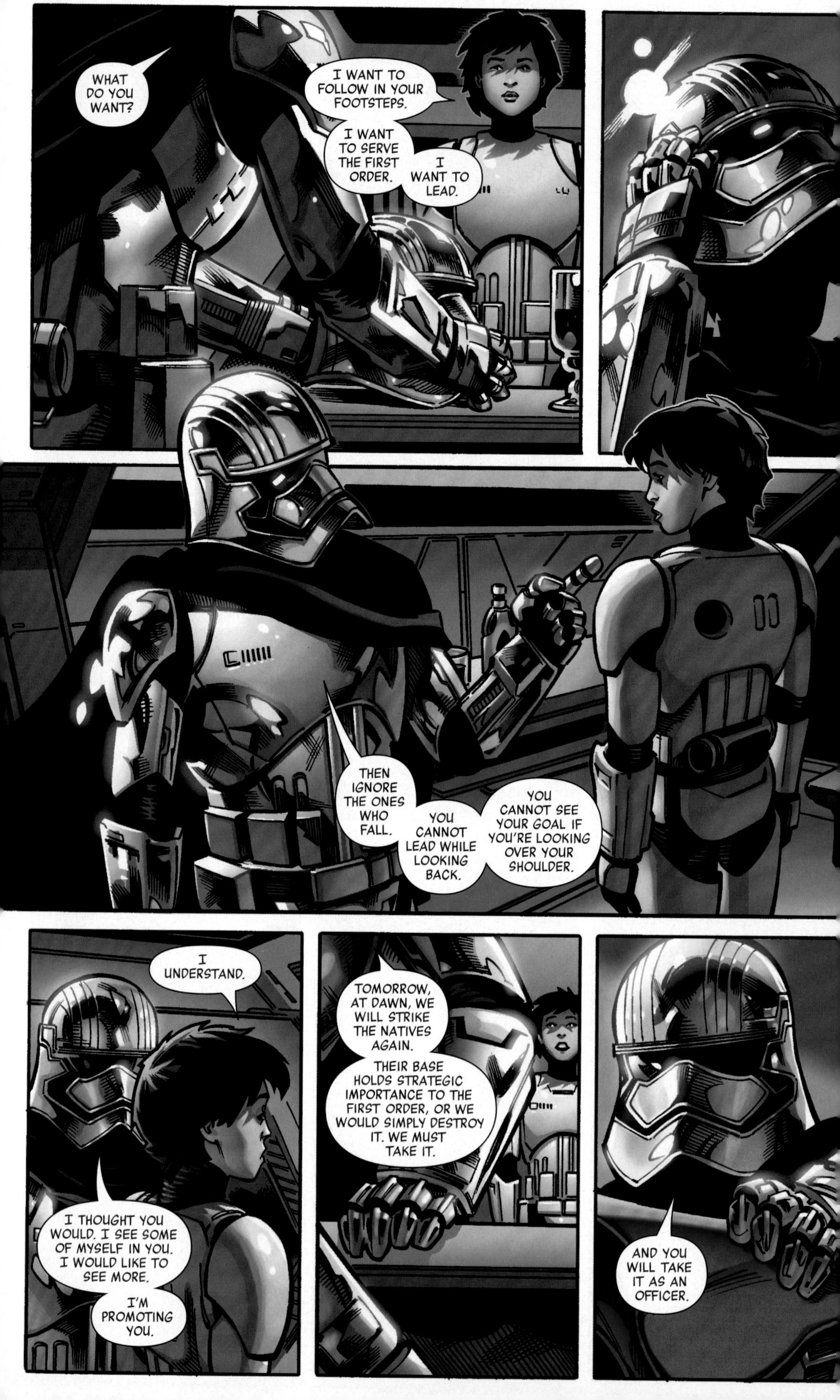
WHAT DO YOU WANT?
I WANT TO FOLLOW IN YOUR FOOTSTEPS.
I WANT TO SERVE THE FIRST ORDER.
I WANT TO LEAD.
THEN IGNORE THE ONES WHO FALL.
YOU CANNOT LEAD WHILE LOOKING BACK.
YOU CANNOT SEE YOUR GOAL IF YOU'RE LOOKING OVER YOUR SHOULDER.
I UNDERSTAND.
I THOUGHT YOU WOULD. I SEE SOME OF MYSELF IN YOU. I WOULD LIKE TO SEE MORE.
I'M PROMOTING YOU.
TOMORROW, AT DAWN, WE WILL STRIKE THE NATIVES AGAIN.
THEIR BASE HOLDS STRATEGIC IMPORTANCE TO THE FIRST ORDER, OR WE WOULD SIMPLY DESTROY IT. WE MUST TAKE IT.
AND YOU WILL TAKE IT AS AN OFFICER.

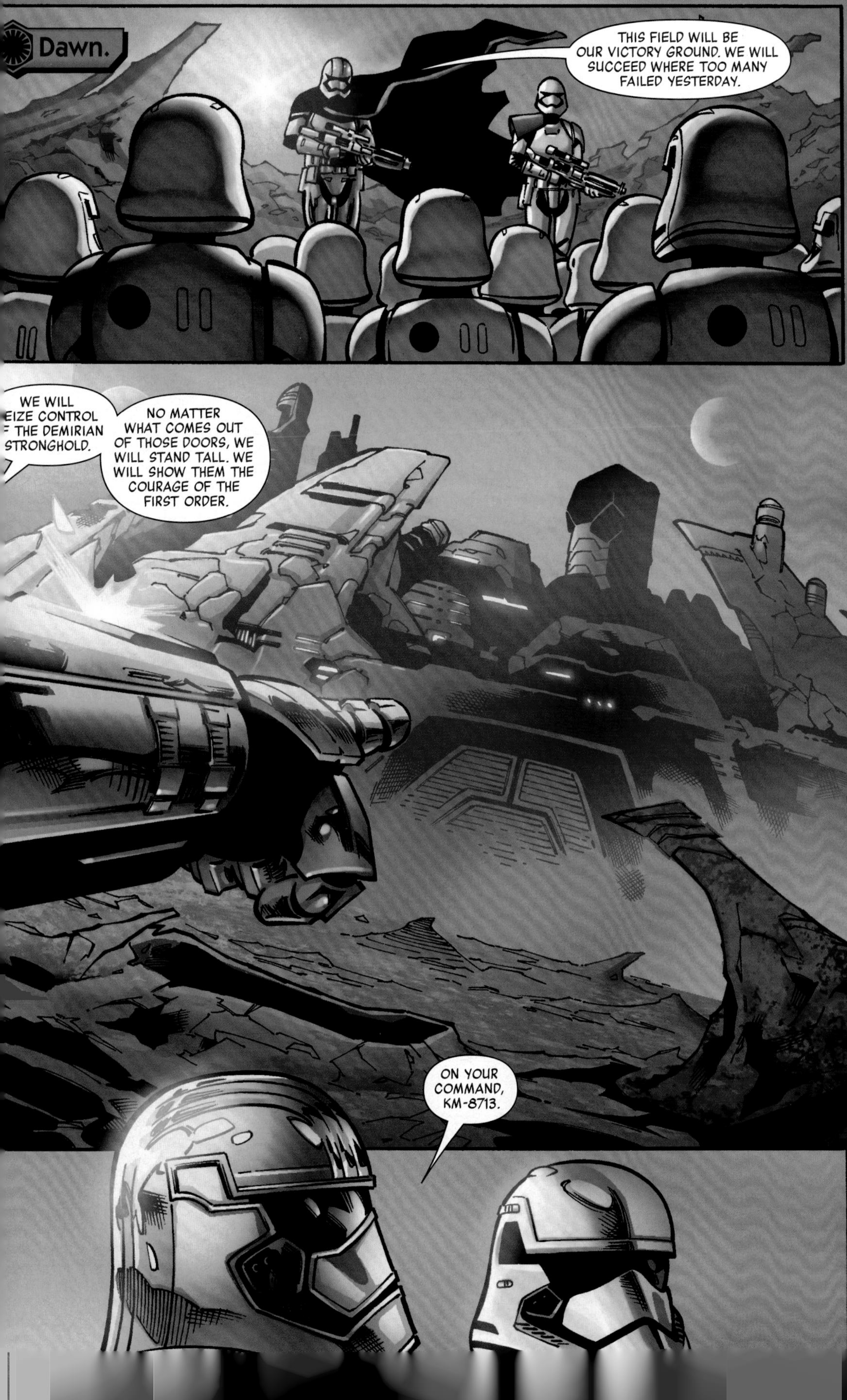

Dawn.
THIS FIELD WILL BE OUR VICTORY GROUND. WE WILL SUCCEED WHERE TOO MANY FAILED YESTERDAY.
WE WILL EIZE CONTROL F THE DEMIRIAN STRONGHOLD.
NO MATTER WHAT COMES OUT OF THOSE DOORS, WE WILL STAND TALL. WE WILL SHOW THEM THE COURAGE OF THE FIRST ORDER.
ON YOUR COMMAND, KM-8713.

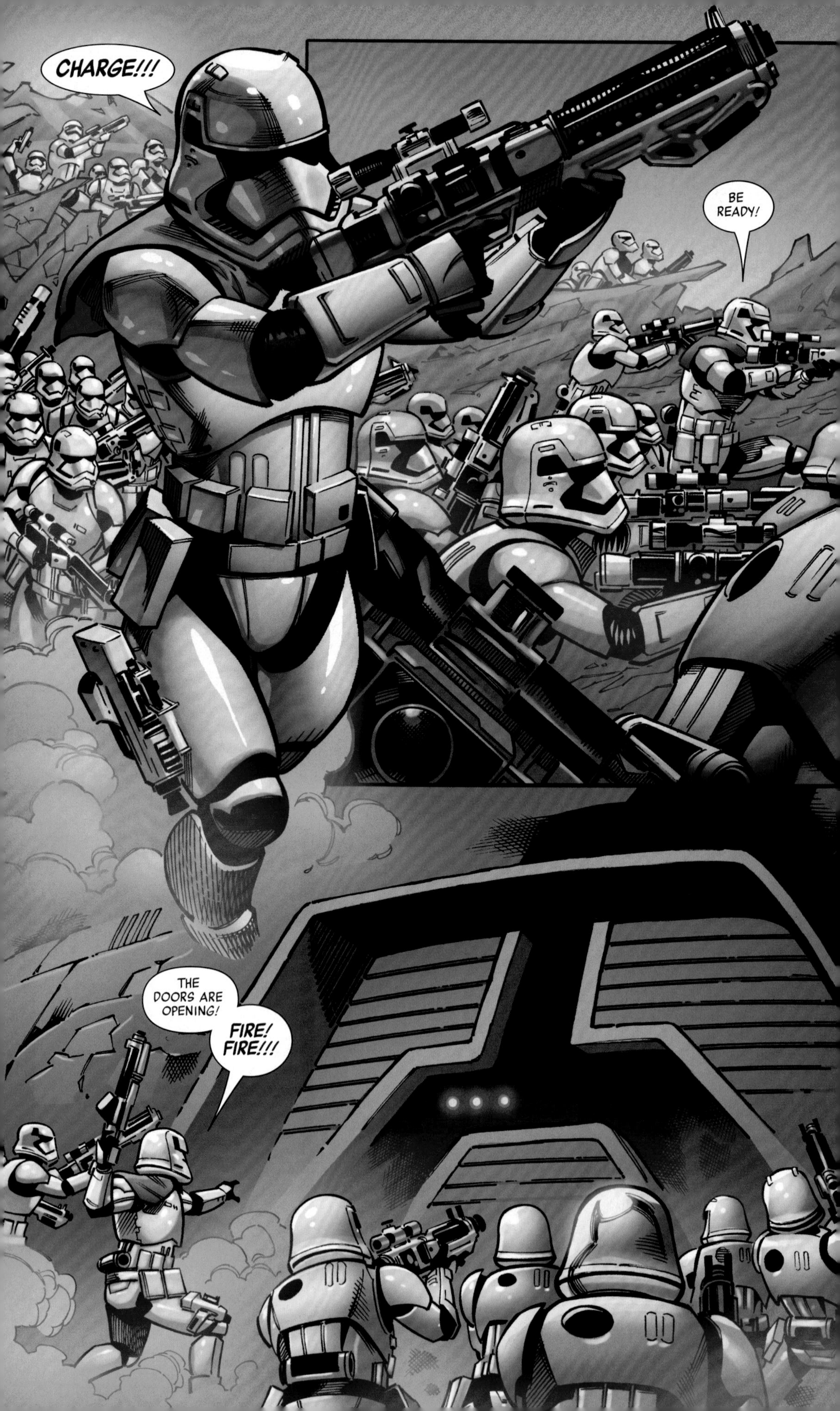
CHARGE!!!
BE READY!
THE DOORS ARE OPENING!
FIRE! FIRE!!!

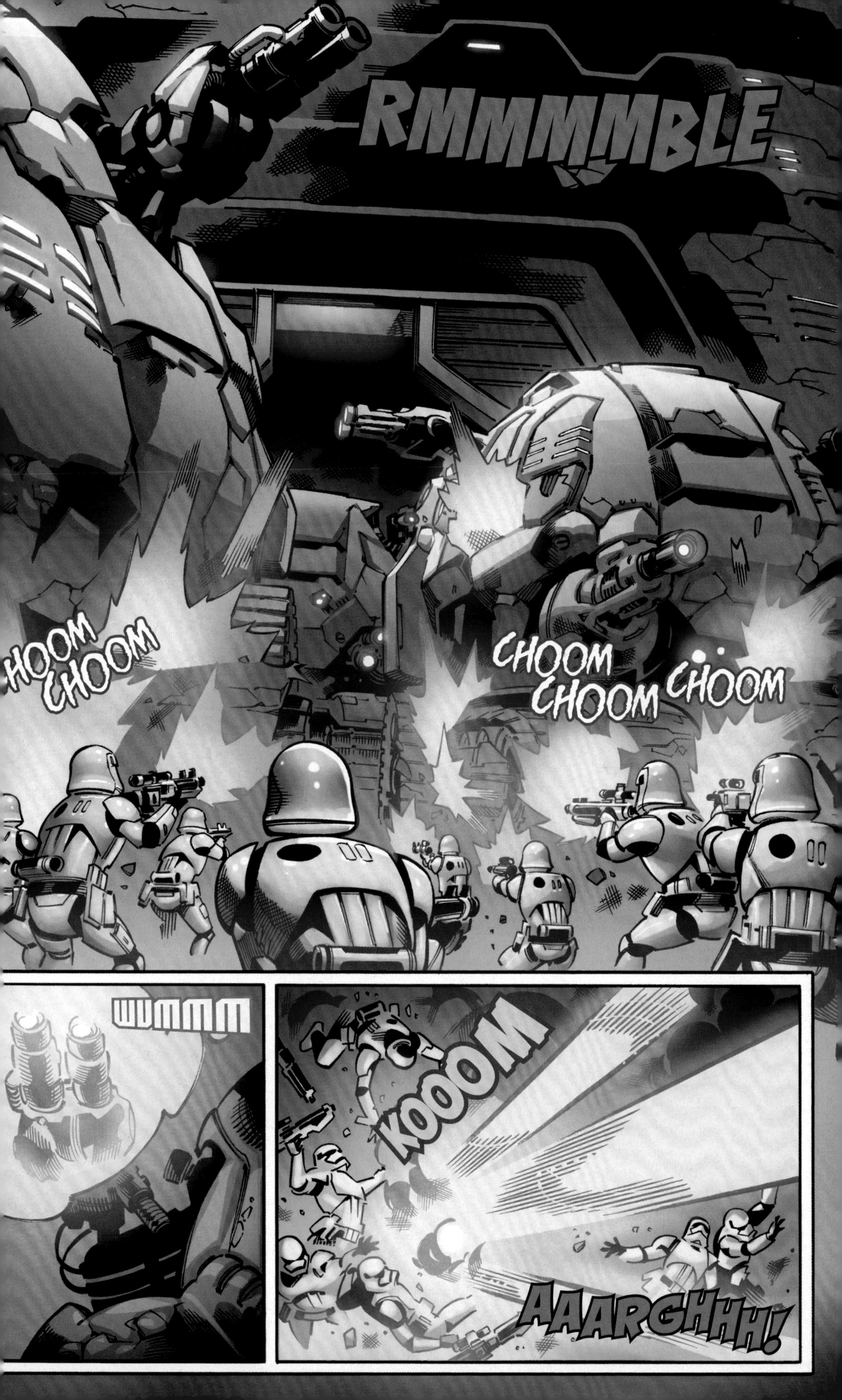
RMMMMMBLE
HOOM
CHOOM
CHOOM
CHOOM
CHOOM
WUMMM
KOOOM
AAARGHHH!

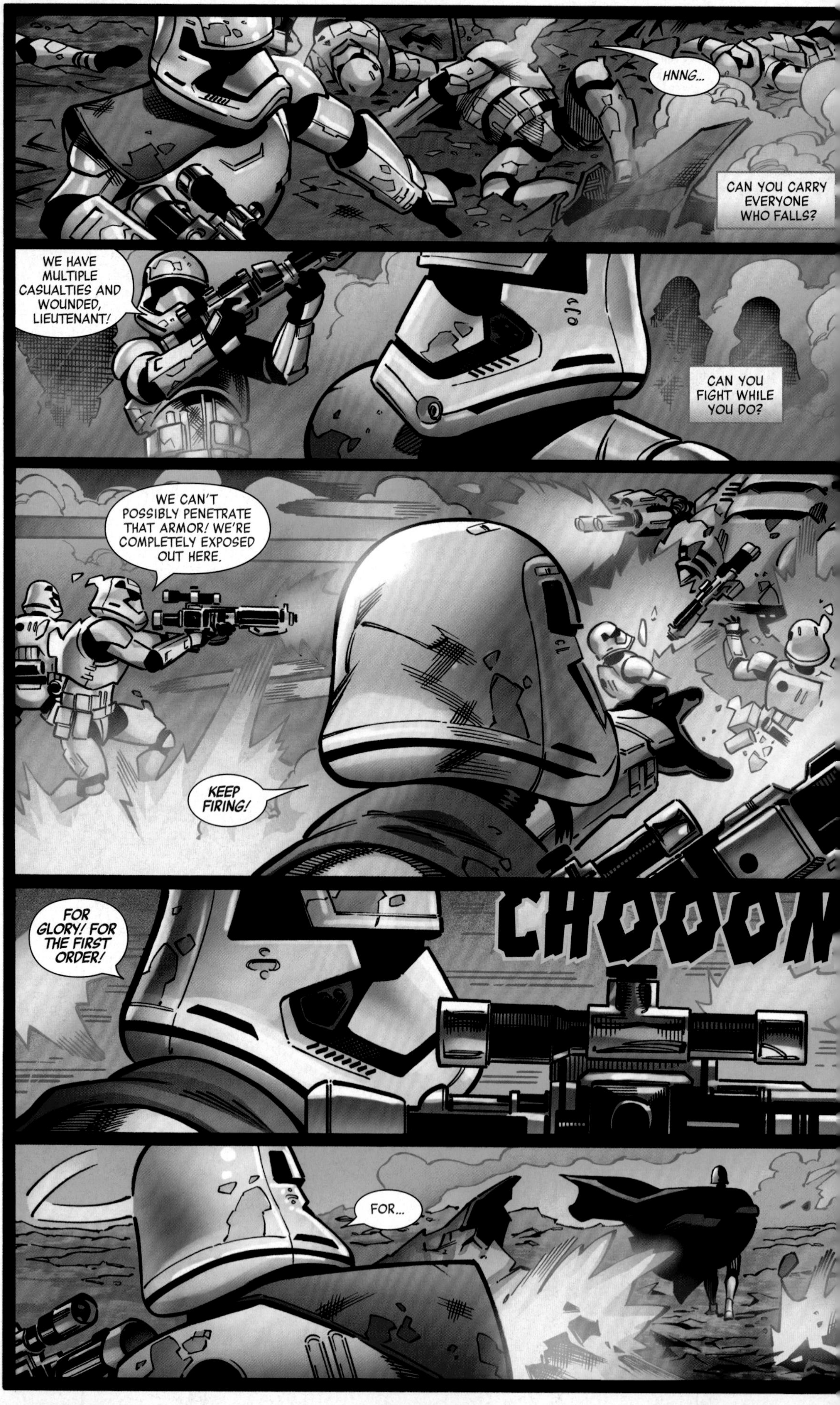
HNNG...
CAN YOU CARRY EVERYONE WHO FALLS?
WE HAVE MULTIPLE CASUALTIES AND WOUNDED, LIEUTENANT!
CAN YOU FIGHT WHILE YOU DO?
WE CAN'T POSSIBLY PENETRATE THAT ARMOR! WE'RE COMPLETELY EXPOSED OUT HERE.
KEEP FIRING!
FOR GLORY! FOR THE FIRST ORDER!
CHOOOM
FOR...

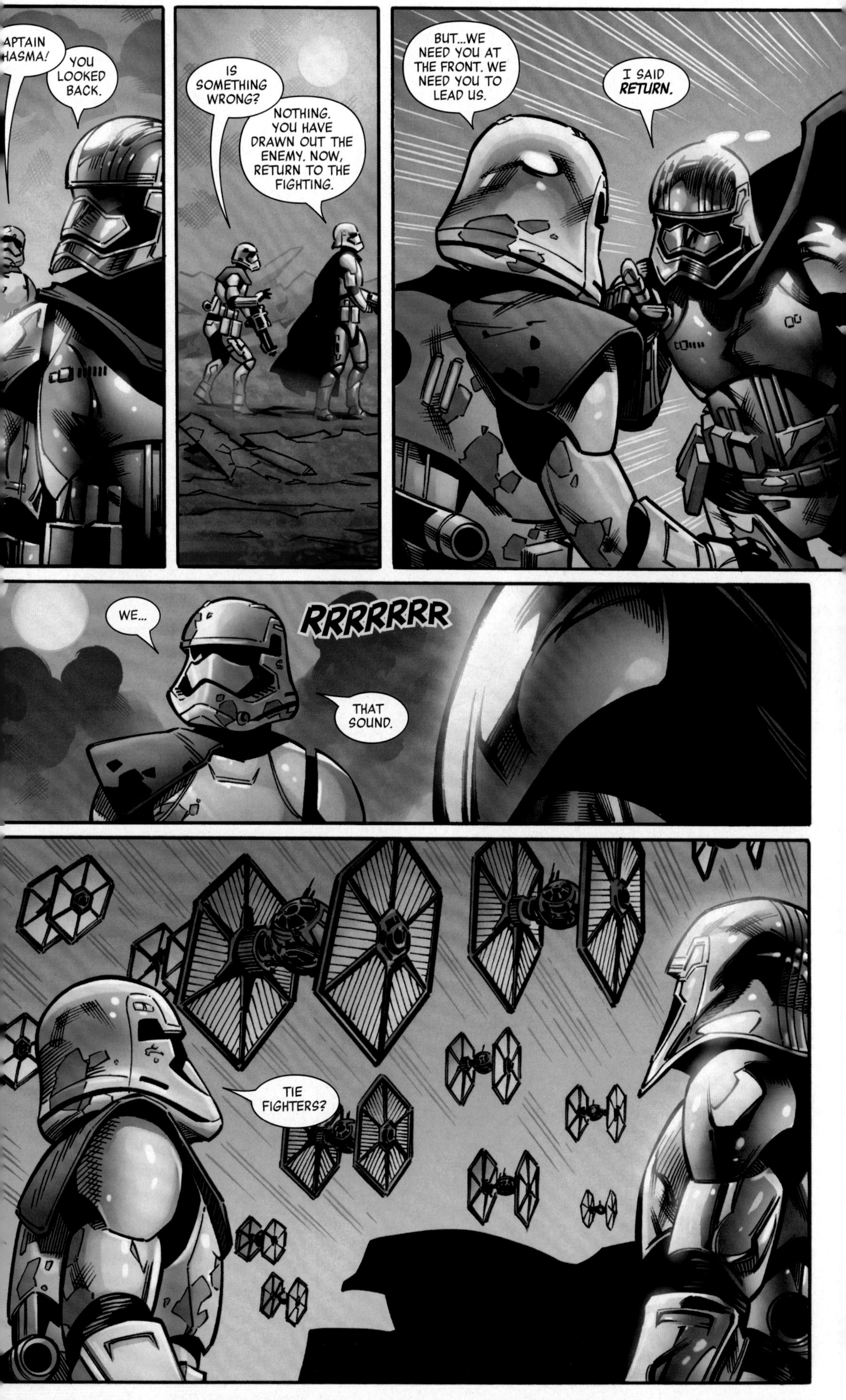
APTAIN
HASMA!
YOU LOOKED BACK.
IS SOMETHING WRONG?
NOTHING. YOU HAVE DRAWN OUT THE ENEMY. NOW, RETURN TO THE FIGHTING.
BUT...WE NEED YOU AT THE FRONT. WE NEED YOU TO LEAD US.
I SAID RETURN.
WE...
RRRRRRR
THAT SOUND.
TIE FIGHTERS?

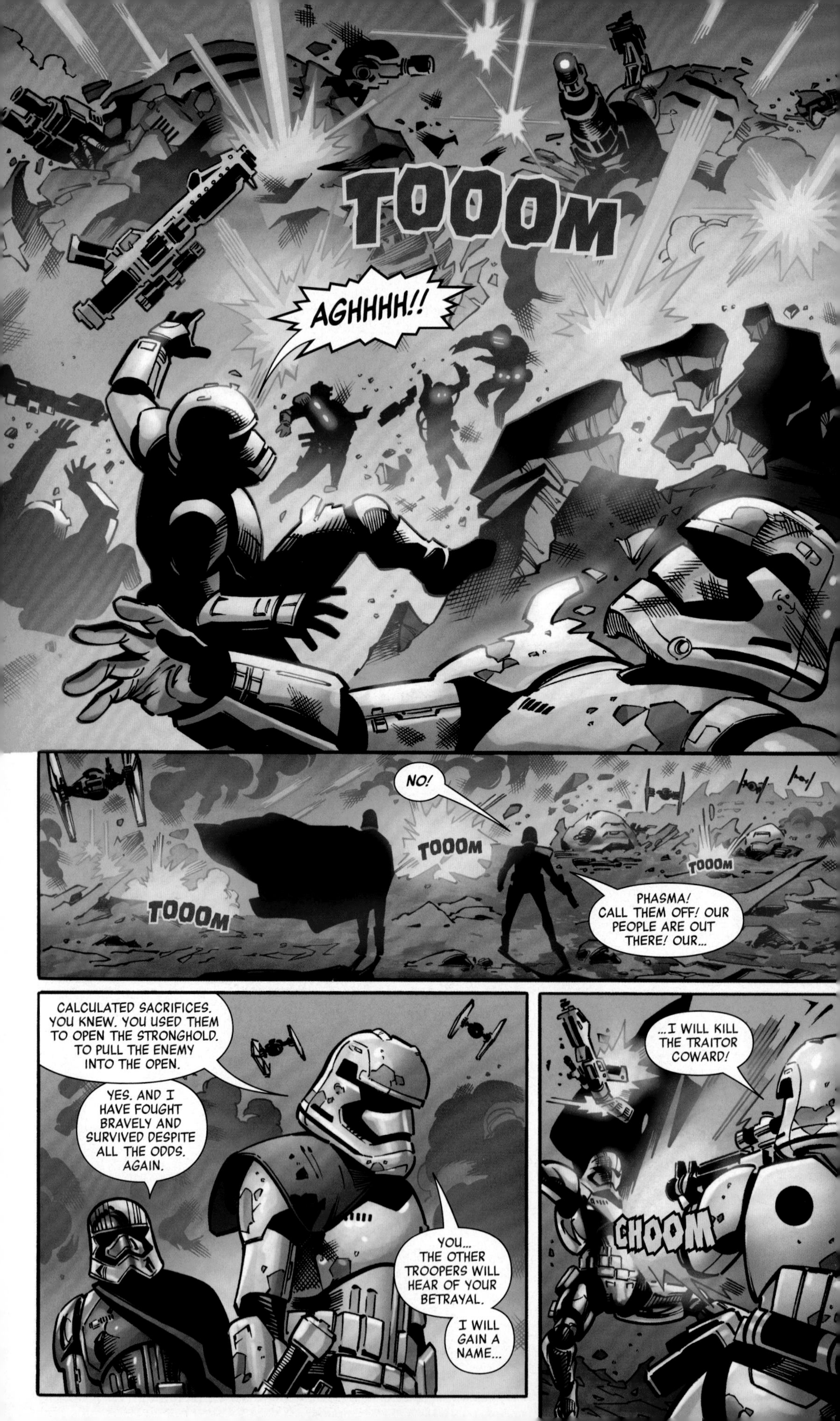
TOOOM
AGHHHH!!
NO!
TOOOM
TOOOM
TOOOM
PHASMA! CALL THEM OFF! OUR PEOPLE ARE OUT THERE! OUR...
CALCULATED SACRIFICES. YOU KNEW. YOU USED THEM TO OPEN THE STRONGHOLD. TO PULL THE ENEMY INTO THE OPEN.
YES. AND I HAVE FOUGHT BRAVELY AND SURVIVED DESPITE ALL THE ODDS. AGAIN.
YOU... THE OTHER TROOPERS WILL HEAR OF YOUR BETRAYAL.
I WILL GAIN A NAME...
...I WILL KILL THE TRAITOR COWARD!
CHOOM

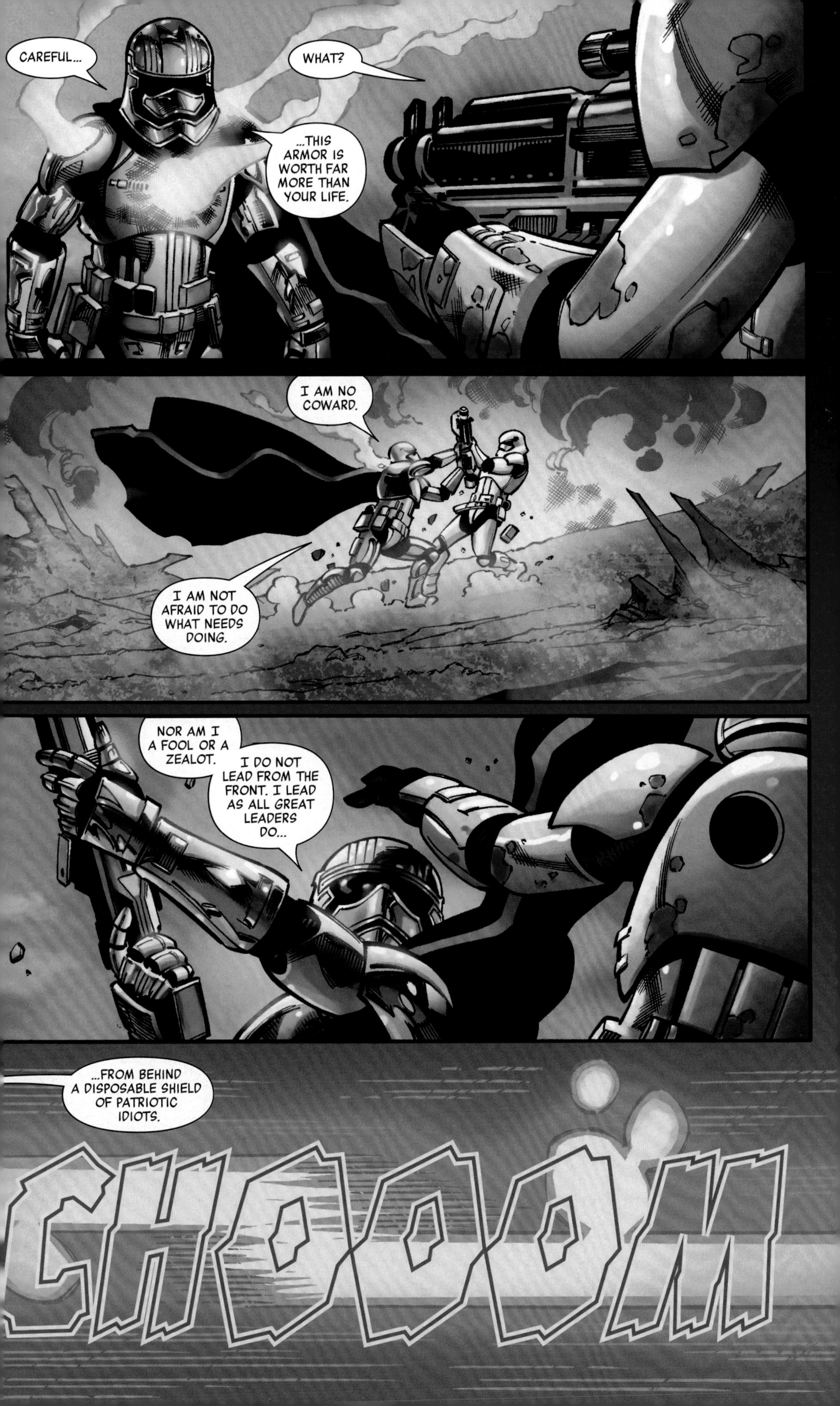
CAREFUL...
WHAT?
...THIS ARMOR IS WORTH FAR MORE THAN YOUR LIFE.
I AM NO COWARD.
I AM NOT AFRAID TO DO WHAT NEEDS DOING.
NOR AM I A FOOL OR A ZEALOT.
I DO NOT LEAD FROM THE FRONT. I LEAD AS ALL GREAT LEADERS DO...
...FROM BEHIND A DISPOSABLE SHIELD OF PATRIOTIC IDIOTS.
CHOOOM

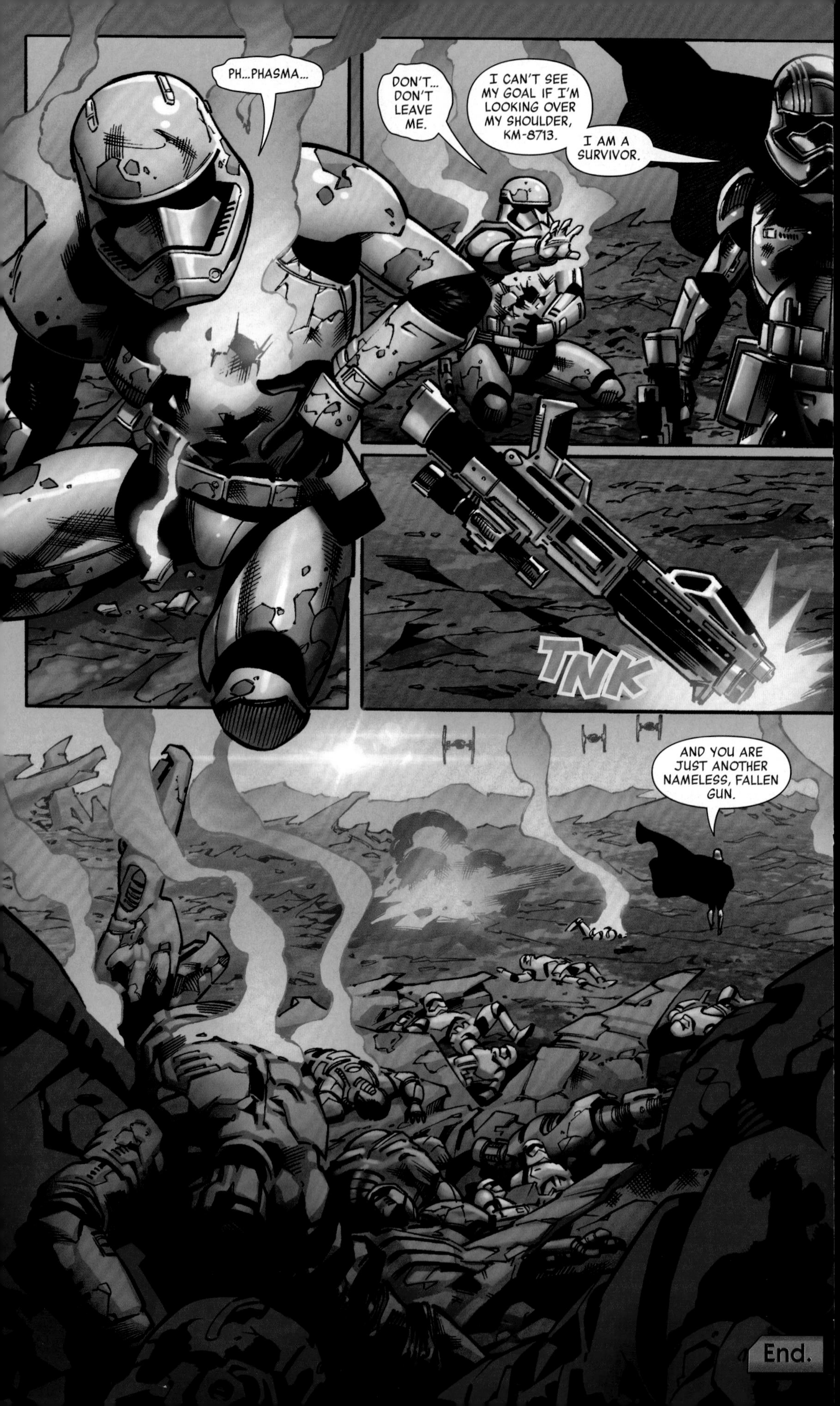
PH...PHASMA...
DON'T... DON'T LEAVE ME.
I CAN'T SEE MY GOAL IF I'M LOOKING OVER MY SHOULDER, KM-8713.
I AM A SURVIVOR.
TNK
AND YOU ARE JUST ANOTHER NAMELESS, FALLEN GUN.
End.

AGE OF RESISTANCE

AGE OF RESISTANCE:
Captain Phasma and Her Origins—In-Universe and Out
By Bryan Young

On the surface, Captain Phasma may look like just a shiny new stormtrooper for the First Order, but when you peel back the layers of the character, something much more complicated—and much more sinister—is revealed. Beneath that chrome armor is a cunning, calculating warrior, willing to murder anyone in her path if they interfere with her life or privacy.

From the moment she appeared in advertising for *The Force Awakens*, Phasma was a fan-favorite, drawing the sort of attention that had previously been reserved for characters like Boba Fett and Darth Vader. When asked by *Entertainment Weekly* about the popularity of Phasma, the actress behind the part, Gwendoline Christie, said, "What I think people are drawn to is that this is a very progressive female character. We see Captain Phasma, and we see the costume from head to toe, and we know that it is a woman. But we are used to, in our media, connecting to female characters via the way that they look, from the way they are made flesh... We are actually connecting to a female character as a human being."

HUMAN BEGINNINGS

Captain Phasma can seem like nothing more than a metal monster, but she has very human beginnings. Thanks to Delilah S. Dawson's novel *Phasma*, we know so much more about Phasma's origin, and it's almost more *Mad Max* than *Star Wars*. In that book, we learned that she came from the planet Parnassos, a world devastated by an unscrupulous industrial concern. To survive, she learned to be ruthless and kill anyone who would oppose

her leadership. Unfortunately, it would turn out that her greatest threat might have been her brother. They put aside their differences for a time to save their people, but ultimately their people weren't as important to Phasma as survival.

Once Phasma set her sights on leaving her home planet, she sold out or killed anyone who stood in her way, women and children included. Brendol Hux, the father of General Hux, was her savior, helping her get away and into the waiting arms of the First Order, who she joined with enthusiasm. But for one so private and so dedicated to the order represented by Snoke's Empire-from-the-ashes, she couldn't let the secrets from the past catch up to her.

It was Vi Moradi, the spy who brought the wounded Resistance to Batuu, who discovered that Phasma went so far as to assassinate Brendol Hux to keep her secrets and consolidate her power.

Ruthless, indeed.

REAL-WORLD ORIGINS

Captain Phasma began life as a male character, but J.J. Abrams opted to switch the gender of the character and bring in a new female villain to the franchise.

Her name, Phasma, came from Abrams himself, who told *Entertainment Weekly*, "Phasma I named because of the amazing chrome design that came from Michael Kaplan's wardrobe team. It reminded me of the ball in *Phantasm*, and I just thought Phasma sounds really

cool." In the universe, however, Phasma got her reflective armor on Parnassos, cobbling it together from salvaged pieces of one of Palpatine's Naboo luxury yachts.

In *The Force Awakens*, J.J. Abrams left Phasma, famously, in the bottom of a garbage chute on Starkiller Base, just before it blew up. This posed a problem for writer/director of *The Last Jedi*, Rian Johnson. "We needed her alive here," he told io9. "Mostly because I wanted to hang out with Gwendoline Christie."

Regardless of his reasons, that decision to bring Phasma back to act as Finn's villainous foil spawned a comic series from Marvel that doubled down on Phasma's murderous need to keep her secrets. In *Star Wars: Captain Phasma*, she works to frame and murder an innocent member of the First Order in hope of keeping a lid on the fact that she's the one who lowered the shields on Starkiller Base.

But as ruthless as Phasma is, Gwendoline Christie still cites Princess Leia as part of her origin. "I was about 6 when I saw *[Star Wars]*," Christie said at the press conference for *The Force Awakens*, "and I remember being so struck by the character of Princess Leia and thinking even then in my infant mind, this seems different to the other women I see in films and feeling very, very inspired by that—inspired by a woman with such tenacity and being so strong-minded."

This serves to prove that Carrie Fisher inspired actresses of every generation, even those who play the most villainous of women in Star Wars.

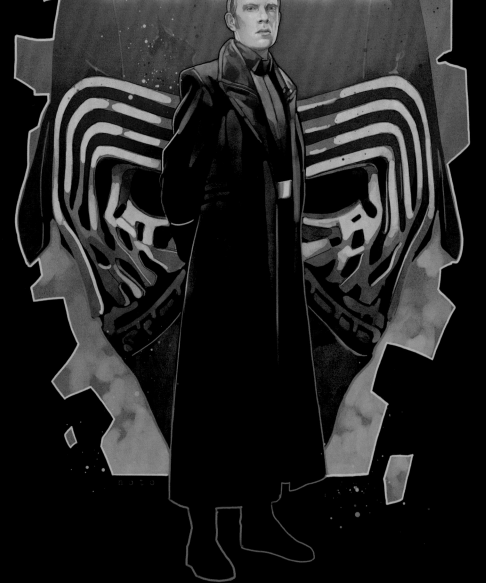

GENERAL HUX

"MAROONED"

Ruthless General Armitage Hux is one of the First Order's most dangerous and trusted leaders, third only to Kylo Ren and the Supreme Leader himself. What made Hux the man he is today? Ambition?

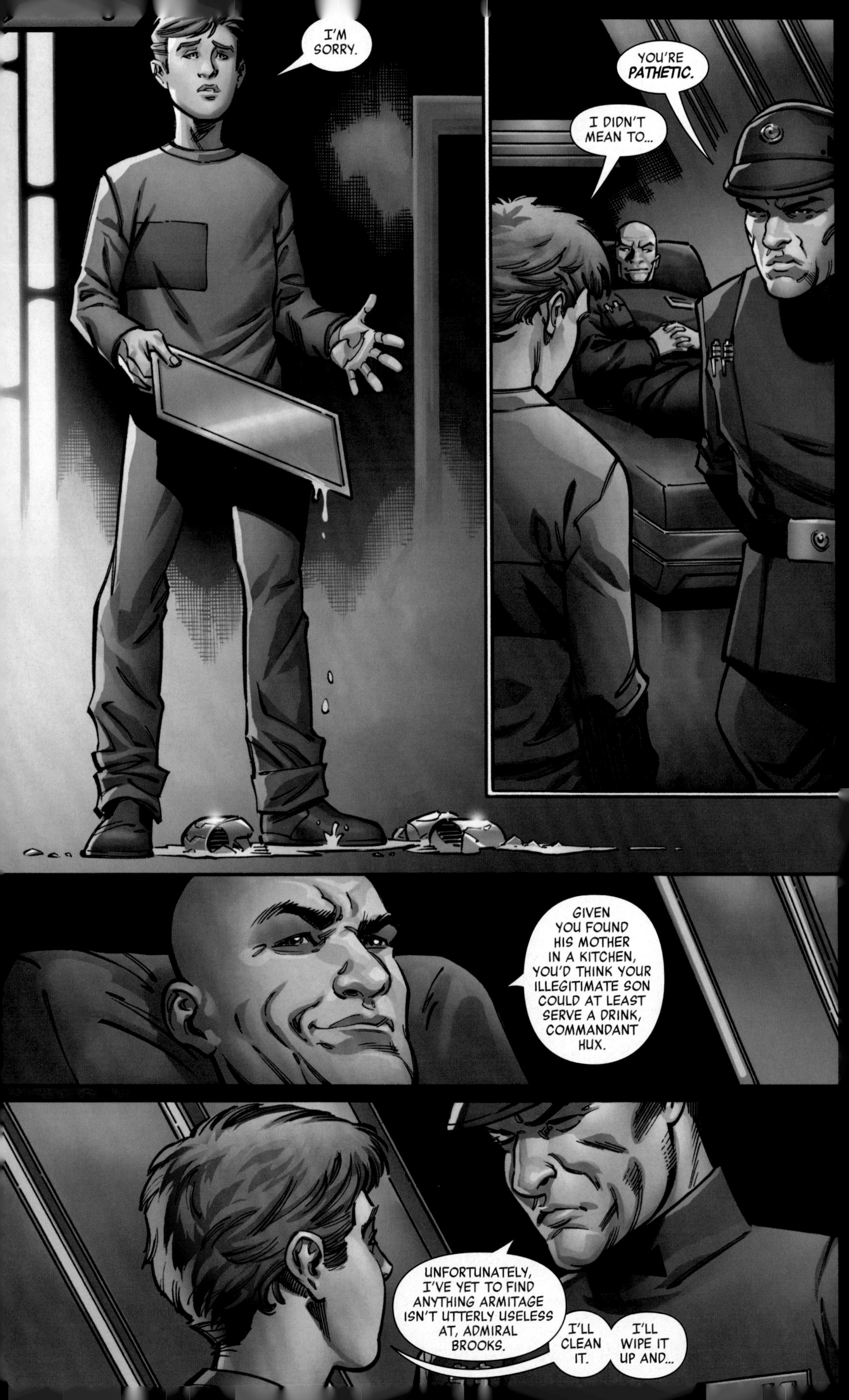
I'M SORRY.
YOU'RE PATHETIC.
I DIDN'T MEAN TO...
GIVEN YOU FOUND HIS MOTHER IN A KITCHEN, YOU'D THINK YOUR ILLEGITIMATE SON COULD AT LEAST SERVE A DRINK, COMMANDANT HUX.
UNFORTUNATELY, I'VE YET TO FIND ANYTHING ARMITAGE ISN'T UTTERLY USELESS AT, ADMIRAL BROOKS.
I'LL CLEAN IT.
I'LL WIPE IT UP AND...

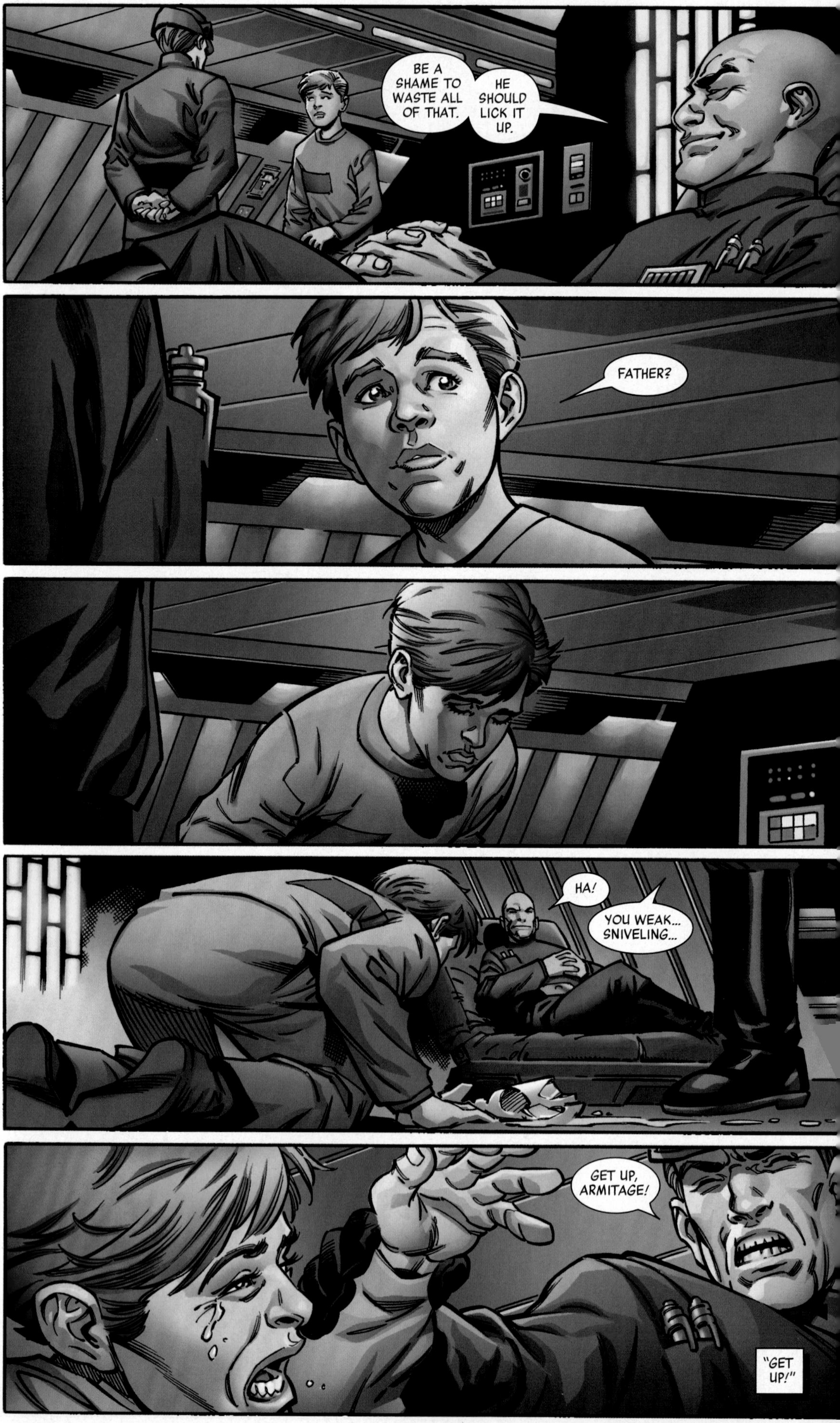
BE A SHAME TO WASTE ALL OF THAT.
HE SHOULD LICK IT UP.
FATHER?
HA!
YOU WEAK... SNIVELING...
GET UP, ARMITAGE!
"GET UP!"

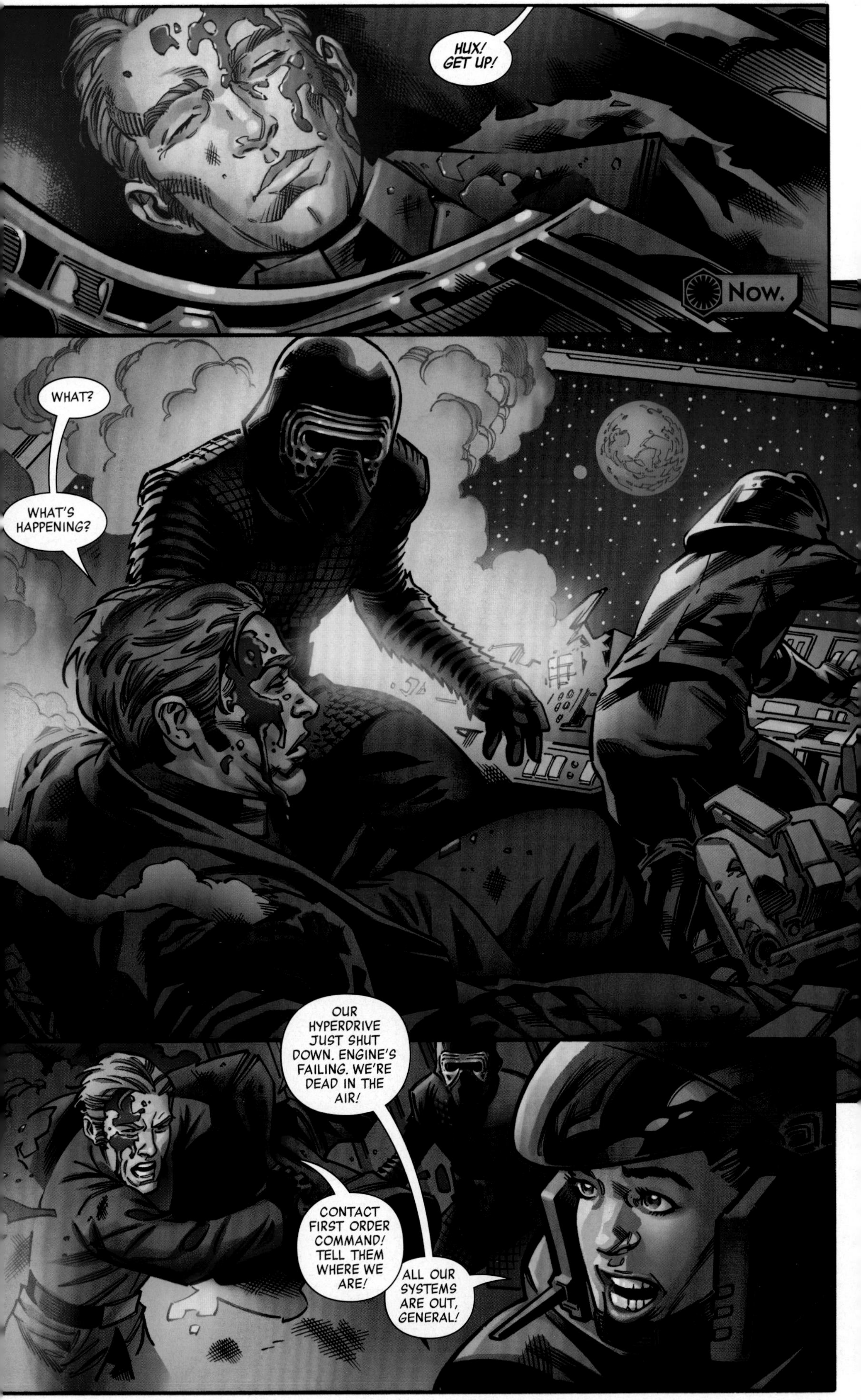
HUX! GET UP!
Now.
WHAT?
WHAT'S HAPPENING?
OUR HYPERDRIVE JUST SHUT DOWN. ENGINE'S FAILING. WE'RE DEAD IN THE AIR!
CONTACT FIRST ORDER COMMAND! TELL THEM WHERE WE ARE!
ALL OUR SYSTEMS ARE OUT, GENERAL!

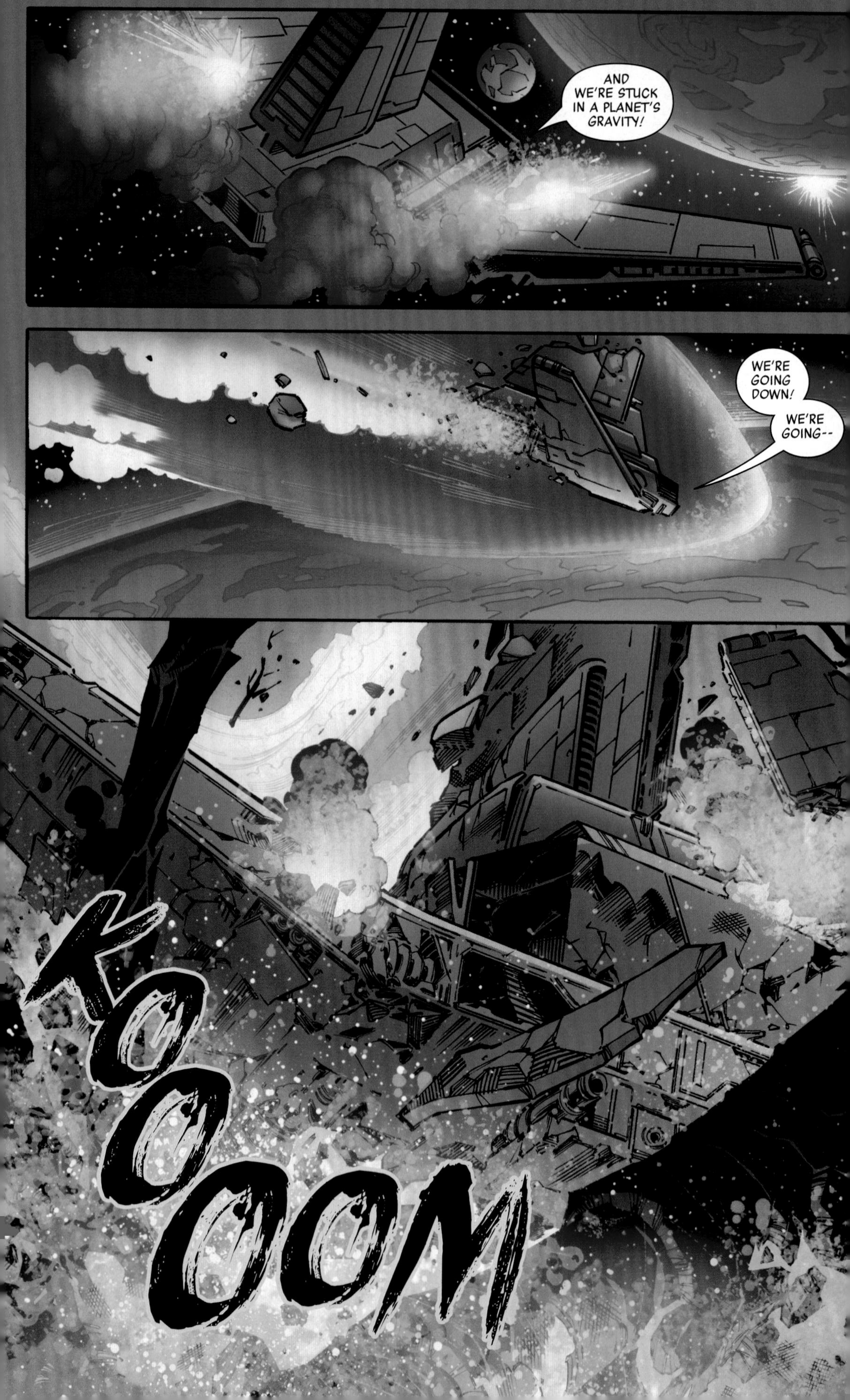
AND WE'RE STUCK IN A PLANET'S GRAVITY!
WE'RE GOING DOWN!
WE'RE GOING--
KOOOOM

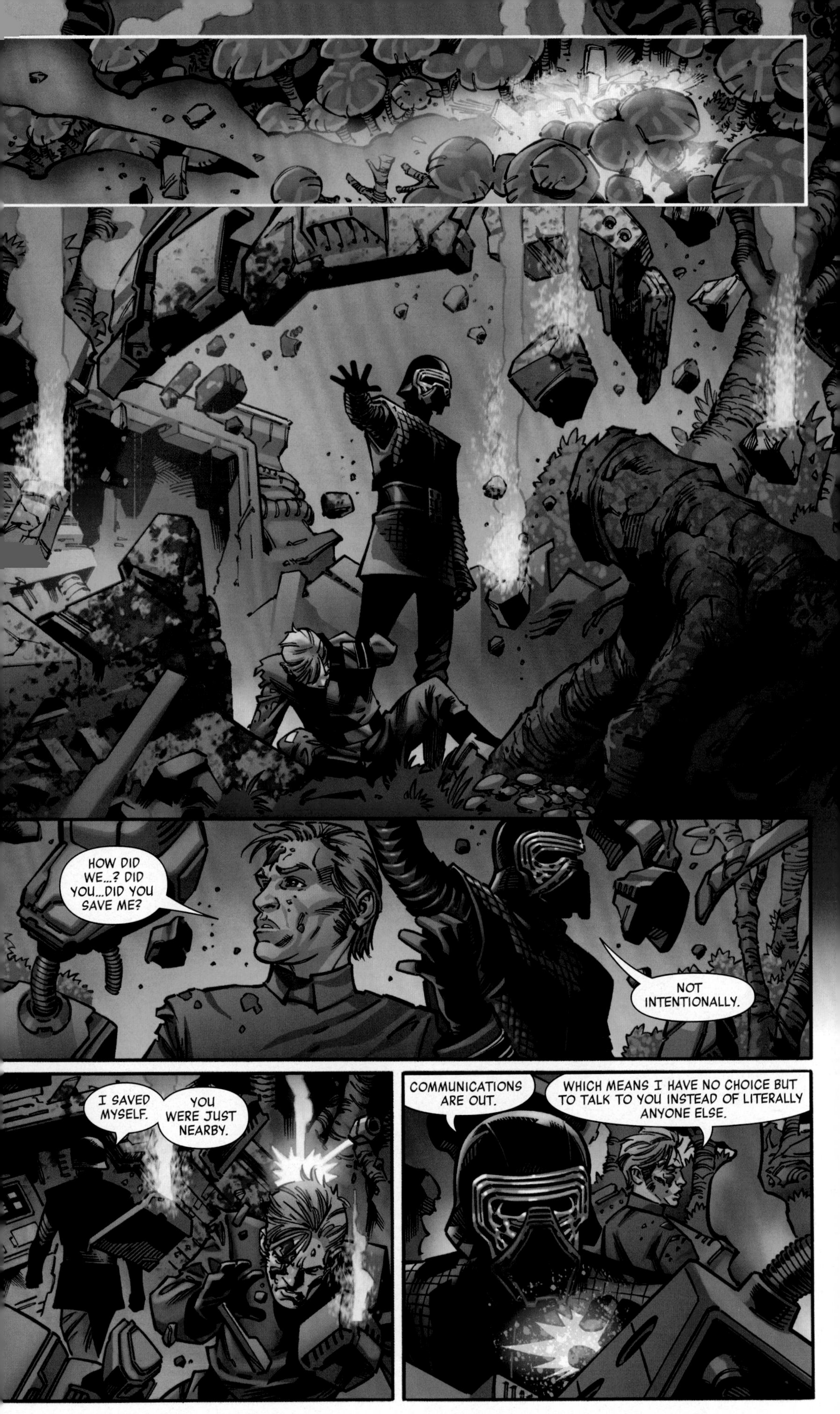
HOW DID WE...? DID YOU...DID YOU SAVE ME?
NOT INTENTIONALLY.
I SAVED MYSELF.
YOU WERE JUST NEARBY.
COMMUNICATIONS ARE OUT.
WHICH MEANS I HAVE NO CHOICE BUT TO TALK TO YOU INSTEAD OF LITERALLY ANYONE ELSE.

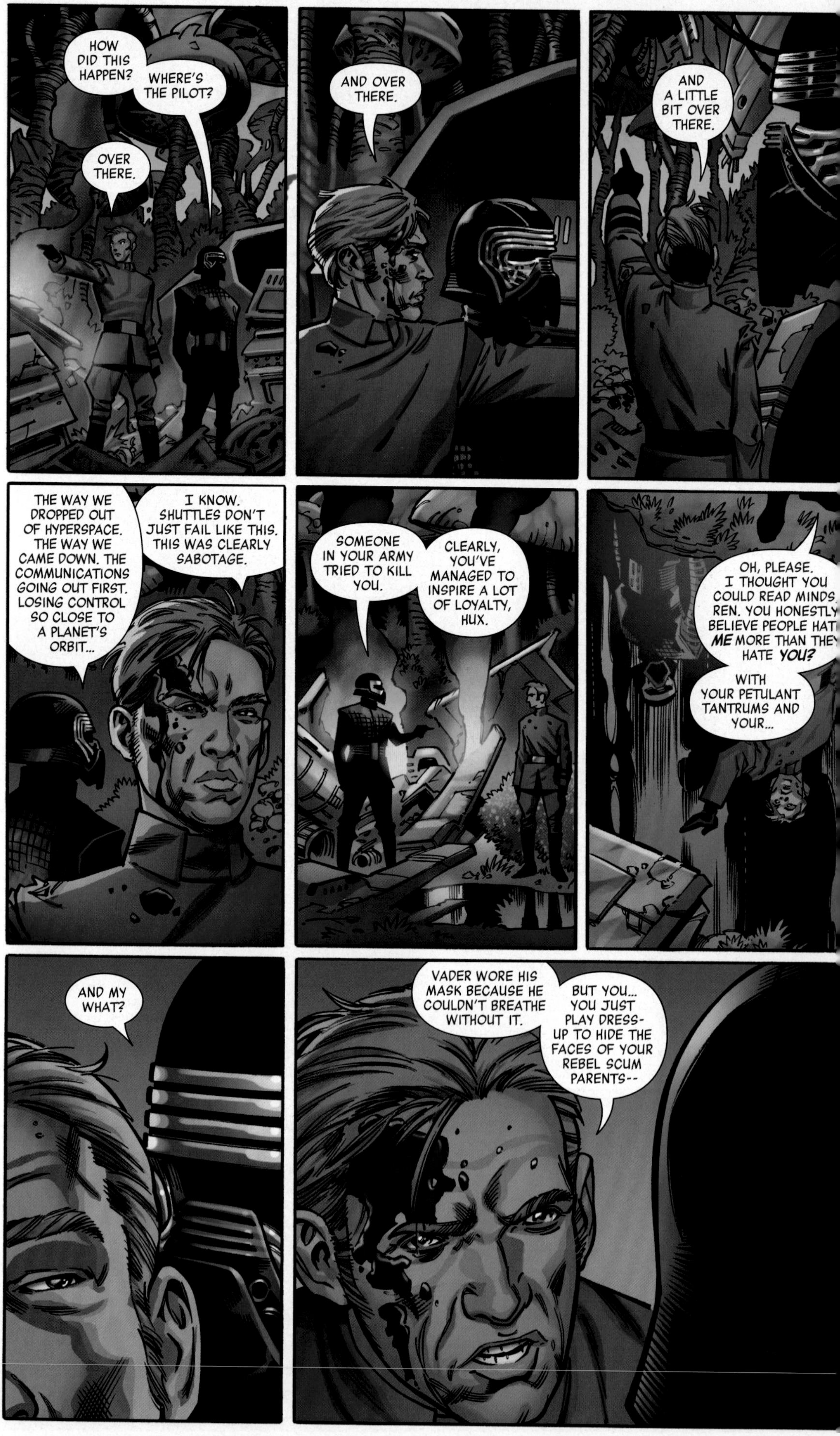
HOW DID THIS HAPPEN?
WHERE'S THE PILOT?
OVER THERE.
AND OVER THERE.
AND A LITTLE BIT OVER THERE.
THE WAY WE DROPPED OUT OF HYPERSPACE. THE WAY WE CAME DOWN. THE COMMUNICATIONS GOING OUT FIRST. LOSING CONTROL SO CLOSE TO A PLANET'S ORBIT...
I KNOW. SHUTTLES DON'T JUST FAIL LIKE THIS. THIS WAS CLEARLY SABOTAGE.
SOMEONE IN YOUR ARMY TRIED TO KILL YOU.
CLEARLY, YOU'VE MANAGED TO INSPIRE A LOT OF LOYALTY, HUX.
OH, PLEASE. I THOUGHT YOU COULD READ MINDS, REN. YOU HONESTLY BELIEVE PEOPLE HATE ***ME*** MORE THAN THEY HATE ***YOU?***
WITH YOUR PETULANT TANTRUMS AND YOUR...
AND MY WHAT?
VADER WORE HIS MASK BECAUSE HE COULDN'T BREATHE WITHOUT IT.
BUT YOU... YOU JUST PLAY DRESS-UP TO HIDE THE FACES OF YOUR REBEL SCUM PARENTS--

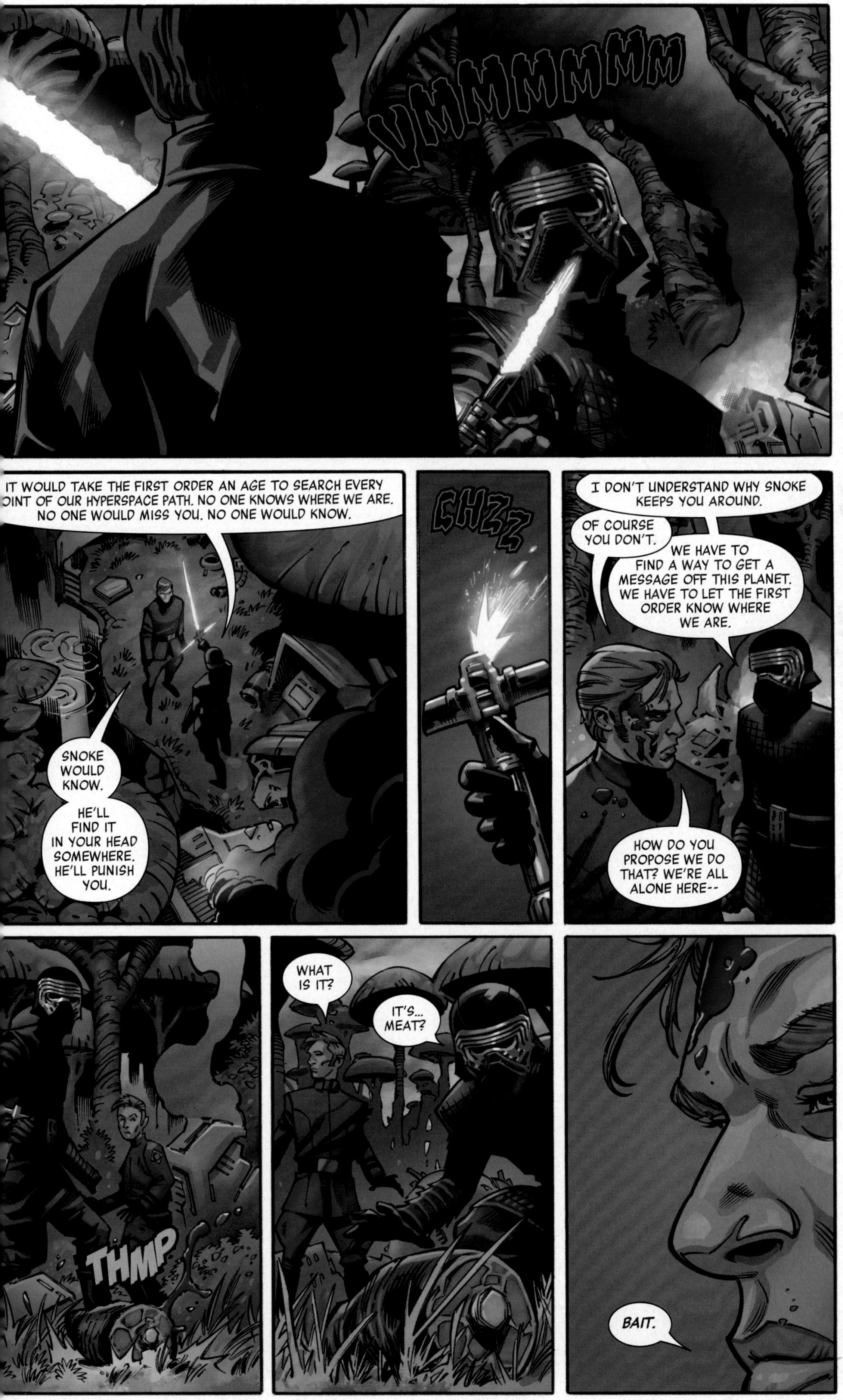
VMMMMMMM
IT WOULD TAKE THE FIRST ORDER AN AGE TO SEARCH EVERY POINT OF OUR HYPERSPACE PATH. NO ONE KNOWS WHERE WE ARE. NO ONE WOULD MISS YOU. NO ONE WOULD KNOW.
SNOKE WOULD KNOW.
HE'LL FIND IT IN YOUR HEAD SOMEWHERE. HE'LL PUNISH YOU.
CHZZ
I DON'T UNDERSTAND WHY SNOKE KEEPS YOU AROUND.
OF COURSE YOU DON'T.
WE HAVE TO FIND A WAY TO GET A MESSAGE OFF THIS PLANET. WE HAVE TO LET THE FIRST ORDER KNOW WHERE WE ARE.
HOW DO YOU PROPOSE WE DO THAT? WE'RE ALL ALONE HERE--
THMP
WHAT IS IT?
IT'S... MEAT?
BAIT.

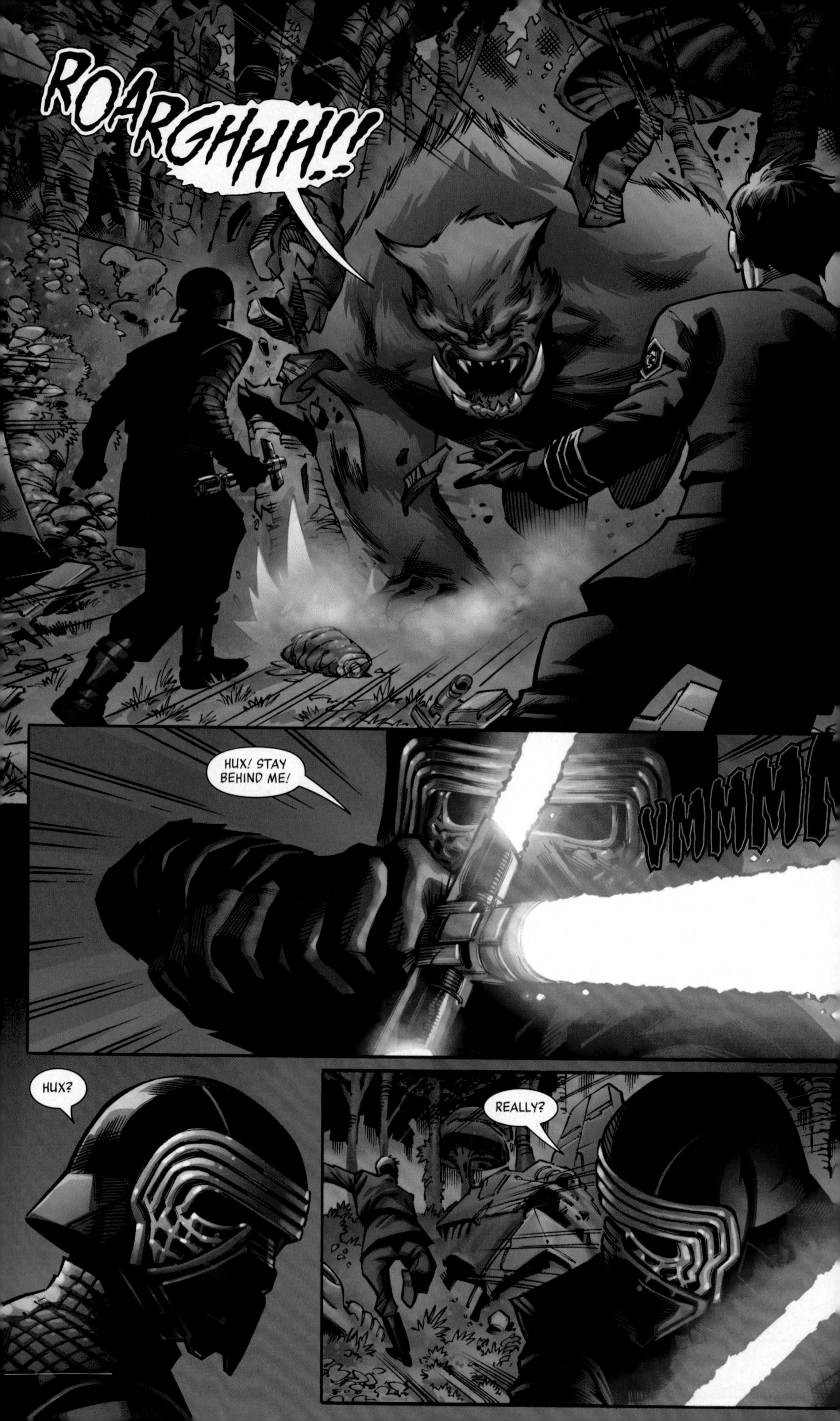
ROARGHHH!!
HUX! STAY BEHIND ME!
VMMMM
HUX?
REALLY?

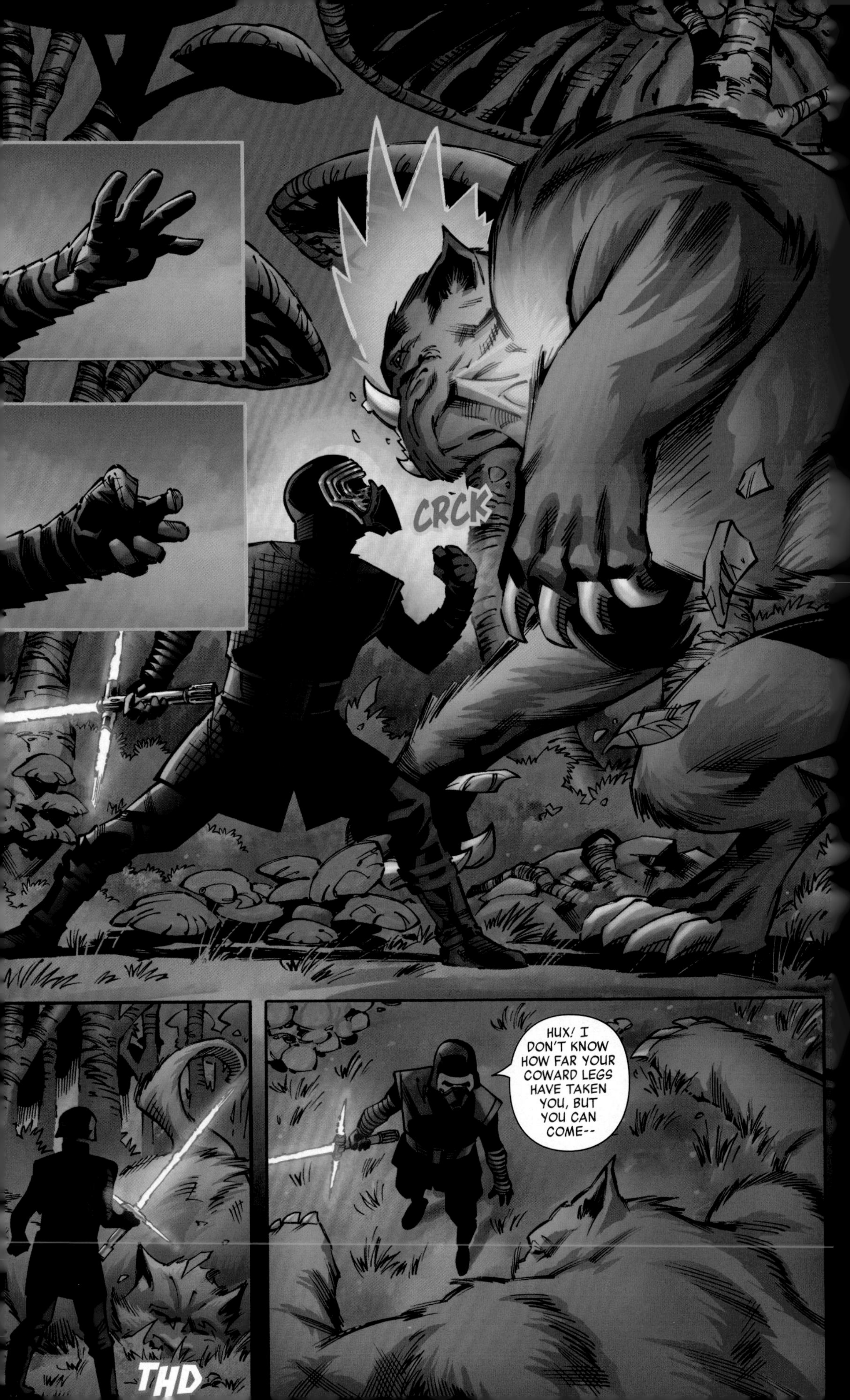
CRCK
THD
HUX! I DON'T KNOW HOW FAR YOUR COWARD LEGS HAVE TAKEN YOU, BUT YOU CAN COME--

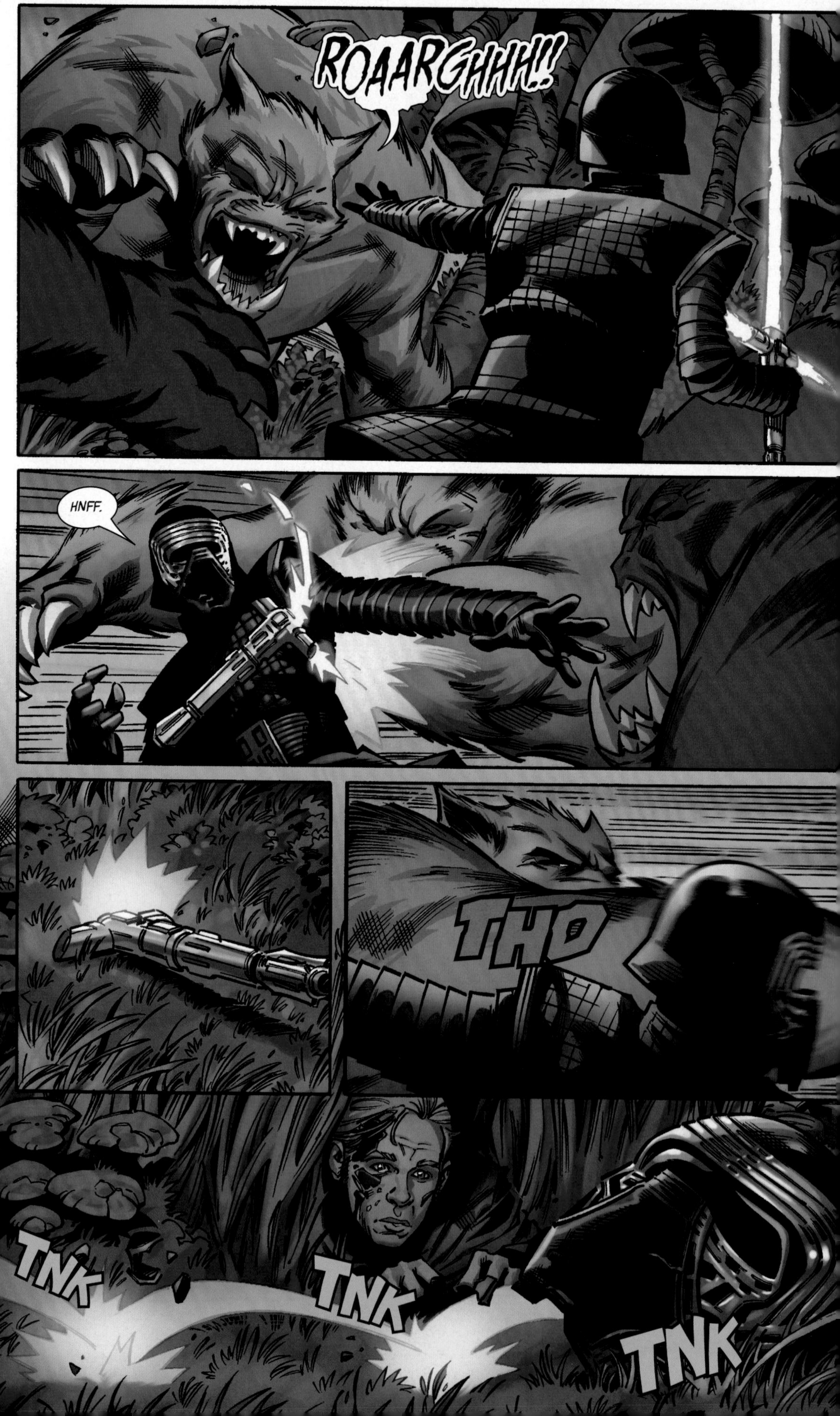
ROAARGHHH!!
HNFF.
THD
TNK
TNK
TNK

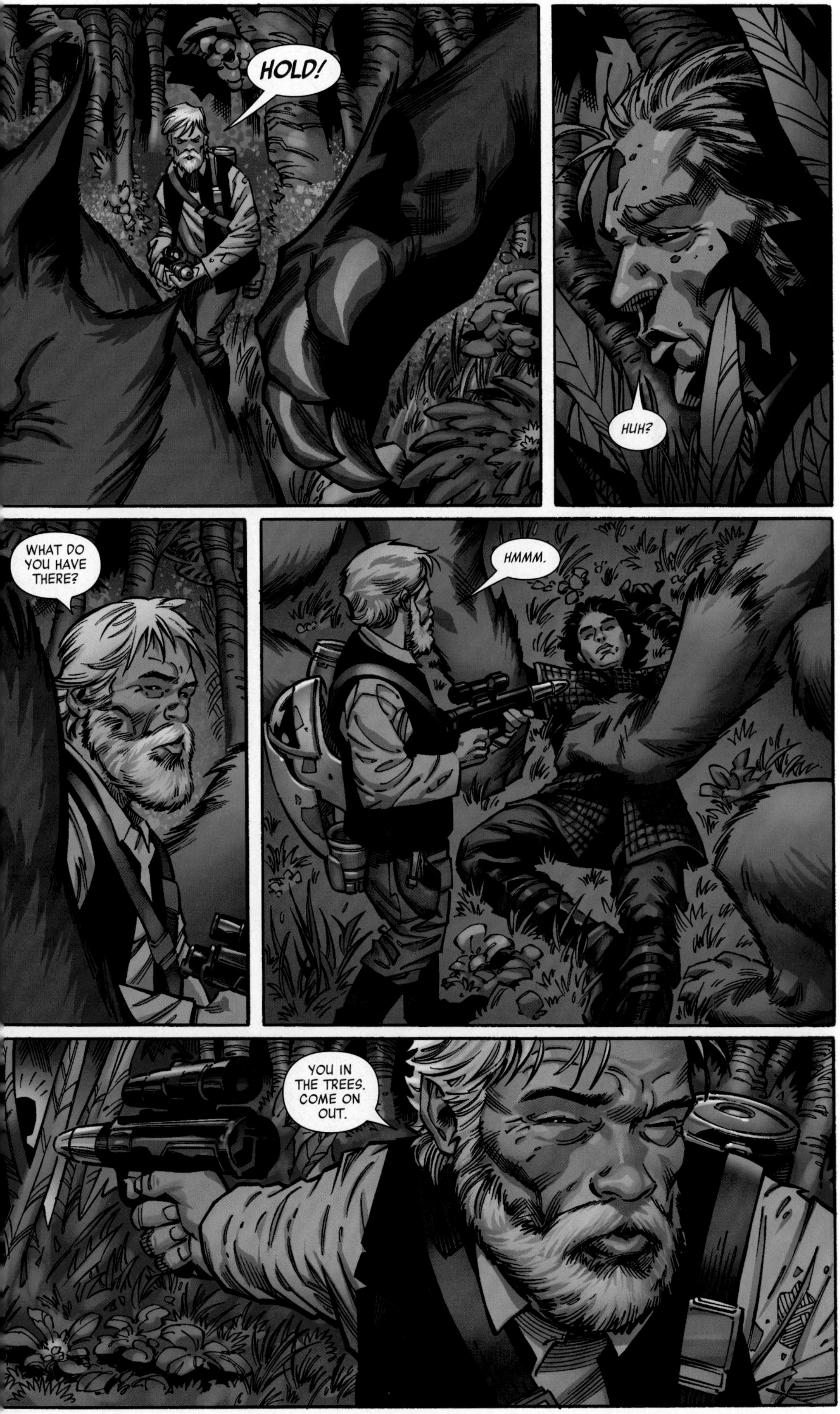
HOLD!
HUH?
WHAT DO YOU HAVE THERE?
HMMM.
YOU IN THE TREES. COME ON OUT.

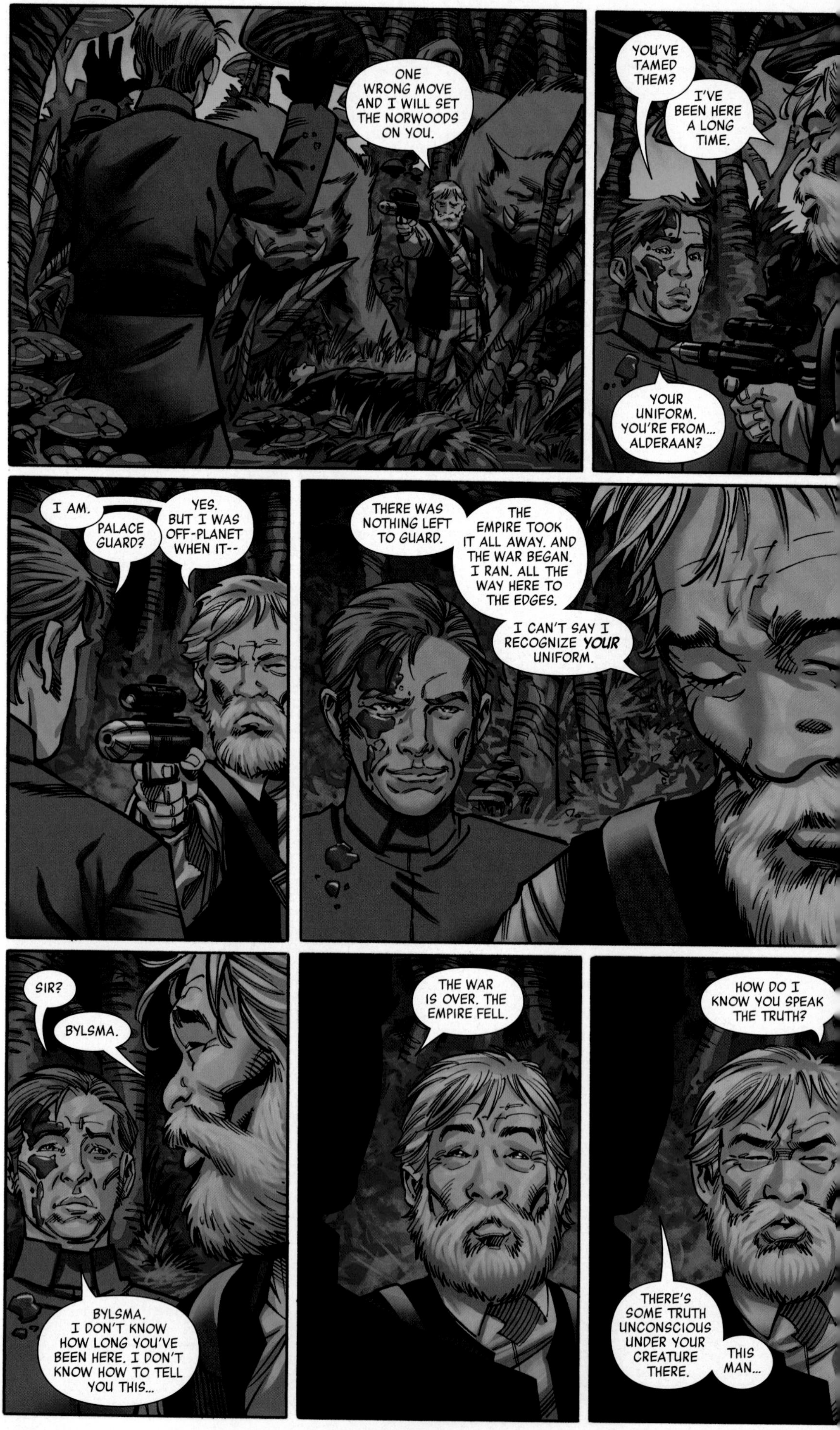
ONE WRONG MOVE AND I WILL SET THE NORWOODS ON YOU.
YOU'VE TAMED THEM?
I'VE BEEN HERE A LONG TIME.
YOUR UNIFORM. YOU'RE FROM... ALDERAAN?
I AM.
PALACE GUARD?
YES. BUT I WAS OFF-PLANET WHEN IT--
THERE WAS NOTHING LEFT TO GUARD.
THE EMPIRE TOOK IT ALL AWAY. AND THE WAR BEGAN. I RAN. ALL THE WAY HERE TO THE EDGES.
I CAN'T SAY I RECOGNIZE **YOUR** UNIFORM.
SIR?
BYLSMA.
BYLSMA. I DON'T KNOW HOW LONG YOU'VE BEEN HERE. I DON'T KNOW HOW TO TELL YOU THIS...
THE WAR IS OVER. THE EMPIRE FELL.
HOW DO I KNOW YOU SPEAK THE TRUTH?
THERE'S SOME TRUTH UNCONSCIOUS UNDER YOUR CREATURE THERE.
THIS MAN...

...HE IS A SON OF ALDERAAN. HIS MOTHER IS *LEIA ORGANA*.

PRINCESS LEIA?

I...I CAN SEE IT.

HIS PARENTS WON THE WAR.

THE DEATH STAR?

DESTROYED. *AND* THE SECOND ONE.

THEY BUILT *ANOTHER* ONE?

THE GALACTIC EMPIRE WAS NEVER RENOWNED FOR ITS CREATIVITY.

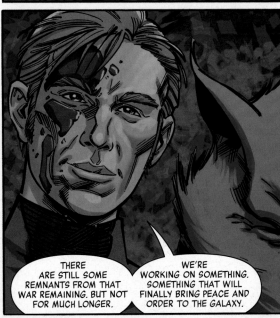

THERE ARE STILL SOME REMNANTS FROM THAT WAR REMAINING. BUT NOT FOR MUCH LONGER.

WE'RE WORKING ON SOMETHING. SOMETHING THAT WILL FINALLY BRING PEACE AND ORDER TO THE GALAXY.

I KNEW HIS GRANDFATHER. AND HIS MOTHER. SHE WAS AN INCREDIBLE WOMAN.

IS HE... IS HE LIKE HER?

HE IS. HE'D DENY IT. BUT HE'S VERY MUCH LIKE HER.

TELL ME. WHY ARE YOU STILL HERE?

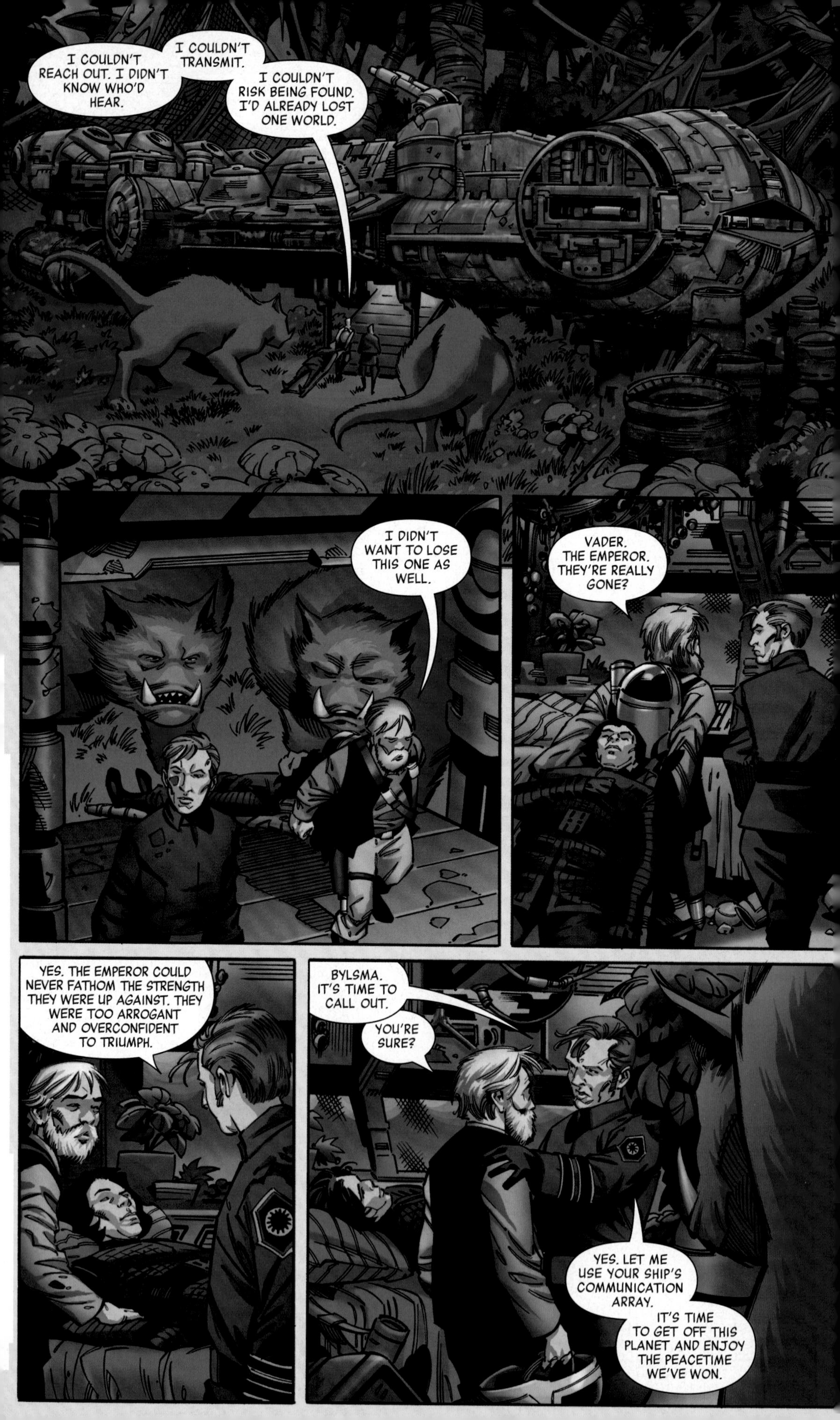
I COULDN'T REACH OUT. I DIDN'T KNOW WHO'D HEAR.
I COULDN'T TRANSMIT.
I COULDN'T RISK BEING FOUND. I'D ALREADY LOST ONE WORLD.
I DIDN'T WANT TO LOSE THIS ONE AS WELL.
VADER. THE EMPEROR. THEY'RE REALLY GONE?
YES. THE EMPEROR COULD NEVER FATHOM THE STRENGTH THEY WERE UP AGAINST. THEY WERE TOO ARROGANT AND OVERCONFIDENT TO TRIUMPH.
BYLSMA. IT'S TIME TO CALL OUT.
YOU'RE SURE?
YES. LET ME USE YOUR SHIP'S COMMUNICATION ARRAY.
IT'S TIME TO GET OFF THIS PLANET AND ENJOY THE PEACETIME WE'VE WON.

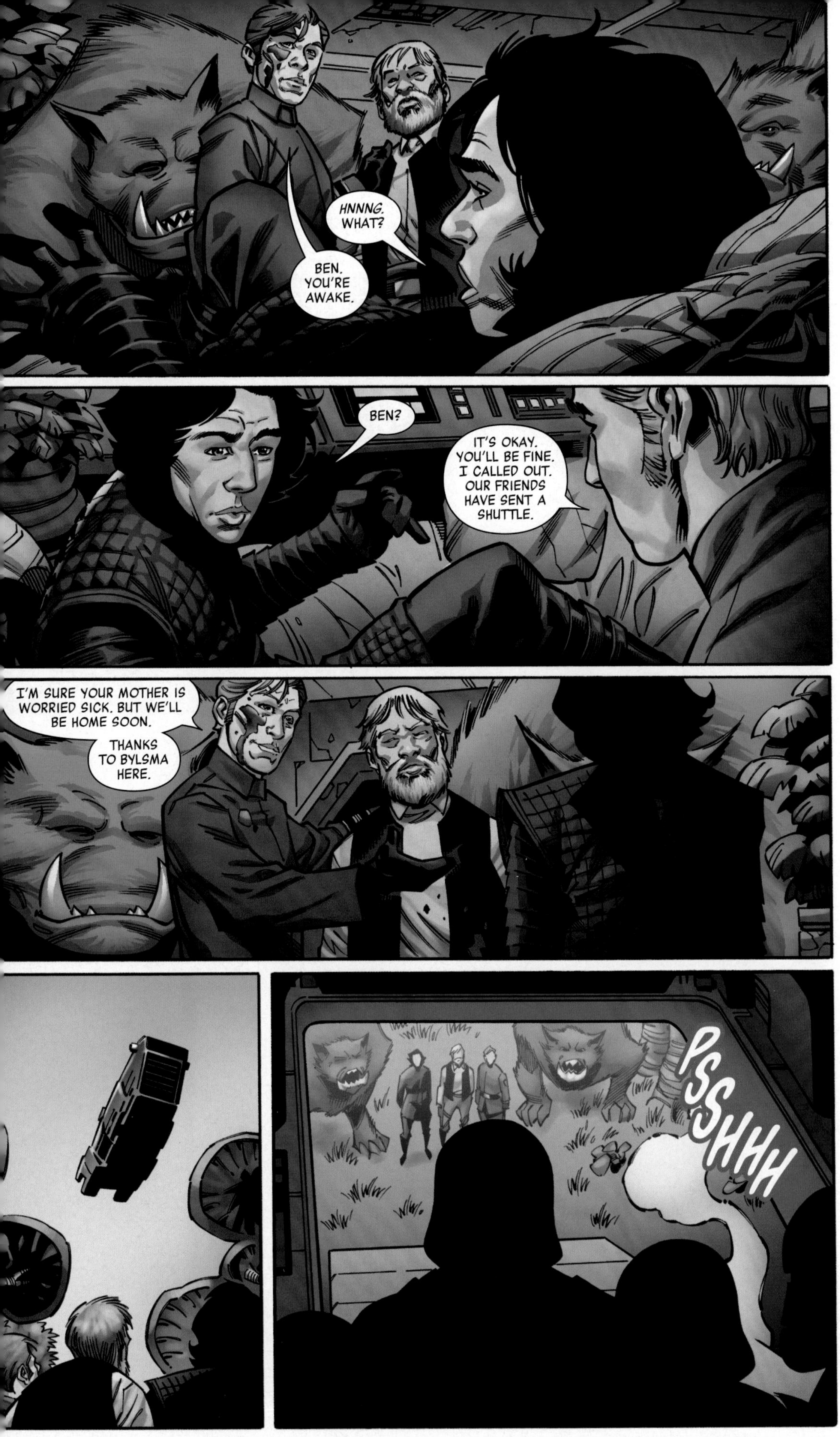
HNNNG. WHAT?
BEN. YOU'RE AWAKE.
BEN?
IT'S OKAY. YOU'LL BE FINE. I CALLED OUT. OUR FRIENDS HAVE SENT A SHUTTLE.
I'M SURE YOUR MOTHER IS WORRIED SICK. BUT WE'LL BE HOME SOON.
THANKS TO BYLSMA HERE.
PSSHHH

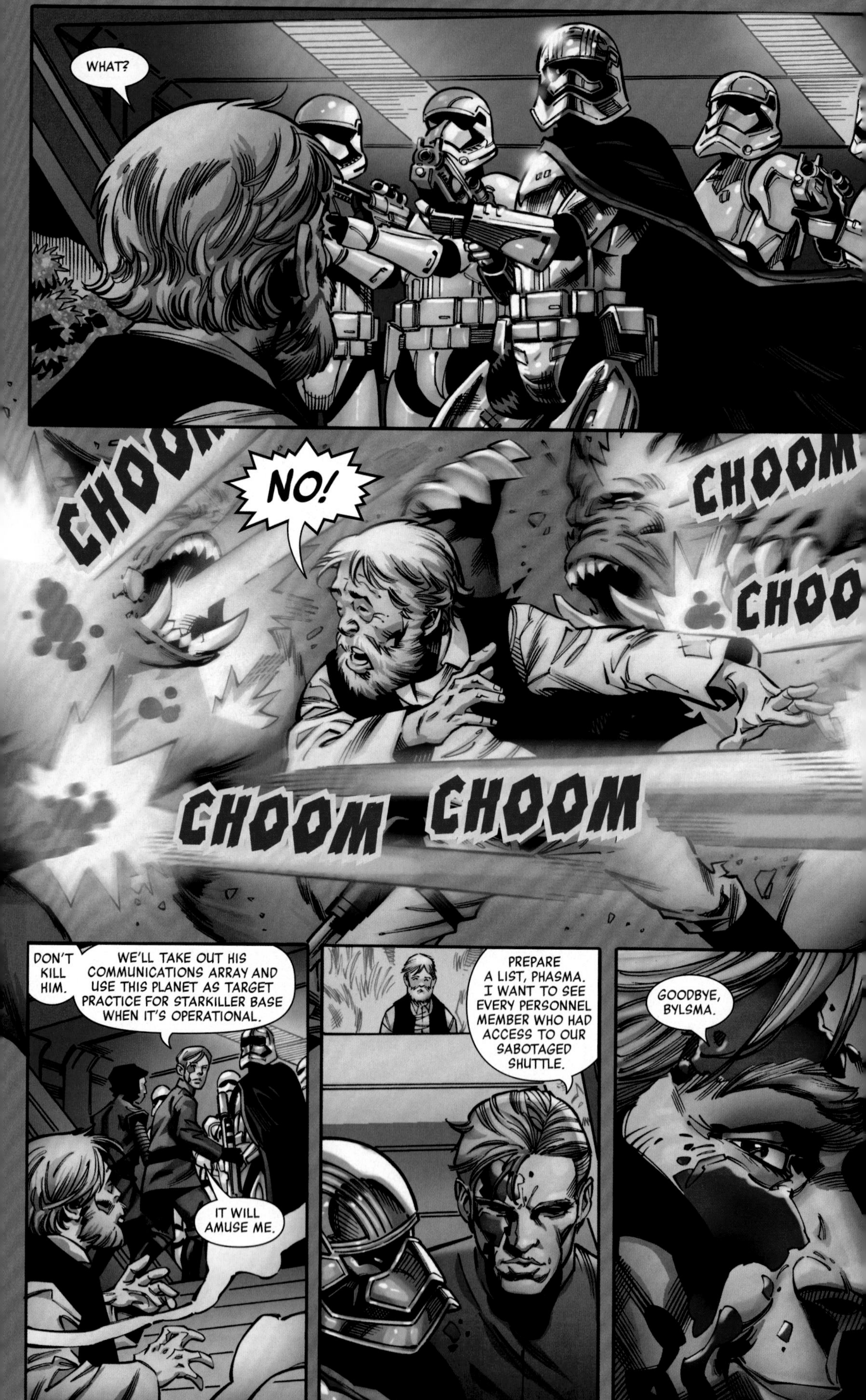
WHAT?
NO!
CHOOM
CHOOM
CHOO
CHOOM CHOOM
DON'T KILL HIM.
WE'LL TAKE OUT HIS COMMUNICATIONS ARRAY AND USE THIS PLANET AS TARGET PRACTICE FOR STARKILLER BASE WHEN IT'S OPERATIONAL.
IT WILL AMUSE ME.
PREPARE A LIST, PHASMA. I WANT TO SEE EVERY PERSONNEL MEMBER WHO HAD ACCESS TO OUR SABOTAGED SHUTTLE.
GOODBYE, BYLSMA.

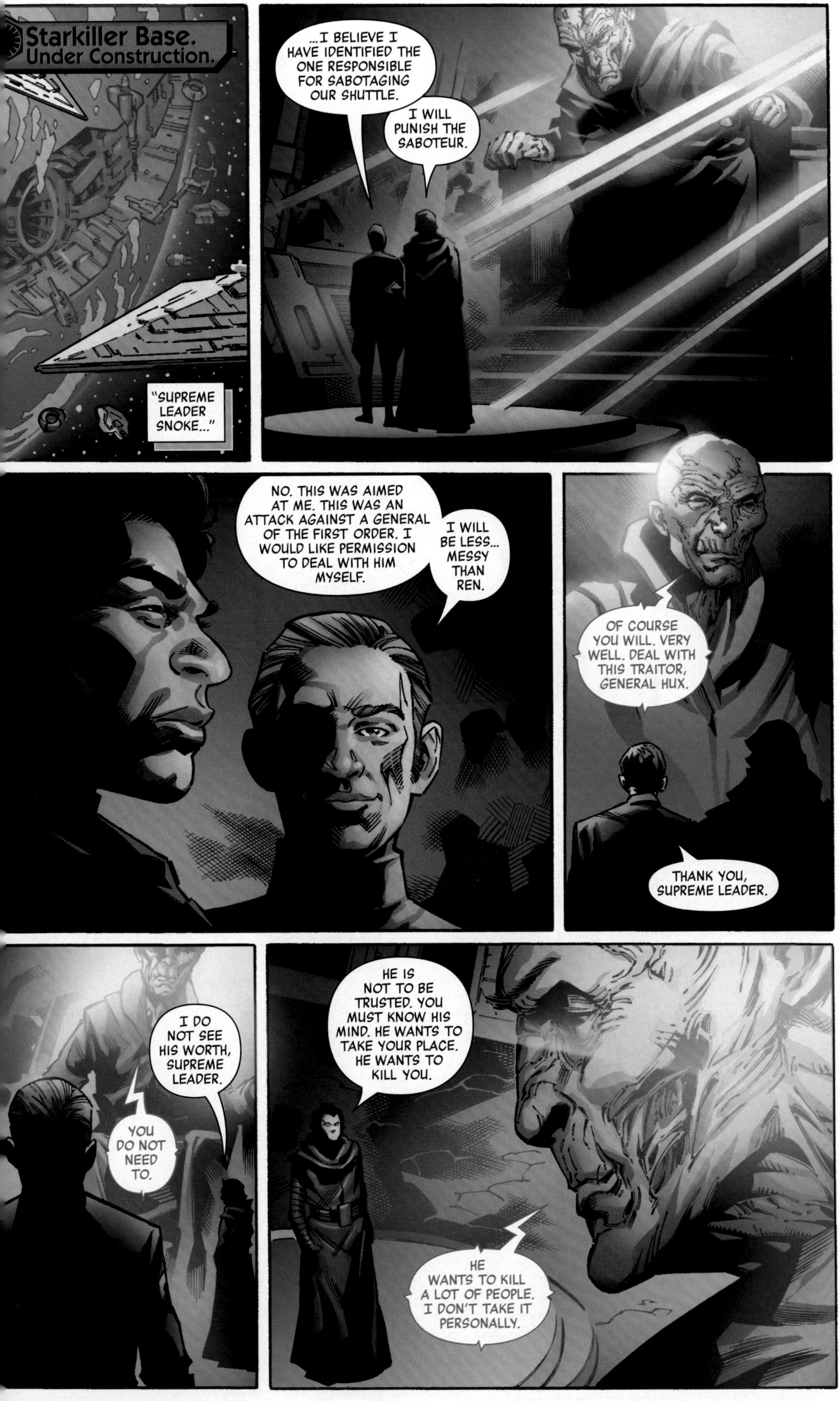
Starkiller Base.
Under Construction.
"SUPREME LEADER SNOKE..."
...I BELIEVE I HAVE IDENTIFIED THE ONE RESPONSIBLE FOR SABOTAGING OUR SHUTTLE.
I WILL PUNISH THE SABOTEUR.
NO. THIS WAS AIMED AT ME. THIS WAS AN ATTACK AGAINST A GENERAL OF THE FIRST ORDER. I WOULD LIKE PERMISSION TO DEAL WITH HIM MYSELF.
I WILL BE LESS... MESSY THAN REN.
OF COURSE YOU WILL. VERY WELL. DEAL WITH THIS TRAITOR, GENERAL HUX.
THANK YOU, SUPREME LEADER.
I DO NOT SEE HIS WORTH, SUPREME LEADER.
YOU DO NOT NEED TO.
HE IS NOT TO BE TRUSTED. YOU MUST KNOW HIS MIND. HE WANTS TO TAKE YOUR PLACE. HE WANTS TO KILL YOU.
HE WANTS TO KILL A LOT OF PEOPLE. I DON'T TAKE IT PERSONALLY.

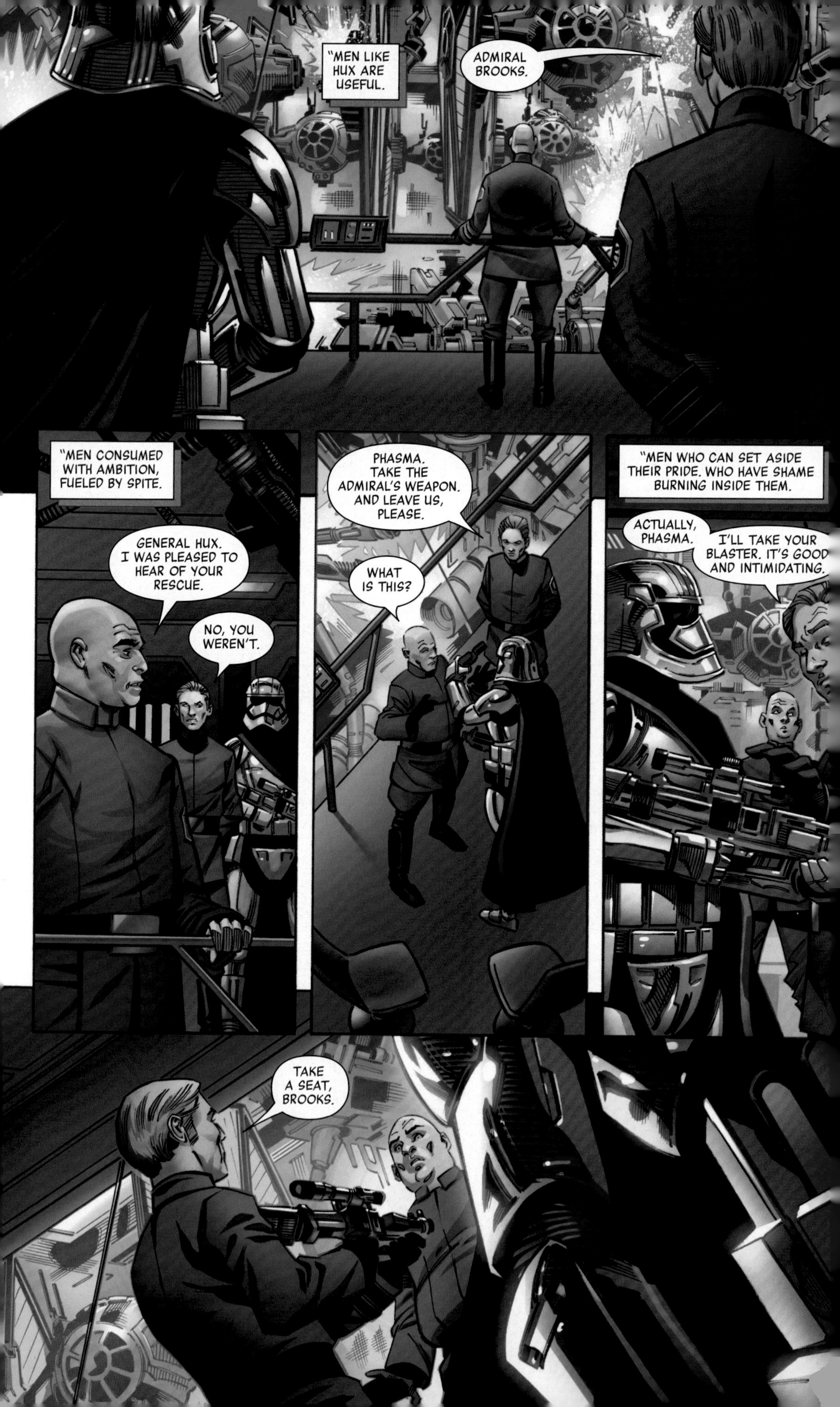
"MEN LIKE HUX ARE USEFUL.
ADMIRAL BROOKS.
"MEN CONSUMED WITH AMBITION, FUELED BY SPITE.
GENERAL HUX. I WAS PLEASED TO HEAR OF YOUR RESCUE.
NO, YOU WEREN'T.
PHASMA. TAKE THE ADMIRAL'S WEAPON. AND LEAVE US, PLEASE.
WHAT IS THIS?
"MEN WHO CAN SET ASIDE THEIR PRIDE. WHO HAVE SHAME BURNING INSIDE THEM.
ACTUALLY, PHASMA.
I'LL TAKE YOUR BLASTER. IT'S GOOD AND INTIMIDATING.
TAKE A SEAT, BROOKS.

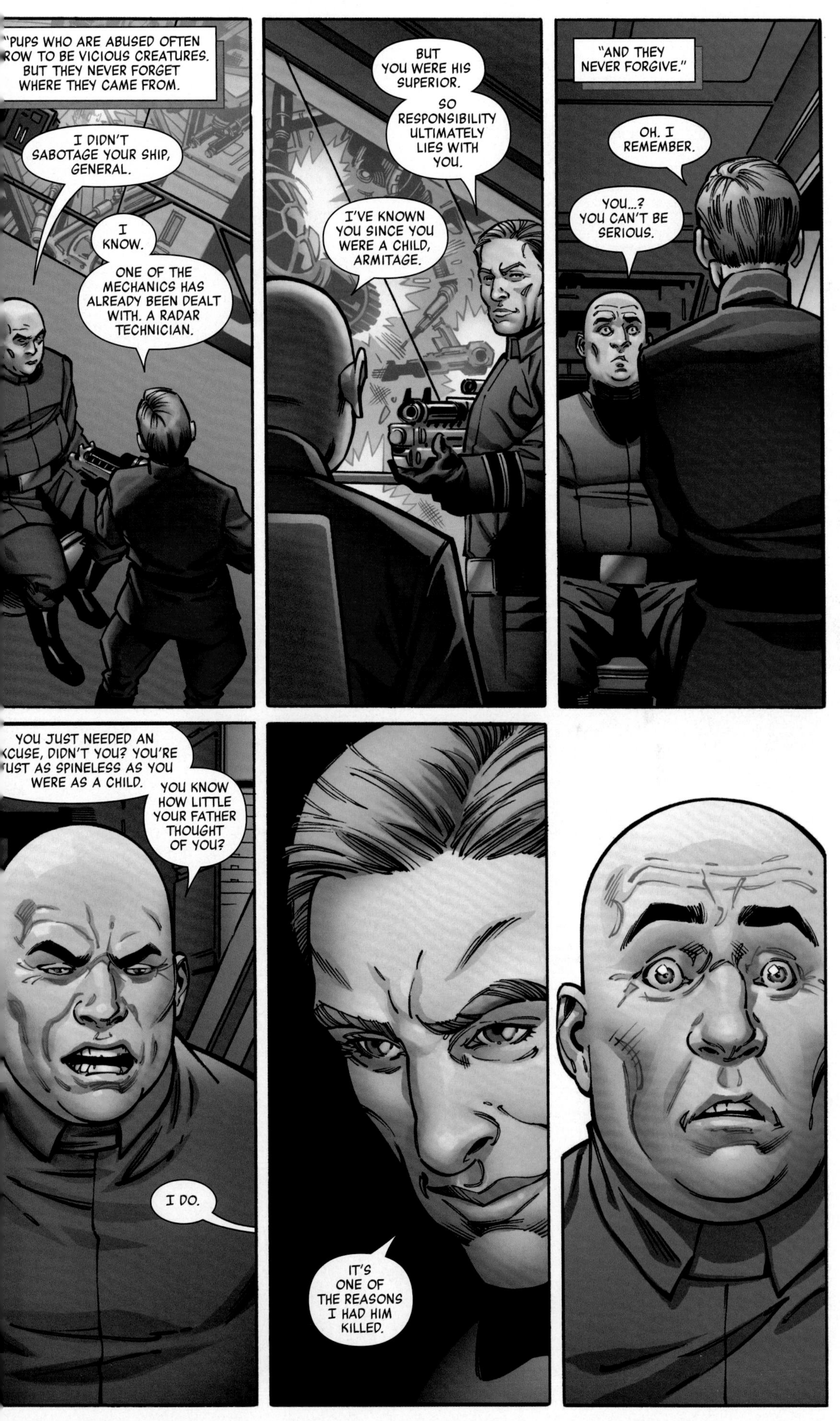

"PUPS WHO ARE ABUSED OFTEN ROW TO BE VICIOUS CREATURES. BUT THEY NEVER FORGET WHERE THEY CAME FROM.
I DIDN'T SABOTAGE YOUR SHIP, GENERAL.
I KNOW.
ONE OF THE MECHANICS HAS ALREADY BEEN DEALT WITH. A RADAR TECHNICIAN.
BUT YOU WERE HIS SUPERIOR.
SO RESPONSIBILITY ULTIMATELY LIES WITH YOU.
I'VE KNOWN YOU SINCE YOU WERE A CHILD, ARMITAGE.
"AND THEY NEVER FORGIVE."
OH. I REMEMBER.
YOU...? YOU CAN'T BE SERIOUS.
YOU JUST NEEDED AN XCUSE, DIDN'T YOU? YOU'RE UST AS SPINELESS AS YOU WERE AS A CHILD.
YOU KNOW HOW LITTLE YOUR FATHER THOUGHT OF YOU?
I DO.
IT'S ONE OF THE REASONS I HAD HIM KILLED.

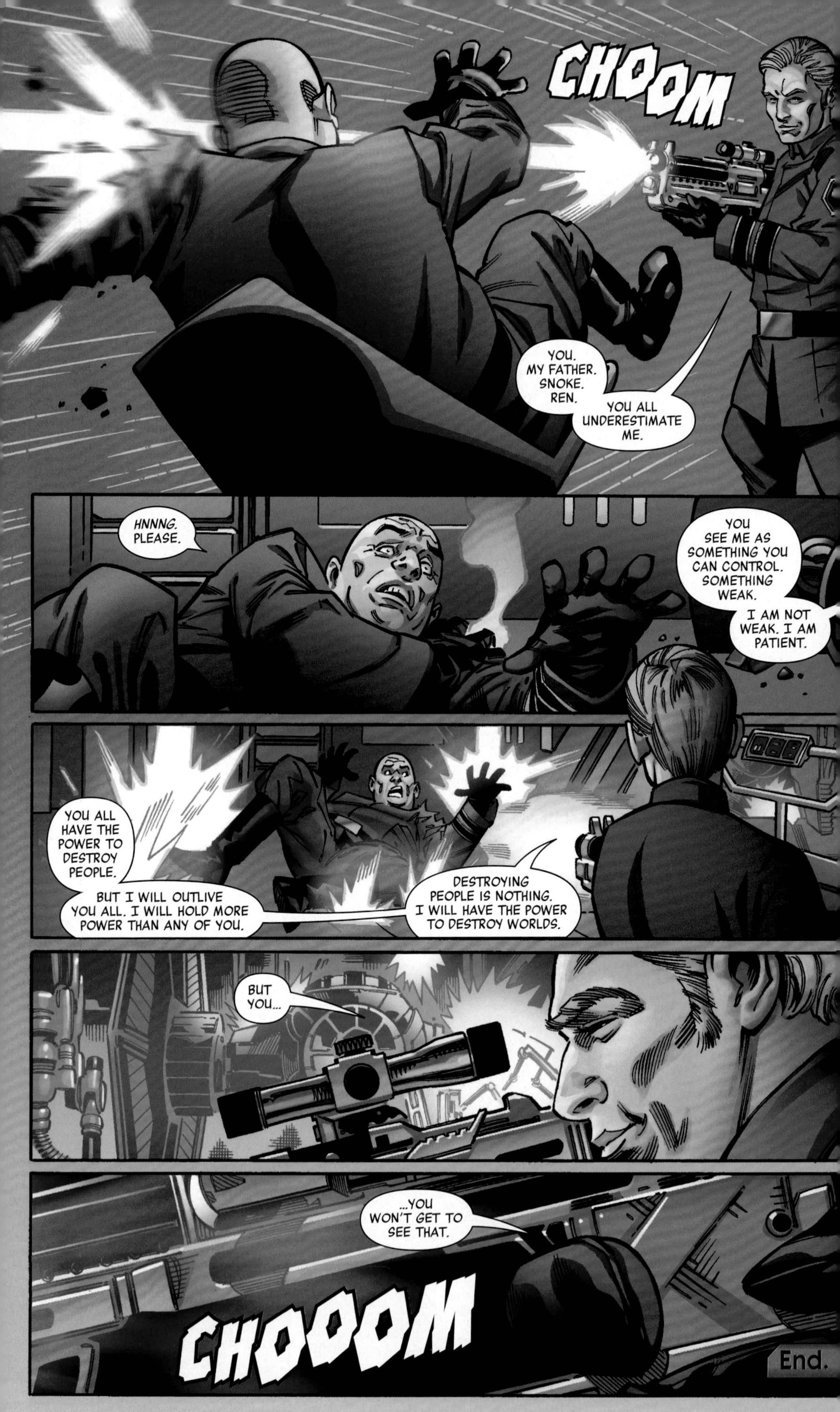
CHOOM
YOU. MY FATHER. SNOKE. REN.
YOU ALL UNDERESTIMATE ME.
HNNNG. PLEASE.
YOU SEE ME AS SOMETHING YOU CAN CONTROL. SOMETHING WEAK.
I AM NOT WEAK. I AM PATIENT.
YOU ALL HAVE THE POWER TO DESTROY PEOPLE.
BUT I WILL OUTLIVE YOU ALL. I WILL HOLD MORE POWER THAN ANY OF YOU.
DESTROYING PEOPLE IS NOTHING. I WILL HAVE THE POWER TO DESTROY WORLDS.
BUT YOU...
...YOU WON'T GET TO SEE THAT.
CHOOOM
End.

AGE OF RESISTANCE -
General Hux: Grudges and Galactic Domination
By Bria LaVorgna

How does a bastard orphan, the son of a kitchen woman and a commandant, dropped in the middle of the Unknown Regions by a shattered Empire, grow up to be a general and a planet killer? Hint: It involved a little bit of murder.

General Armitage Hux is not a nice man. Instead, he is what his upbringing and the galaxy made him: ruthless and hell-bent on proving himself no matter how long it takes or what the cost. While nothing can excuse ordering the destruction of an entire star system and the murder of everyone on those planets, it's difficult to see how he could have possibly become anything else, except perhaps a mere cog in the First Order wheel.

Even from a young age, Armitage's role was made clear to him. The Empire may have needed children, and the First Order doubly so, but that didn't mean Commandant Brendol Hux treated his illegitimate son kindly. Instead, he referred to his child as being "a weak-willed boy...thin as a slip of paper and just as useless," and his abuses hardly stopped there. It's no wonder why Armitage wasn't broken up about coordinating his father's death with

Captain Phasma. Perhaps the only person who engaged with a young Armitage with any sort of respect was Grand Admiral Rae Sloane. After the Battle of Jakku, she made a deal with him: He would protect her from the vicious orphans who would become the first class of new stormtroopers, and in return, she would protect him from his father. Precisely how far and how long that protection went is unknown, but she certainly delivered the message to Brendol rather pointedly. With her fists.

There is an ironic duality to how Hux is viewed within the First Order, especially once he achieved the rank of general. To the legions of stormtroopers, he is above them and better than them in every way, the heir to Brendol's legacy and in charge of the trooper education program. Among the officers and elite, though, respect is somewhat lacking. Snoke refers to him as a useful yet rabid cur, and older ranking officers who were a part of the Empire chafe at having to serve under someone so inexperienced. Captain Canady even referred to Hux as a "bloody idiot." With respect from one side and disdain from the other, it's little wonder why there are so few whom Hux actually trusts.

At least with Kylo Ren, the dynamic between the two men is straightforward: an intense, openly antagonistic rivalry without pretense. By the end of *The Last Jedi*, the competition is as dead as Snoke as Kylo takes the throne after a forceful reminder to Armitage regarding his strength and powers. They are no longer equals, and Hux must bow. But, if Kylo is smart, he'll keep an eye out for the knife Hux keeps up his sleeve.

Domhnall Gleeson summed his character up succinctly in an interview with the *Huffington Post*: "He knows that he's always on the edge of losing everything. He's just desperate to maintain position and to improve, and as a result he's just a very nasty piece of work." After the destruction of Starkiller Base, Hux was repeatedly knocked down (literally) and kicked (metaphorically). It is a situation that makes him more dangerous than any of his enemies within the First Order could possibly imagine. When the day finally comes that he's pushed too far, it won't just be the Resistance in the line of fire.

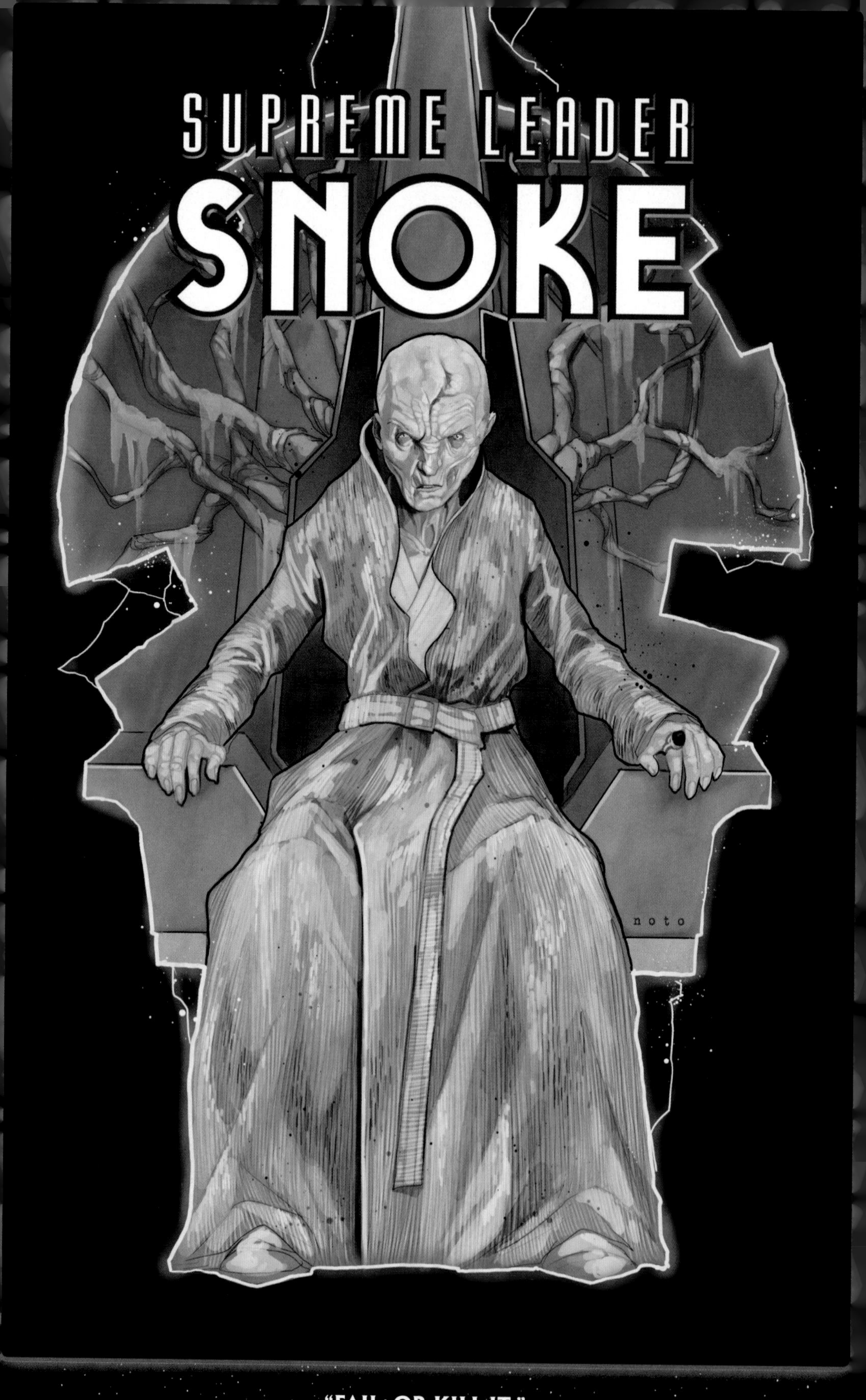
SUPREME LEADER
SNOKE
noto

"FAIL. OR KILL IT."

From the ashes of the evil Galactic Empire rises the First Order, a villainous sect of fanatics united by their Supreme Leader, Snoke. With a promising new apprentice and the limitless power of the dark side of the Force to command, Snoke is poised to crush the New Republic and take over the galaxy.

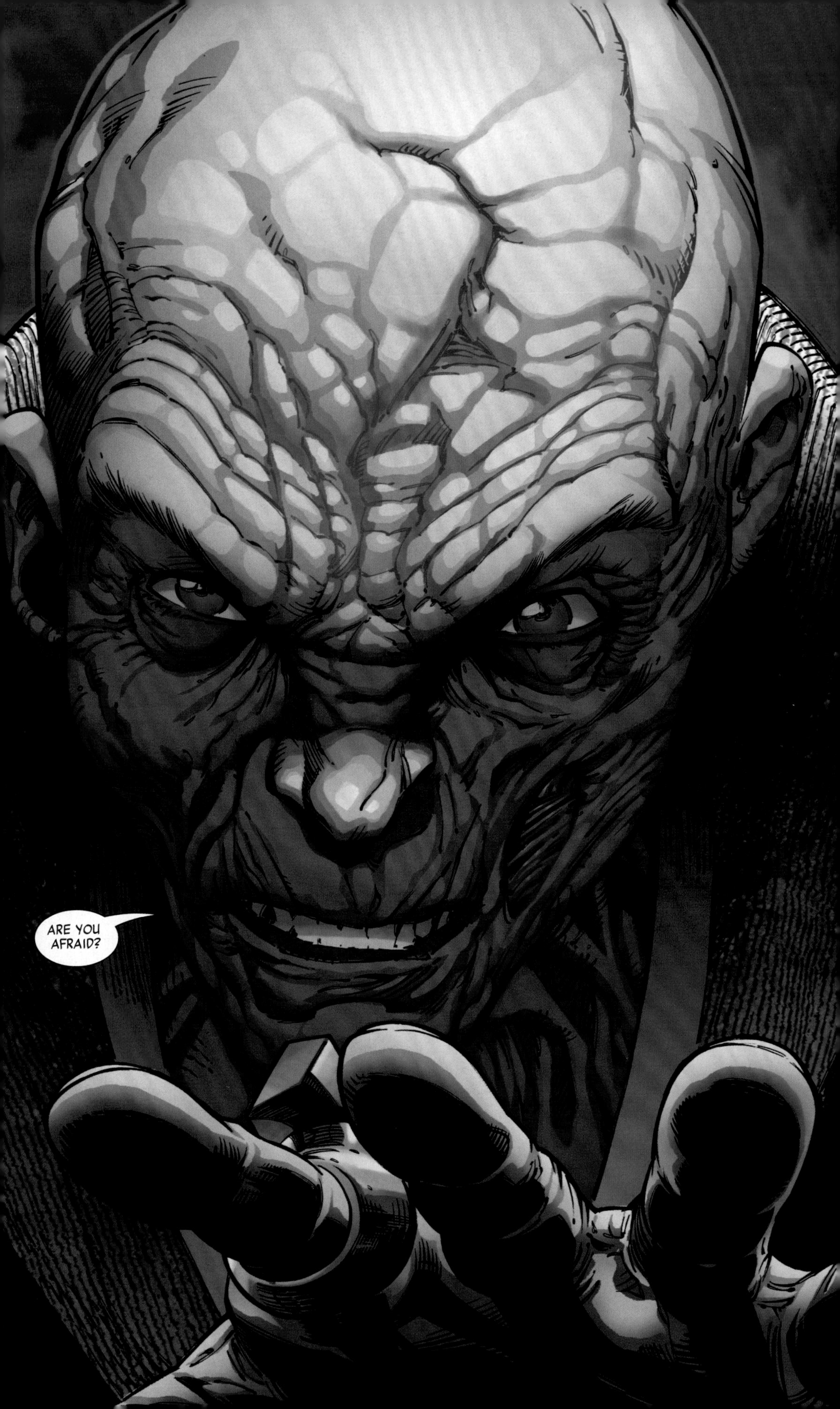

ARE YOU AFRAID?

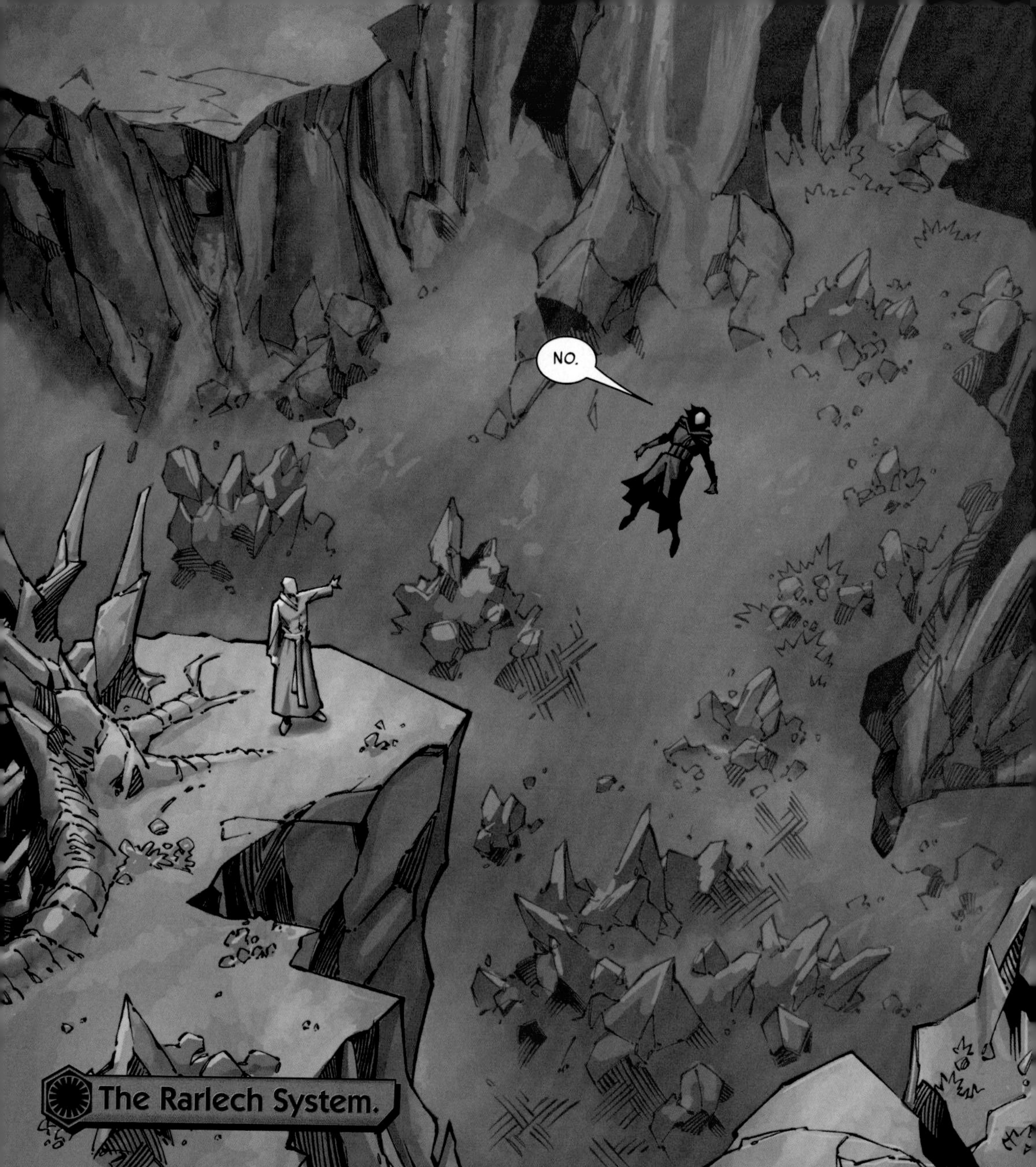
NO.
The Rarlech System.

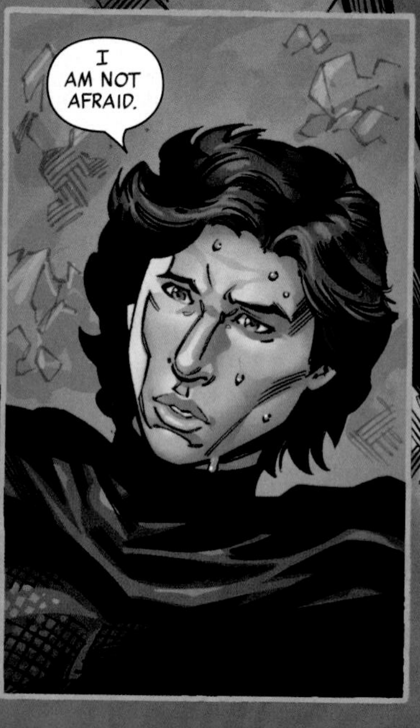
I AM NOT AFRAID.

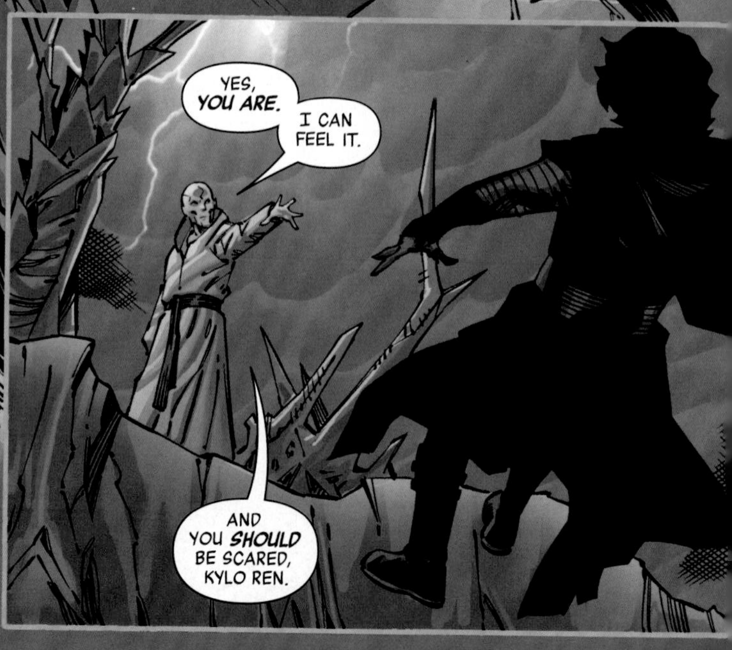
YES, YOU ARE.
I CAN FEEL IT.
AND YOU SHOULD BE SCARED, KYLO REN.

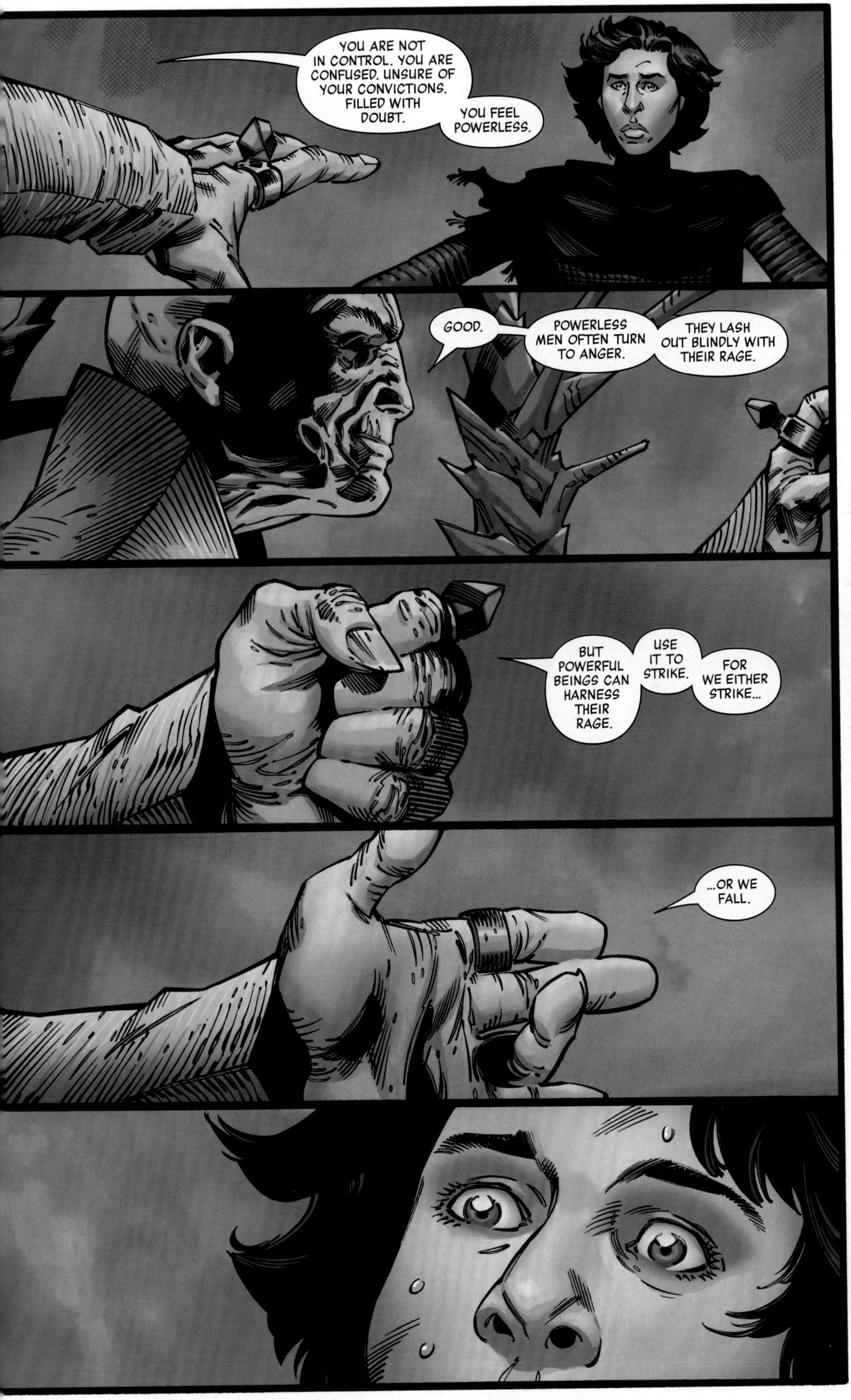
YOU ARE NOT IN CONTROL. YOU ARE CONFUSED. UNSURE OF YOUR CONVICTIONS. FILLED WITH DOUBT.
YOU FEEL POWERLESS.
GOOD.
POWERLESS MEN OFTEN TURN TO ANGER.
THEY LASH OUT BLINDLY WITH THEIR RAGE.
BUT POWERFUL BEINGS CAN HARNESS THEIR RAGE.
USE IT TO STRIKE.
FOR WE EITHER STRIKE...
...OR WE FALL.

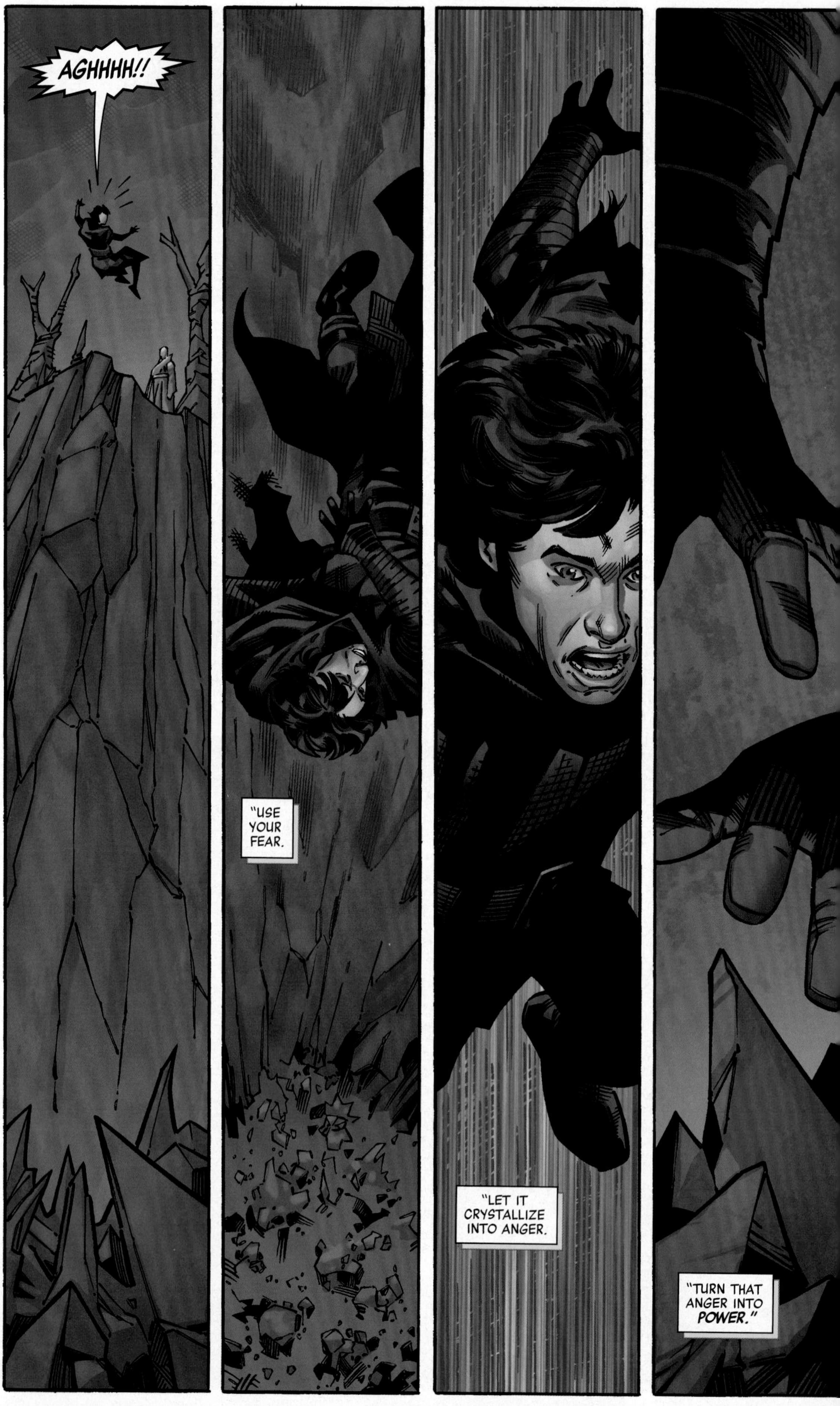
AGHHHH!!
"USE YOUR FEAR.
"LET IT CRYSTALLIZE INTO ANGER.
"TURN THAT ANGER INTO POWER."

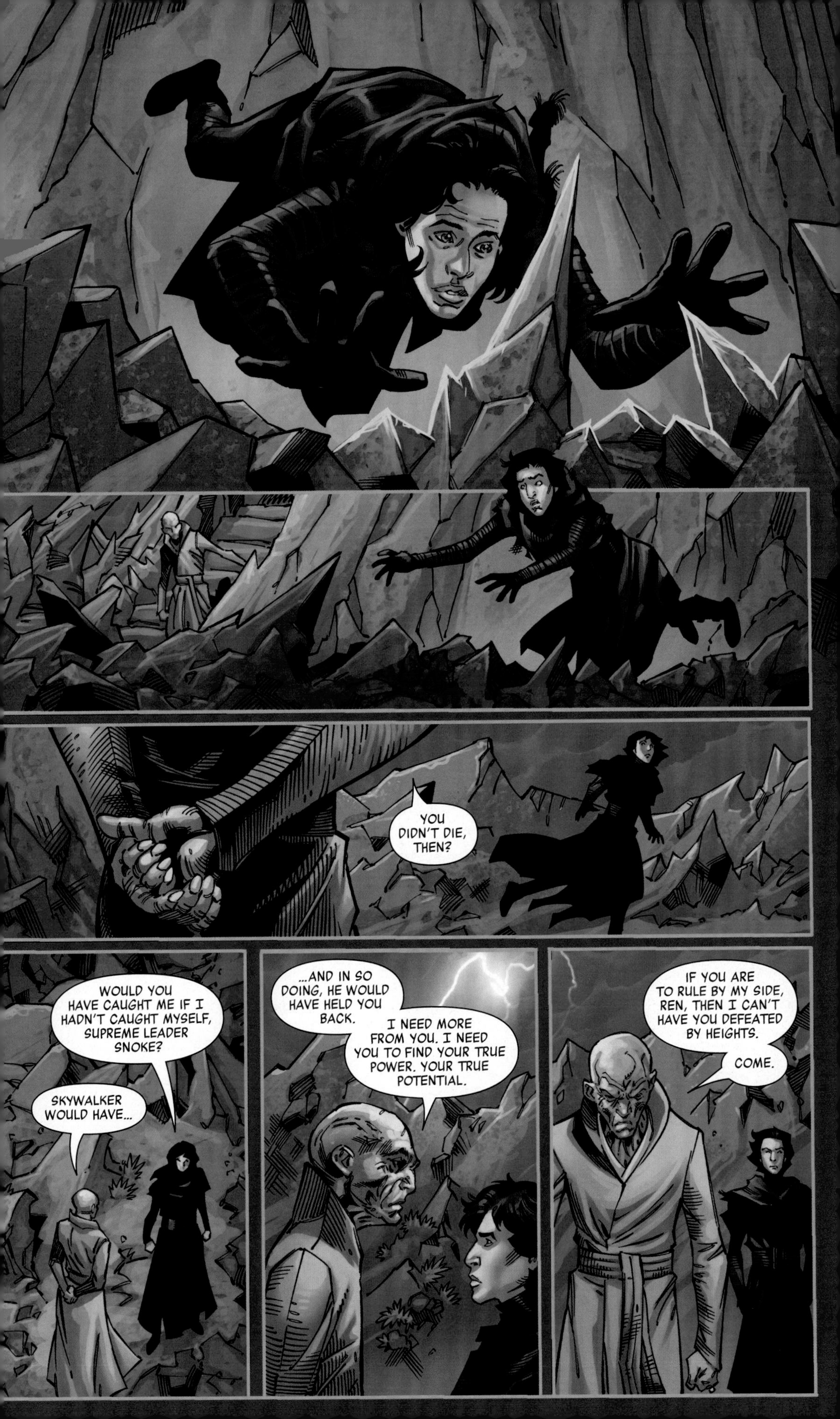
YOU DIDN'T DIE, THEN?
WOULD YOU HAVE CAUGHT ME IF I HADN'T CAUGHT MYSELF, SUPREME LEADER SNOKE?
SKYWALKER WOULD HAVE...
...AND IN SO DOING, HE WOULD HAVE HELD YOU BACK.
I NEED MORE FROM YOU. I NEED YOU TO FIND YOUR TRUE POWER. YOUR TRUE POTENTIAL.
IF YOU ARE TO RULE BY MY SIDE, REN, THEN I CAN'T HAVE YOU DEFEATED BY HEIGHTS.
COME.

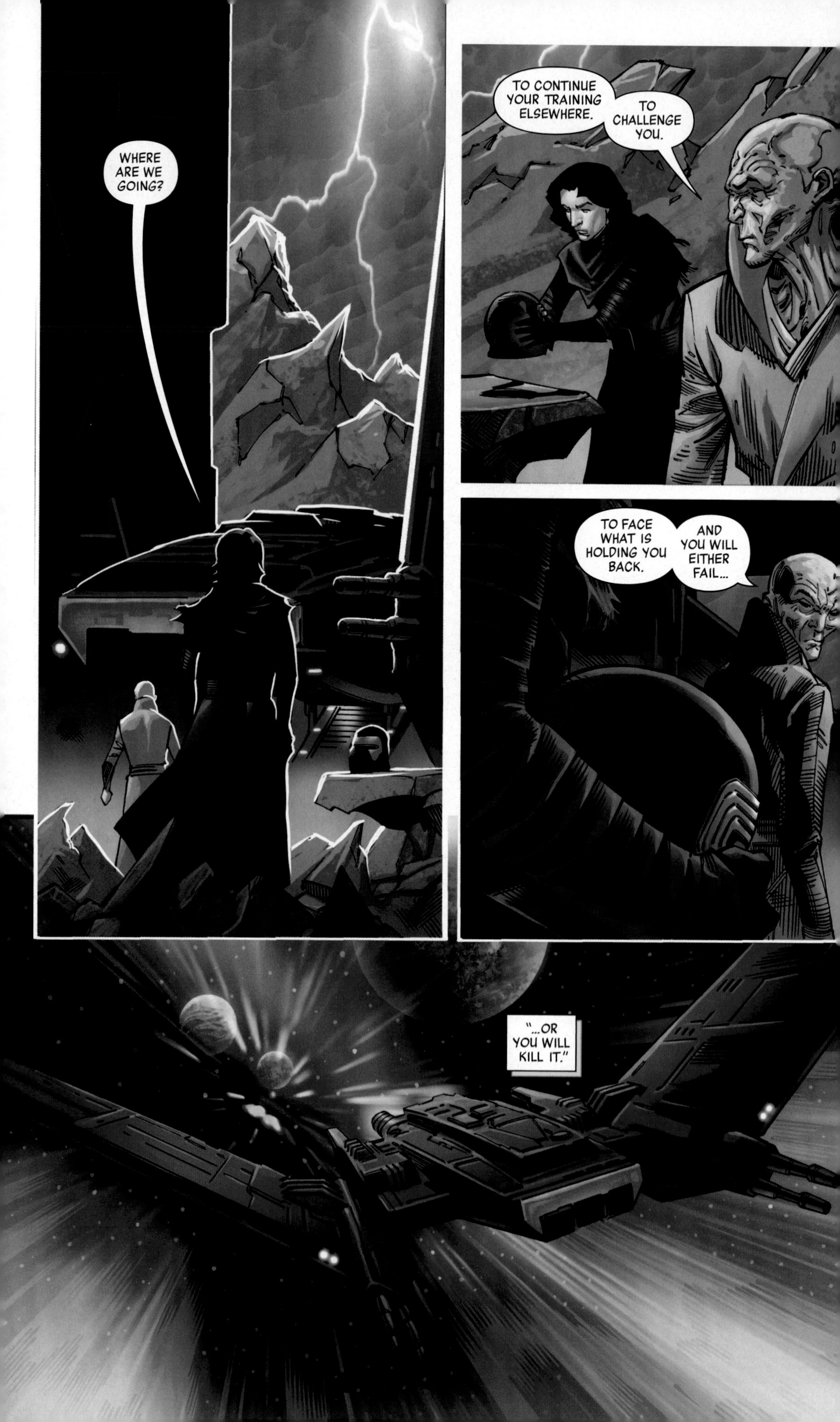
WHERE ARE WE GOING?
TO CONTINUE YOUR TRAINING ELSEWHERE.
TO CHALLENGE YOU.
TO FACE WHAT IS HOLDING YOU BACK.
AND YOU WILL EITHER FAIL...
"...OR YOU WILL KILL IT."

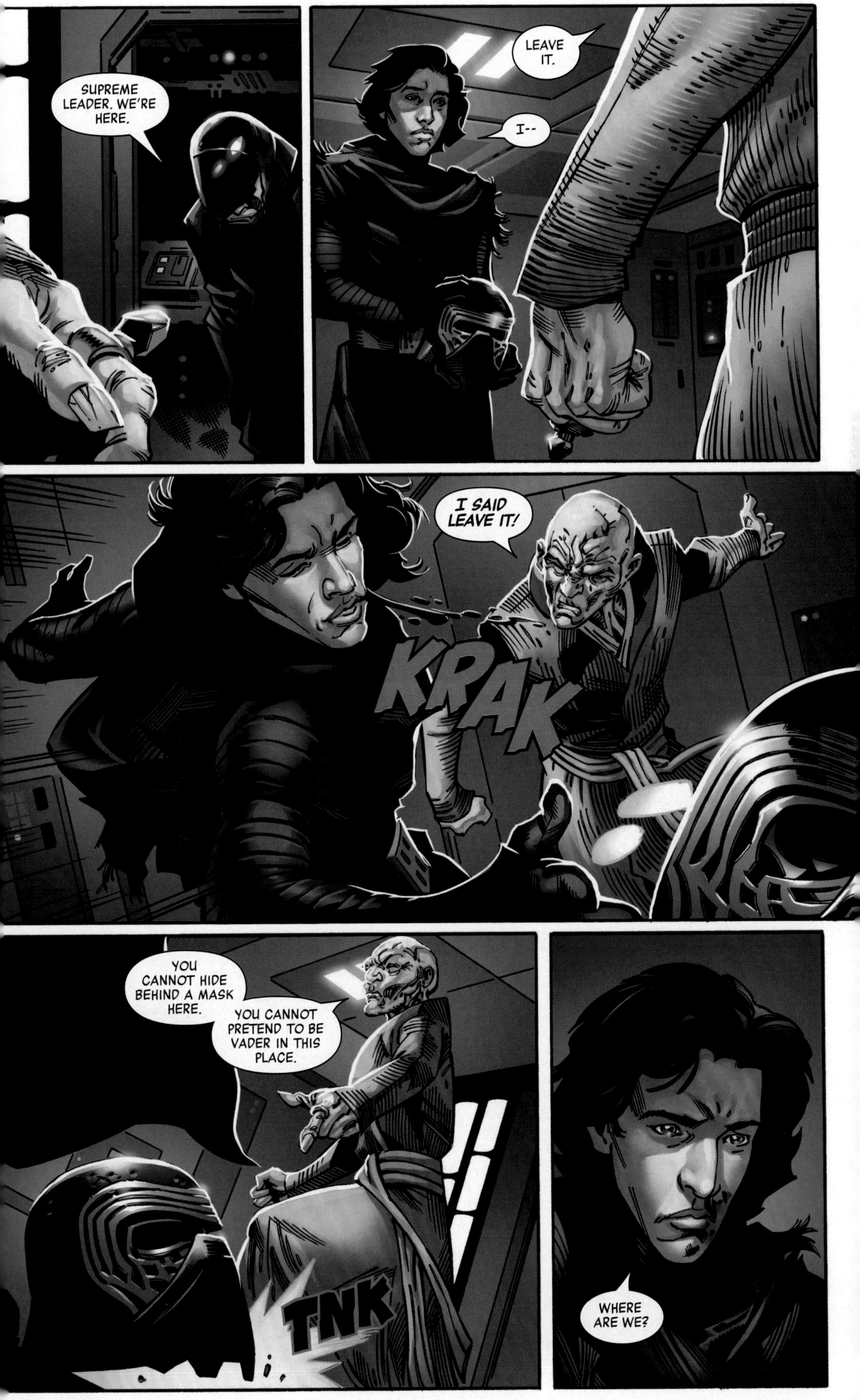
SUPREME LEADER. WE'RE HERE.
LEAVE IT.
I--
I SAID LEAVE IT!
KRAK
YOU CANNOT HIDE BEHIND A MASK HERE.
YOU CANNOT PRETEND TO BE VADER IN THIS PLACE.
TNK
WHERE ARE WE?

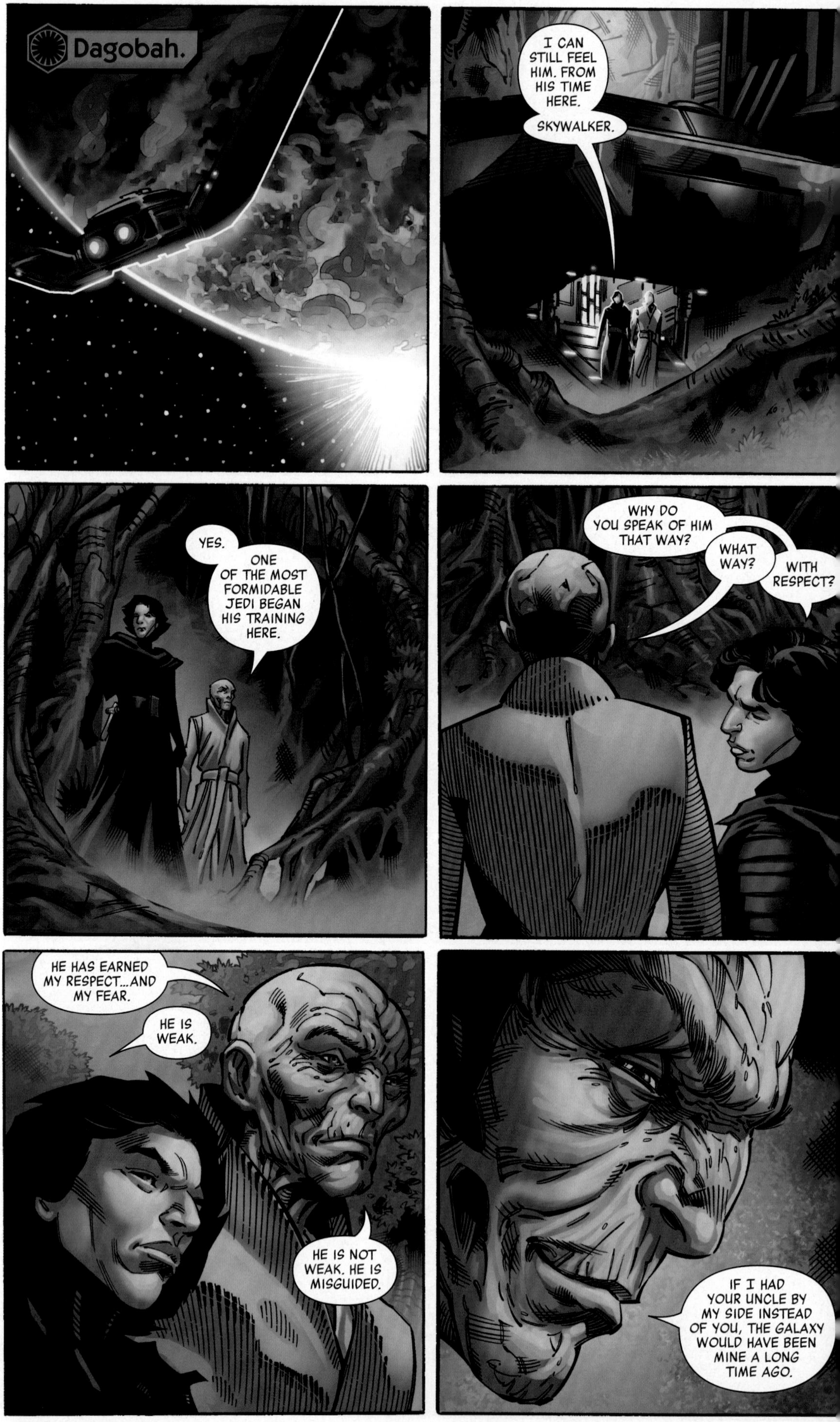
Dagobah.
I CAN STILL FEEL HIM. FROM HIS TIME HERE.
SKYWALKER.
YES.
ONE OF THE MOST FORMIDABLE JEDI BEGAN HIS TRAINING HERE.
WHY DO YOU SPEAK OF HIM THAT WAY?
WHAT WAY?
WITH RESPECT?
HE HAS EARNED MY RESPECT...AND MY FEAR.
HE IS WEAK.
HE IS NOT WEAK. HE IS MISGUIDED.
IF I HAD YOUR UNCLE BY MY SIDE INSTEAD OF YOU, THE GALAXY WOULD HAVE BEEN MINE A LONG TIME AGO.

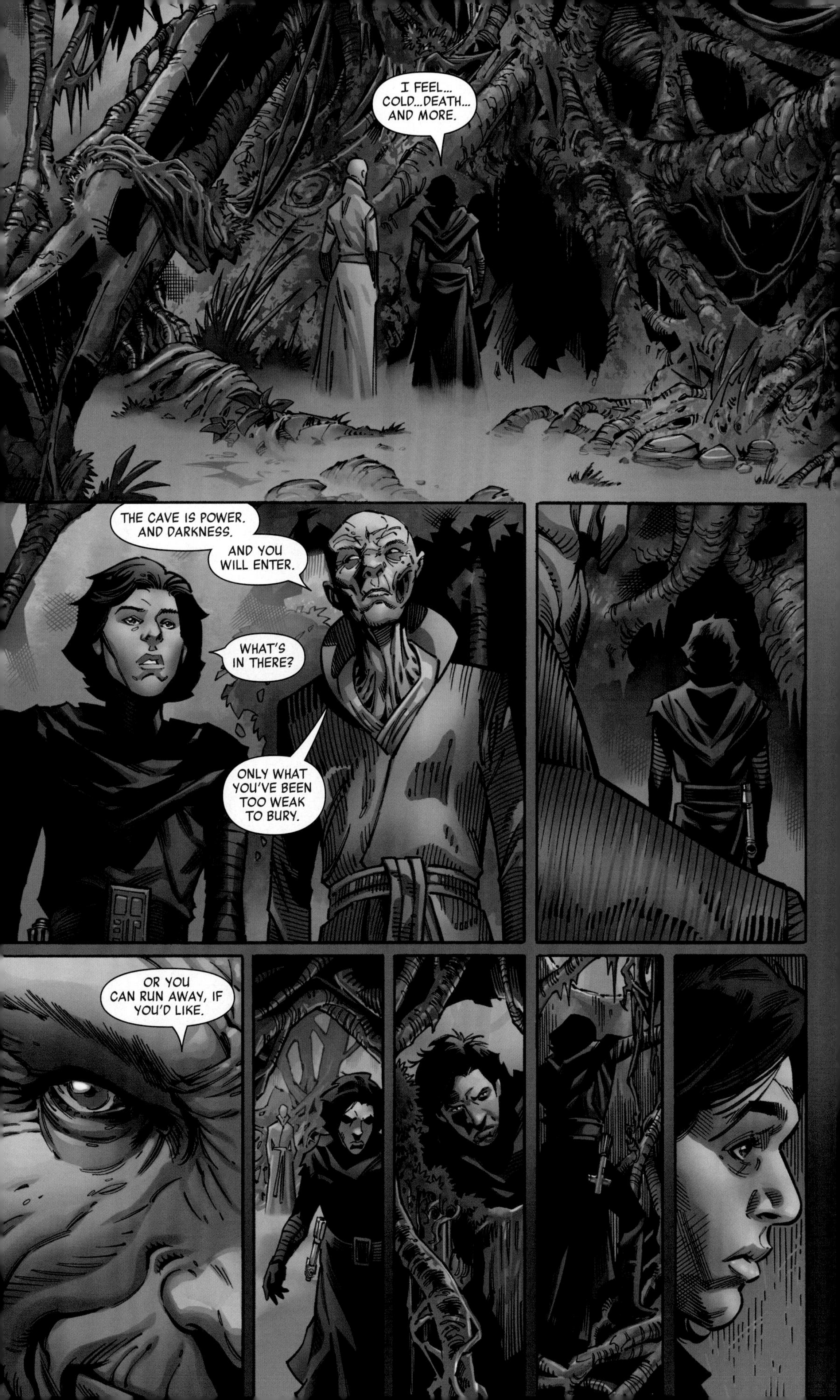
I FEEL... COLD...DEATH... AND MORE.
THE CAVE IS POWER. AND DARKNESS.
AND YOU WILL ENTER.
WHAT'S IN THERE?
ONLY WHAT YOU'VE BEEN TOO WEAK TO BURY.
OR YOU CAN RUN AWAY, IF YOU'D LIKE.

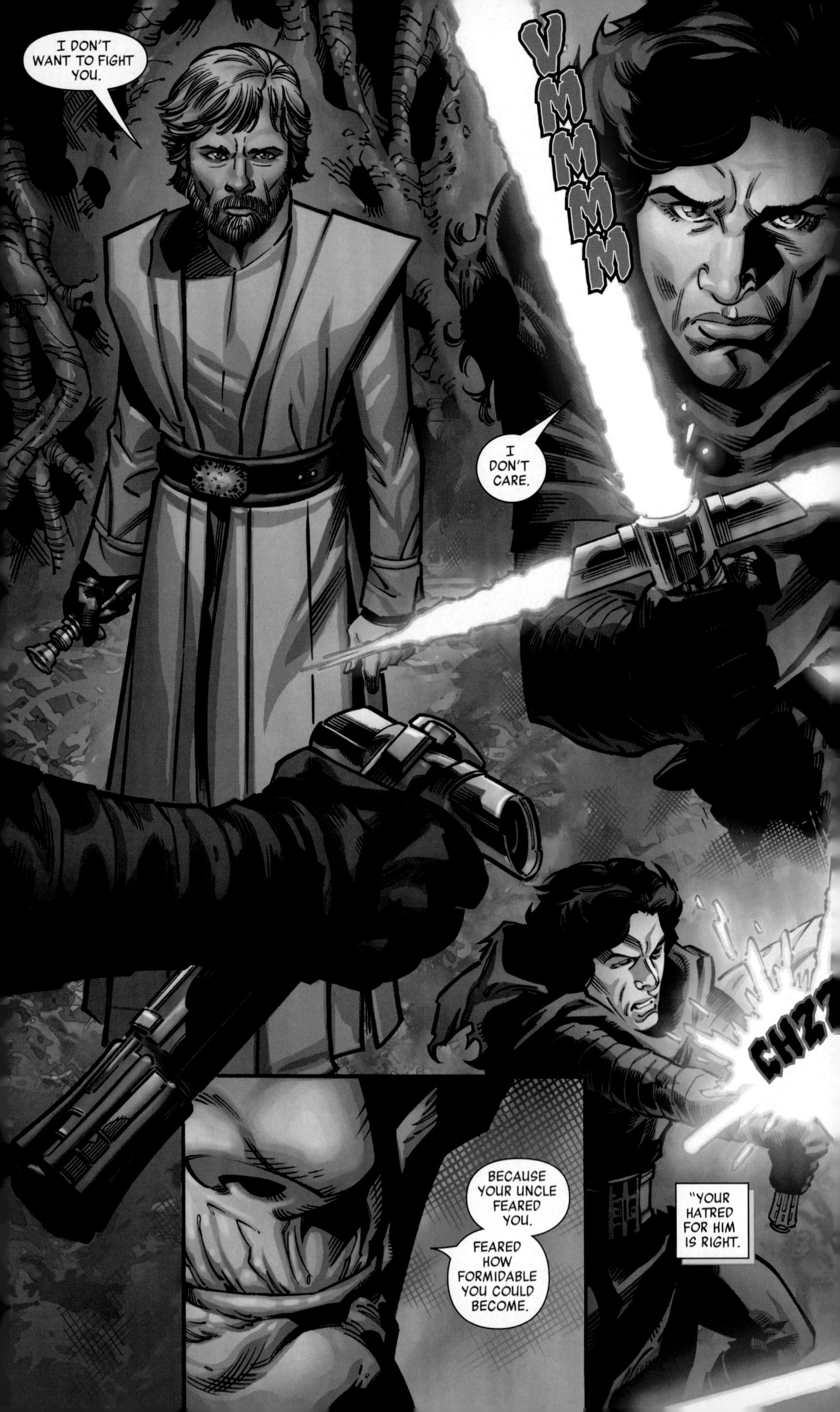
I DON'T WANT TO FIGHT YOU.
VMMMMMM
I DON'T CARE.
CHZZ
BECAUSE YOUR UNCLE FEARED YOU.
FEARED HOW FORMIDABLE YOU COULD BECOME.
"YOUR HATRED FOR HIM IS RIGHT.

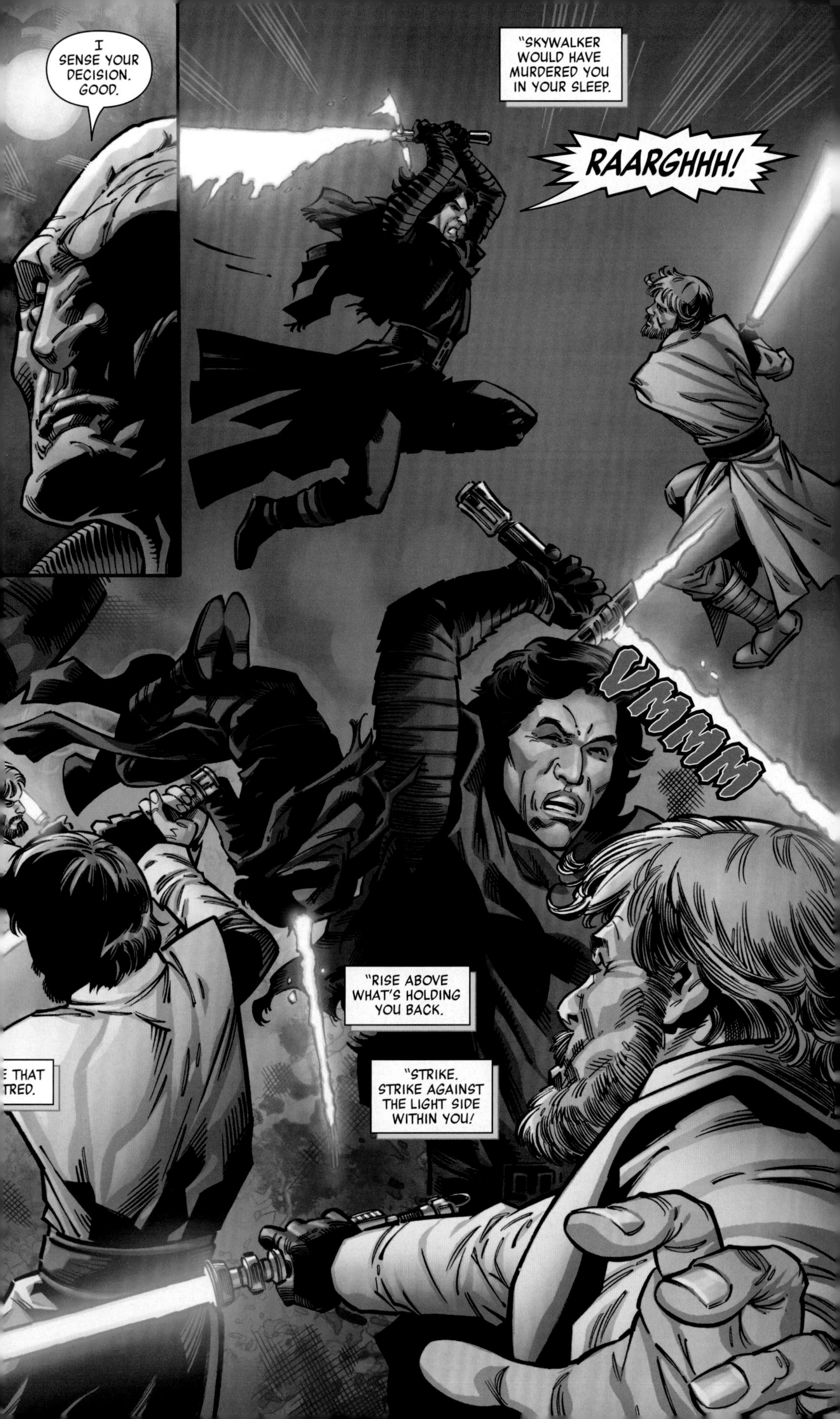
I SENSE YOUR DECISION. GOOD.
"SKYWALKER WOULD HAVE MURDERED YOU IN YOUR SLEEP.
RAARGHHH!
VMMMM
"RISE ABOVE WHAT'S HOLDING YOU BACK.
"STRIKE. STRIKE AGAINST THE LIGHT SIDE WITHIN YOU!

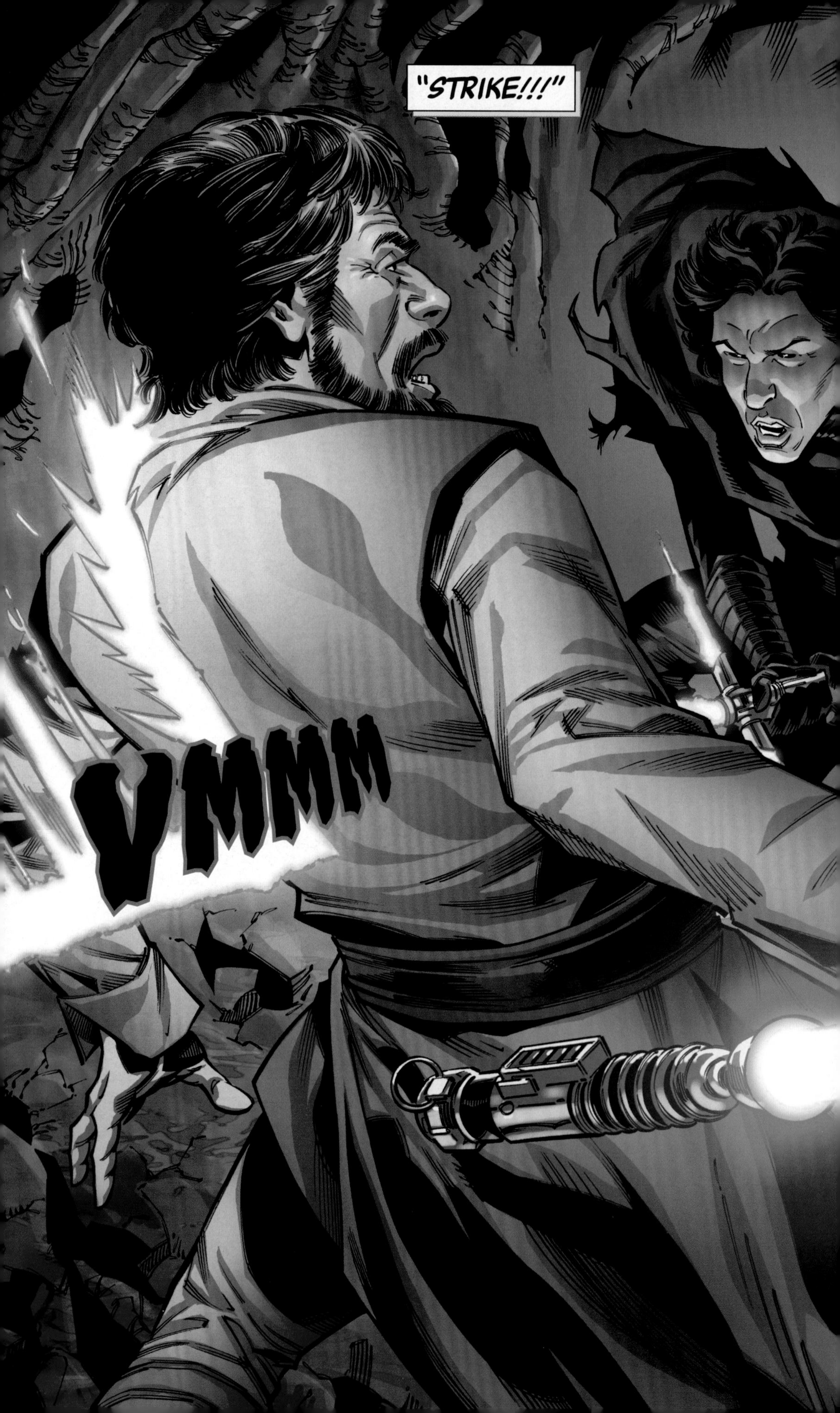
"STRIKE!!!"
VMMM

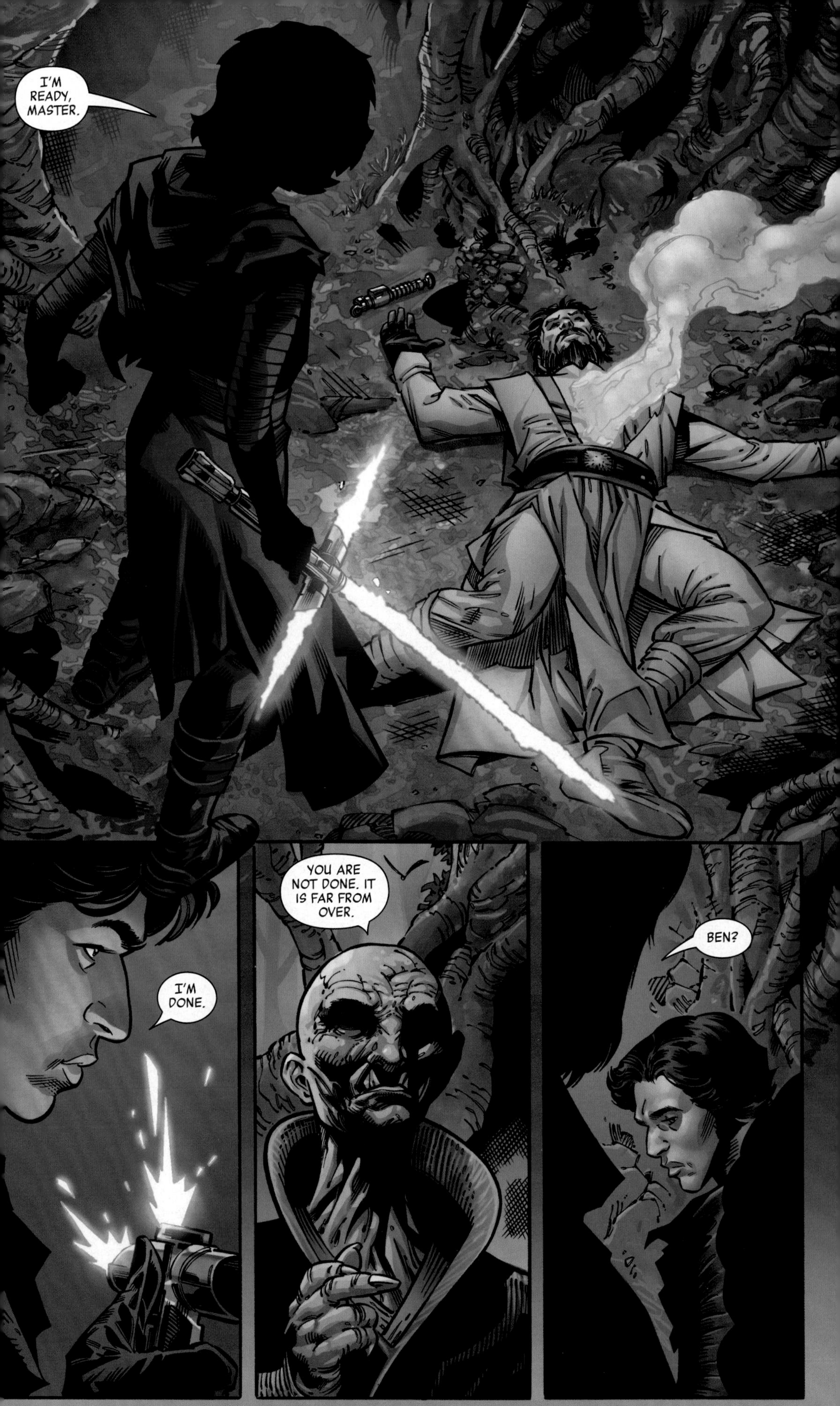
I'M READY, MASTER.
I'M DONE.
YOU ARE NOT DONE. IT IS FAR FROM OVER.
BEN?

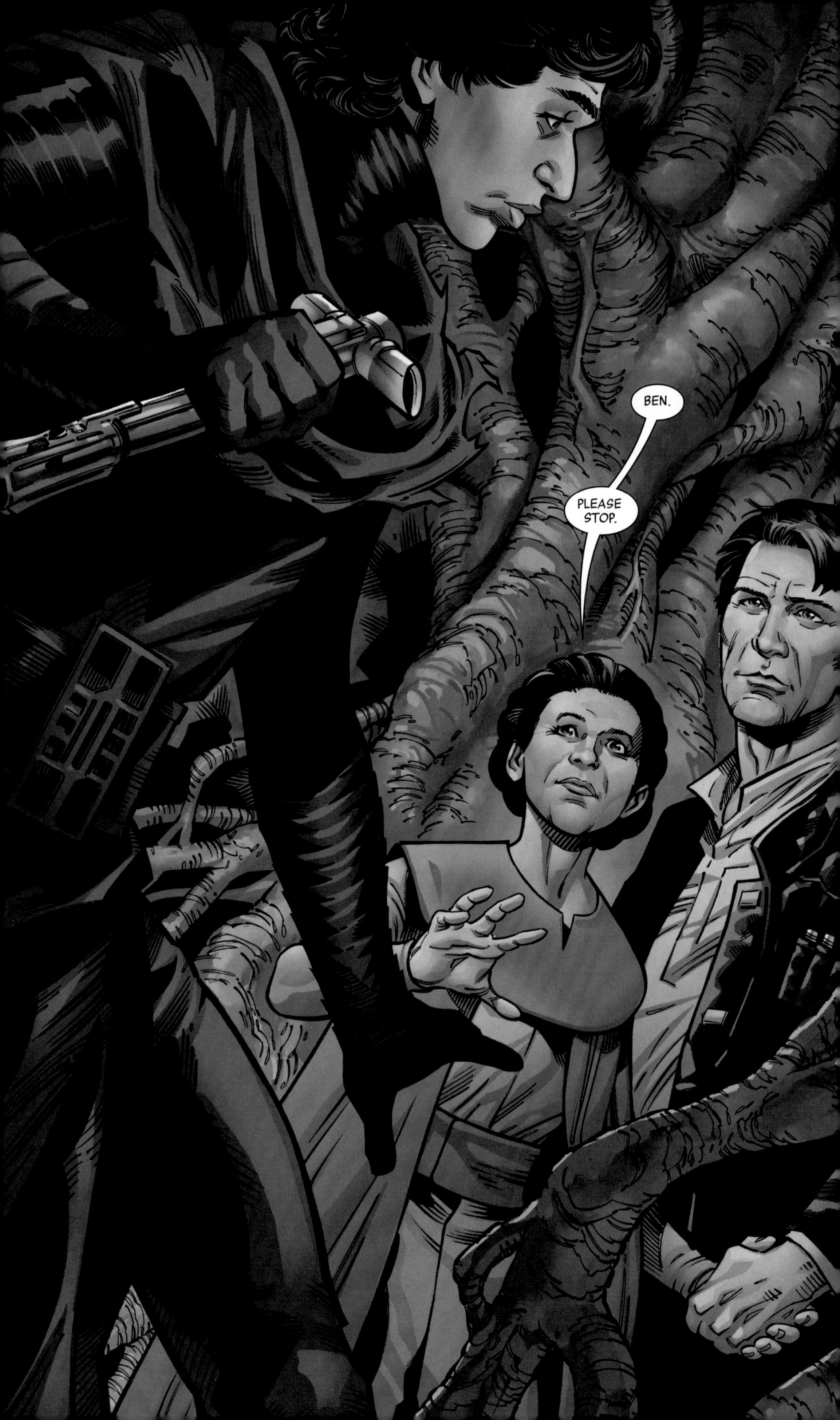
BEN.
PLEASE STOP.

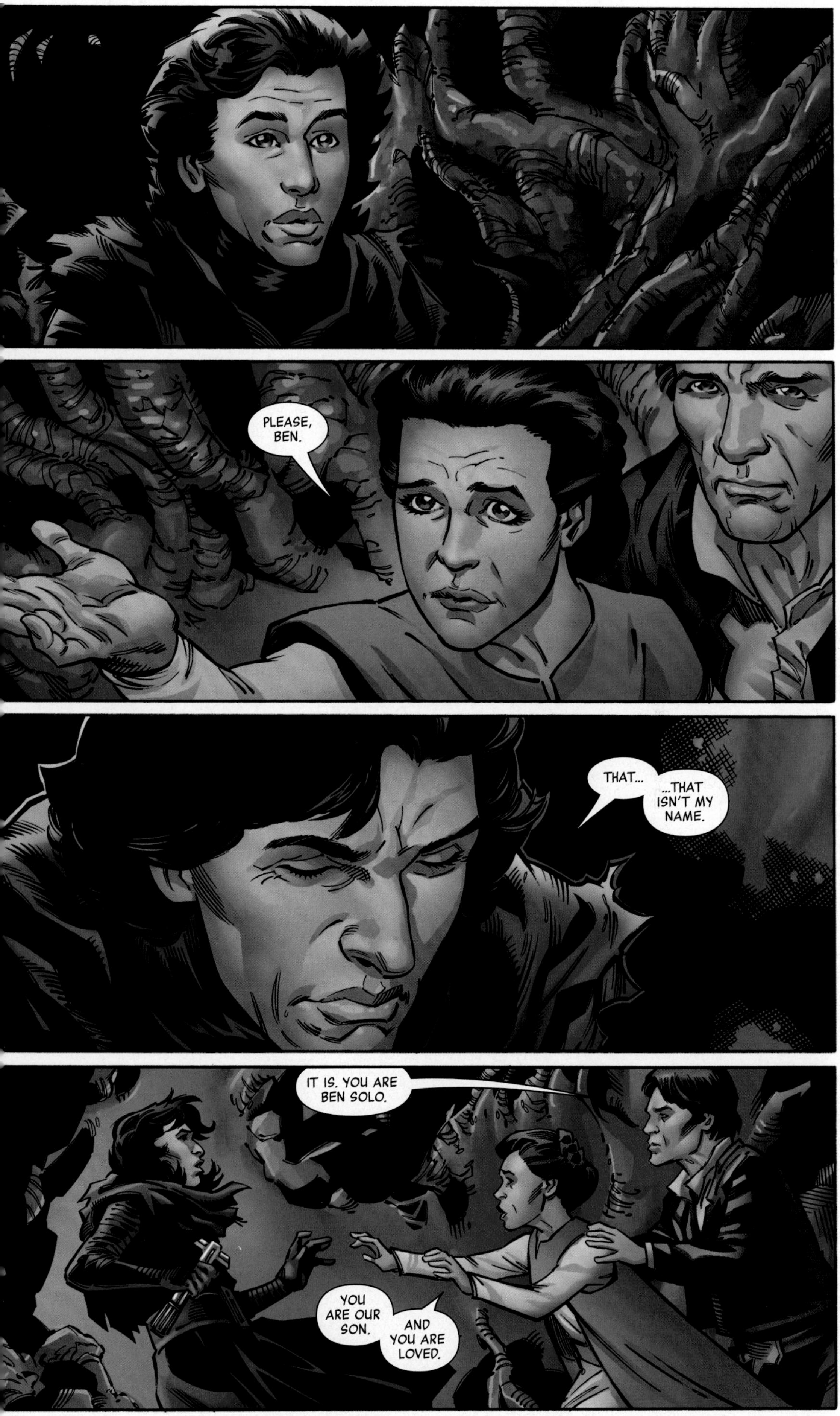
PLEASE, BEN.
THAT...
...THAT ISN'T MY NAME.
IT IS. YOU ARE BEN SOLO.
YOU ARE OUR SON.
AND YOU ARE LOVED.

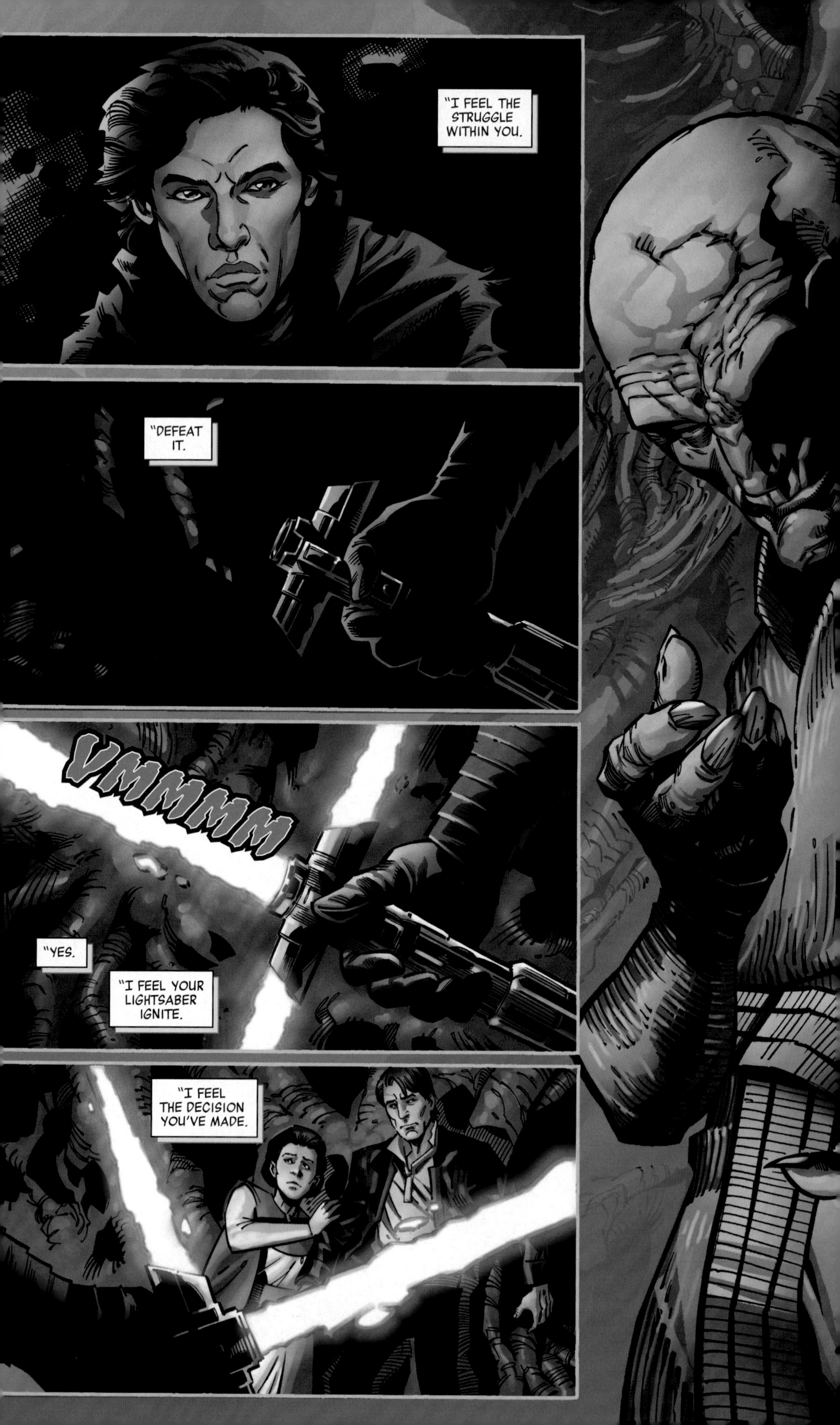
"I FEEL THE STRUGGLE WITHIN YOU.
"DEFEAT IT.
VMMMMM
"YES.
"I FEEL YOUR LIGHTSABER IGNITE.
"I FEEL THE DECISION YOU'VE MADE.

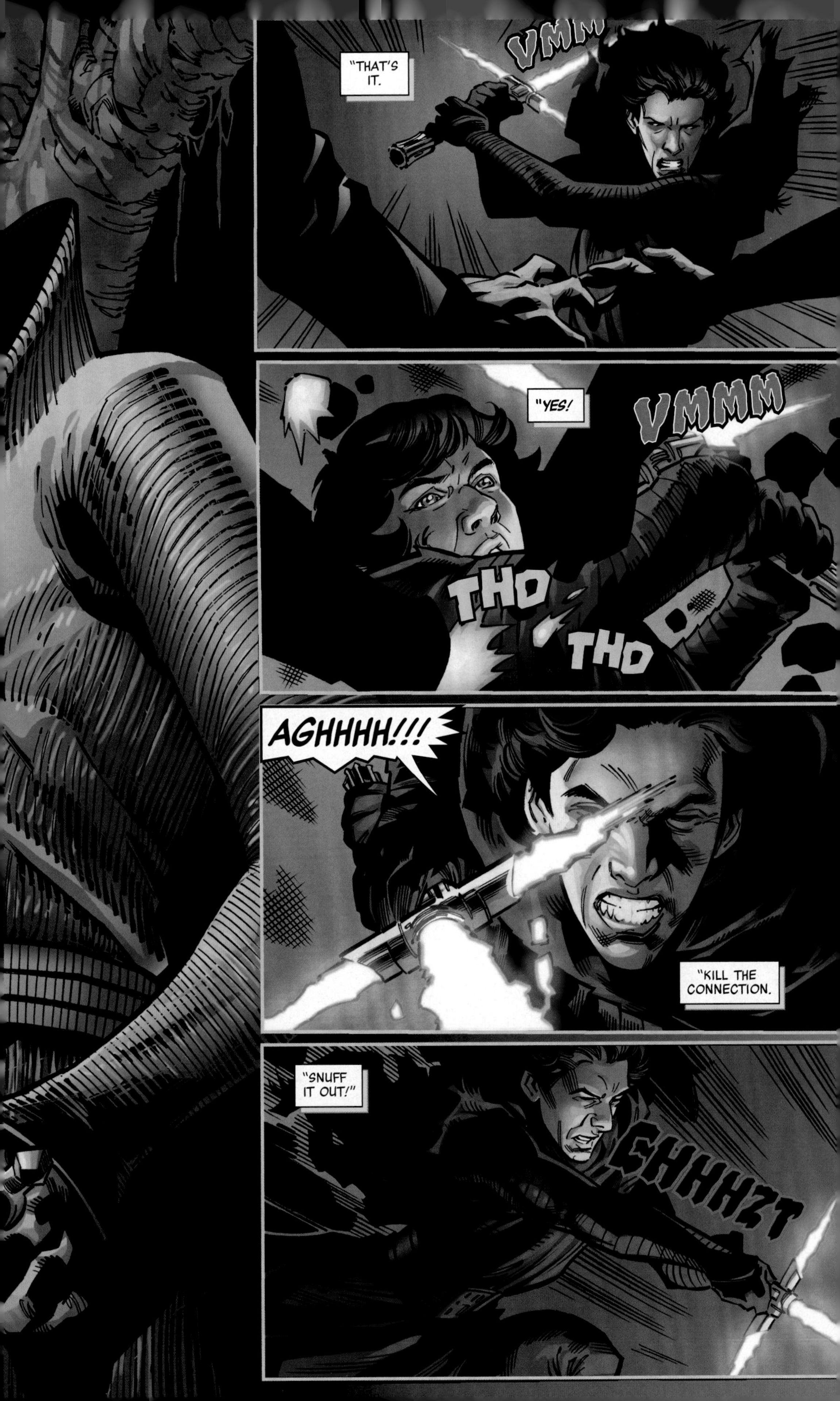

"THAT'S IT.
VMM
"YES!
VMMM
THO
THO
AGHHHH!!!
"KILL THE CONNECTION.
"SNUFF IT OUT!"
CHHHZT

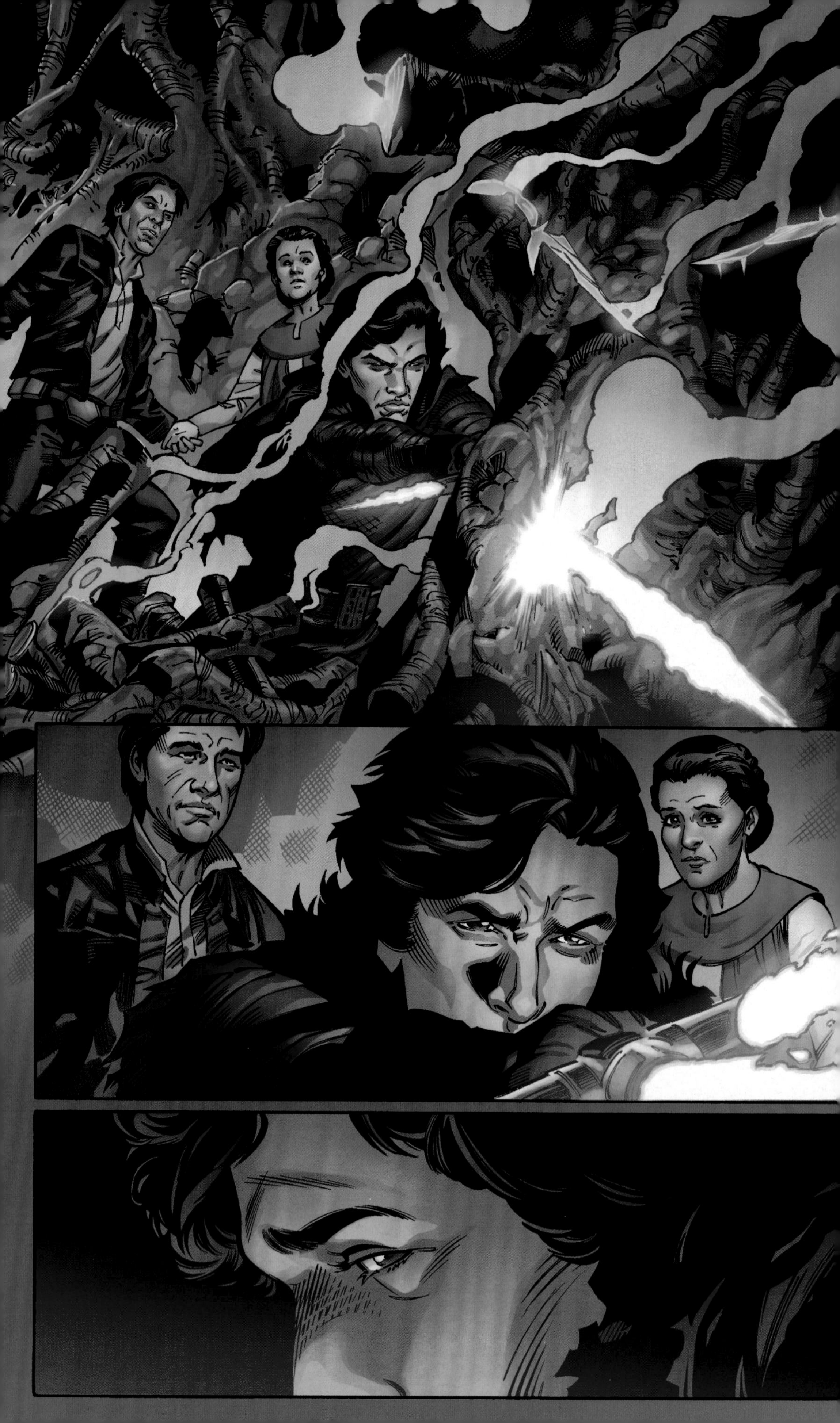

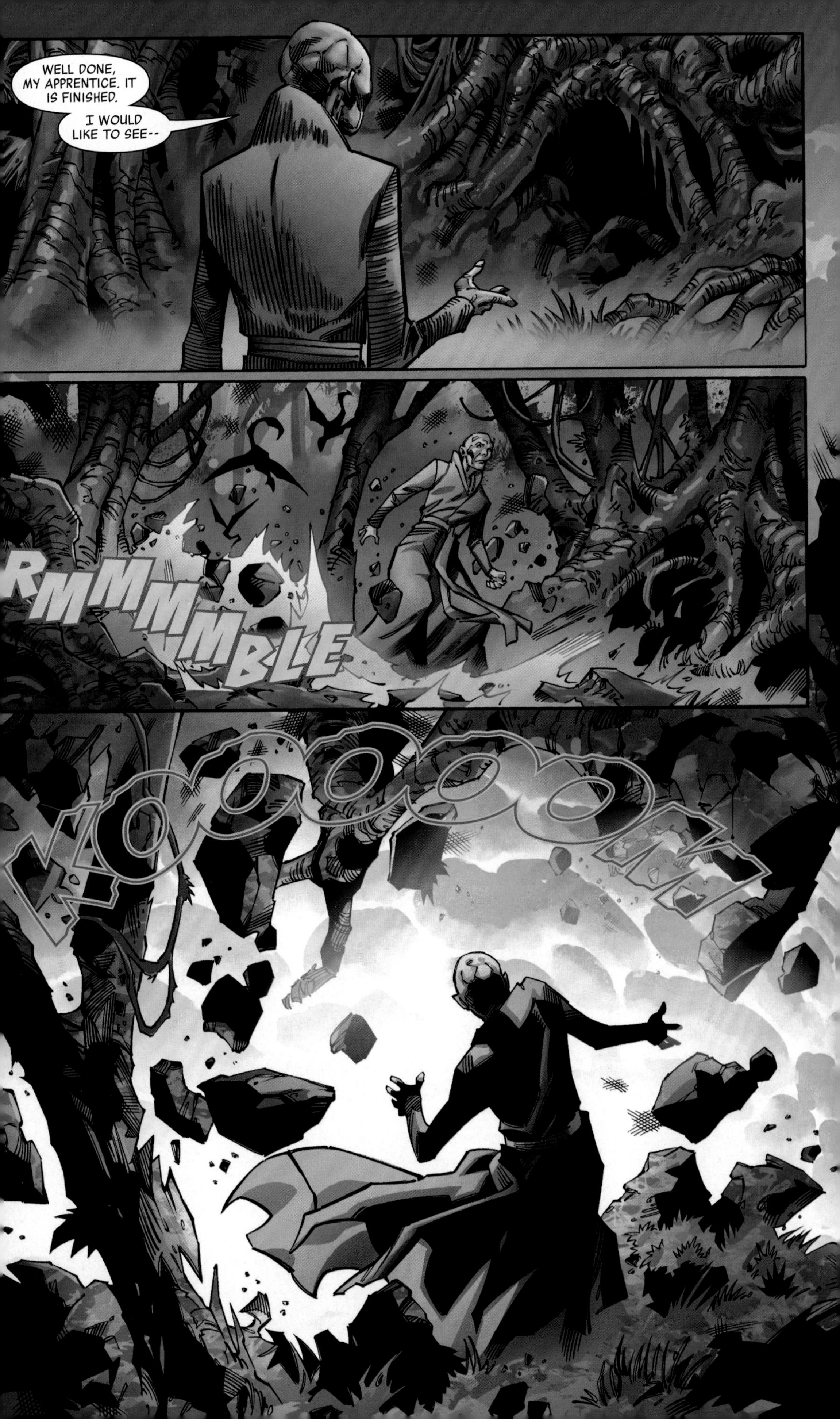
WELL DONE, MY APPRENTICE. IT IS FINISHED.
I WOULD LIKE TO SEE--
RMMMMMBLE
KOOOOOOOM

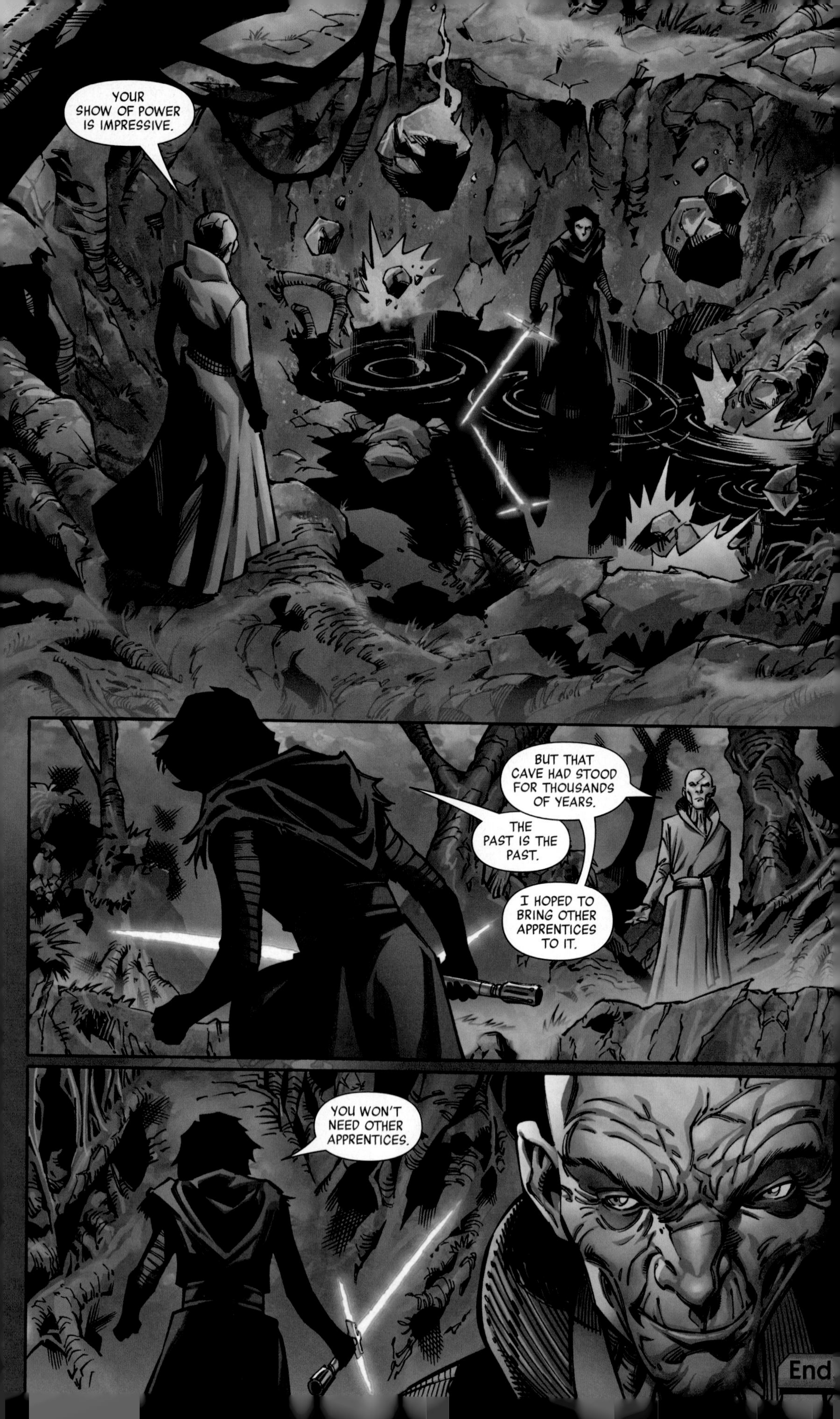
YOUR SHOW OF POWER IS IMPRESSIVE.
BUT THAT CAVE HAD STOOD FOR THOUSANDS OF YEARS.
THE PAST IS THE PAST.
I HOPED TO BRING OTHER APPRENTICES TO IT.
YOU WON'T NEED OTHER APPRENTICES.
End

STAR WARS

AGE OF RESISTANCE

Art by Ivan Manzella

AGE OF RESISTANCE
Darkness Rises: Supreme Leader Snoke and His Conquest of the Universe
By Bryan Young

There's not much known about Supreme Leader Snoke. He's an enigma whose existence brings about more questions than have been answered. How did he know the secret of Darth Vader's identity in order to turn Ben Solo's young heart? How did Snoke know of Yoda's refuge on Dagobah in order to train his new apprentice there? Are these things he learned from personal knowledge and interactions? Are they things he's plucked out of the heads of passersby using the Force?

All of these things are a mystery. Perhaps they always will be.

Talking to Conan O'Brien, Andy Serkis--who played Snoke in *The Force Awakens* and *The Last Jedi*--said, "Snoke, any great leader, likes a lot of mystery around them, but some leaders like Snoke--that mystery helps them be more powerful. But [after the events of *The Force Awakens*] he's under threat and has a lot of fear."

According to Serkis, that fear--fear of his own plight and instilling fear in others--is partly where Snoke draws his power from.

THE WIZARD OF OZ

The idea of controlling by fear is an old one. *Star Wars* got some of its cinematic inspiration of this concept from *The Wizard of Oz.* "When George made *A New*

Hope, he was influenced very much by Kurosawa and by Flash Gordon and by *The Wizard of Oz*," the *Star Wars* screenwriter Lawrence Kasdan said at the world press conference for *The Force Awakens*. "And I think that all those movies, you can feel them in *A New Hope*, and everything that's in *A New Hope* has come down through the movies to this day."

As far as Snoke, the parallels to the actual Wizard of Oz couldn't be clearer. He appears at first as a giant apparition, ruling by fear. Everyone in his command is afraid of his power, from his lowly stormtroopers to his chief general, Hux. Though Snoke has abilities in the Force, perhaps abilities beyond what viewers had ever seen previously, his chief tool is his mystery and fear, used to instill loyalty--to a point.

It's this fear that Snoke uses to manipulate Kylo Ren into doing his bidding. "He's using you for your power," Han Solo tells his son in *The Force Awakens.* "He'll crush you."

And maybe he would have, had Kylo not crushed him first.

KILLING SNOKE

In a film packed with epic moments, few could reach the heights of the throne room scene in *The Last Jedi,*

which would prove to be the final confrontation between Kylo Ren and Snoke. Audiences had no idea that Snoke would suffer the fate he did at the hands of his apprentice. Audiences in theaters gasped when Kylo Ren ignited Rey's lightsaber and were shocked to their cores when he pulled it through Snoke's gold-robed body. And who could forget the collective cheer when Rey caught the saber in her hand and we realized we would be treated to the team-up we'd all dreamed of: Rey fighting back-to-back with Ben Solo.

Speaking to *Entertainment Weekly*, writer/director Rian Johnson talked about how he was trying to come up with ways to test Kylo Ren the most. He wanted to lead him to be a more complex character, trying to find his own way by the end of the film. "That made me realize the most interesting thing would be to eliminate that dynamic between the 'emperor' and pupil, so that all bets are off going into the next one."

And as we look at what could be possible as we learn more about Snoke and take into account what might be happening in *The Rise of Skywalker*, given Palpatine's involvement, it's clear that Rian Johnson is right. All bets are off.

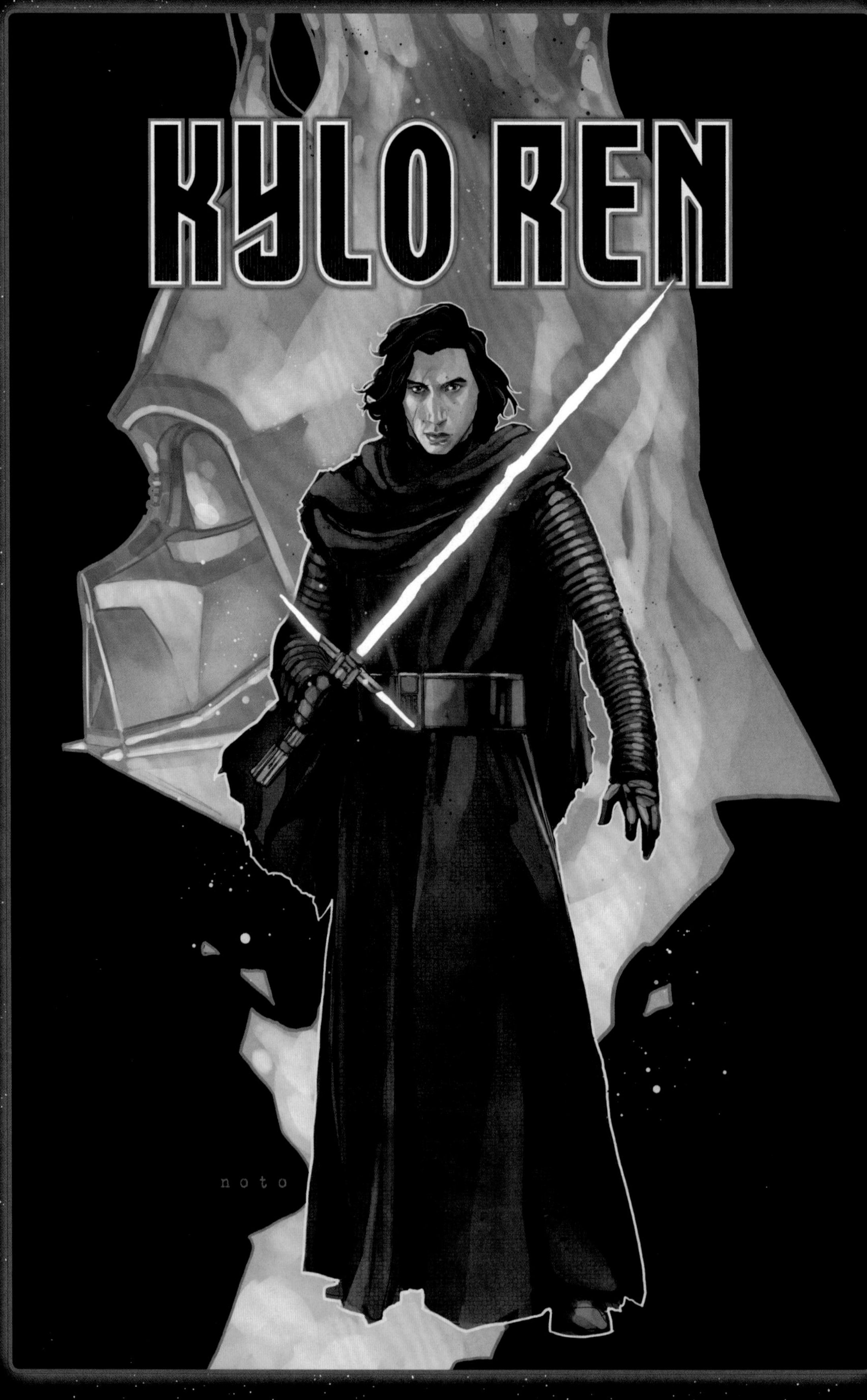
KYLO REN
noto

"OUT OF THE SHADOW"

The son of Princess Leia Organa and smuggler Han Solo, Ben Solo was once one of the most promising of the new generation of Jedi. That is, until his uncle, Jedi Master Luke Skywalker, sensed the dark side in Ben. Since then, Ben has abandoned the ways of the Jedi. As Kylo Ren of the villainous First Order, he now walks a dark path.

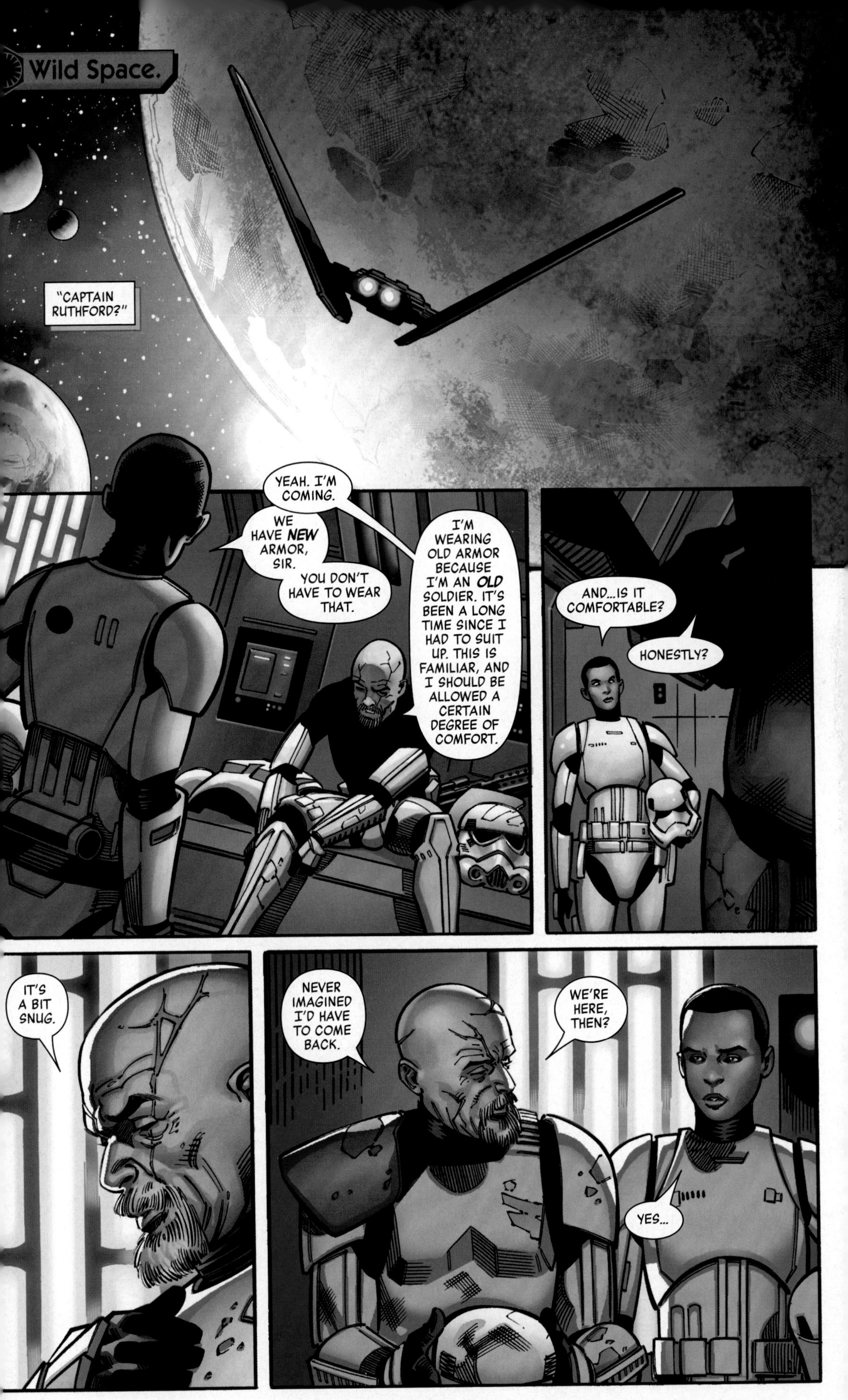
Wild Space.
"CAPTAIN RUTHFORD?"
YEAH. I'M COMING.
WE HAVE **NEW** ARMOR, SIR.
YOU DON'T HAVE TO WEAR THAT.
I'M WEARING OLD ARMOR BECAUSE I'M AN **OLD** SOLDIER. IT'S BEEN A LONG TIME SINCE I HAD TO SUIT UP. THIS IS FAMILIAR, AND I SHOULD BE ALLOWED A CERTAIN DEGREE OF COMFORT.
AND...IS IT COMFORTABLE?
HONESTLY?
IT'S A BIT SNUG.
NEVER IMAGINED I'D HAVE TO COME BACK.
WE'RE HERE, THEN?
YES...

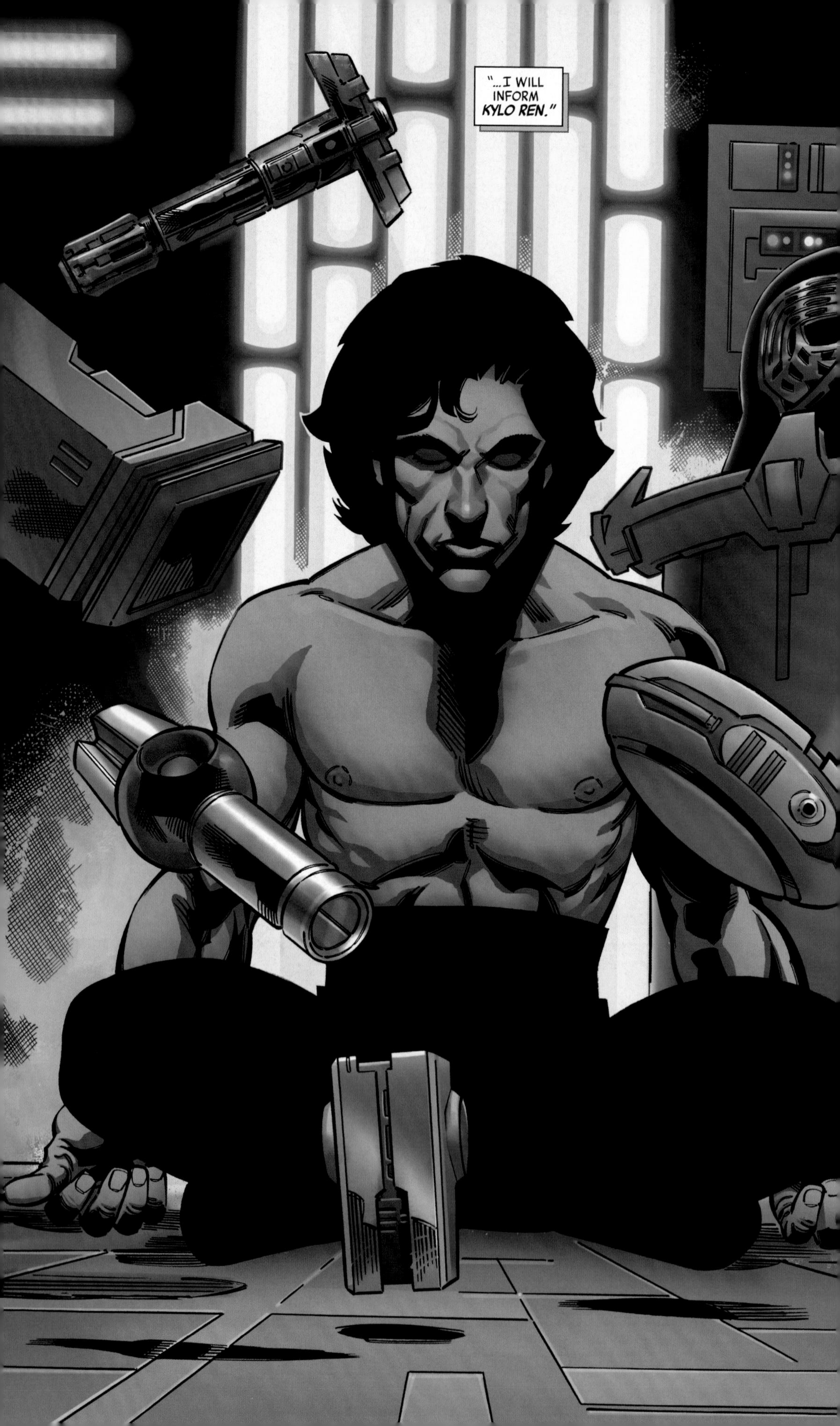
"...I WILL INFORM KYLO REN."

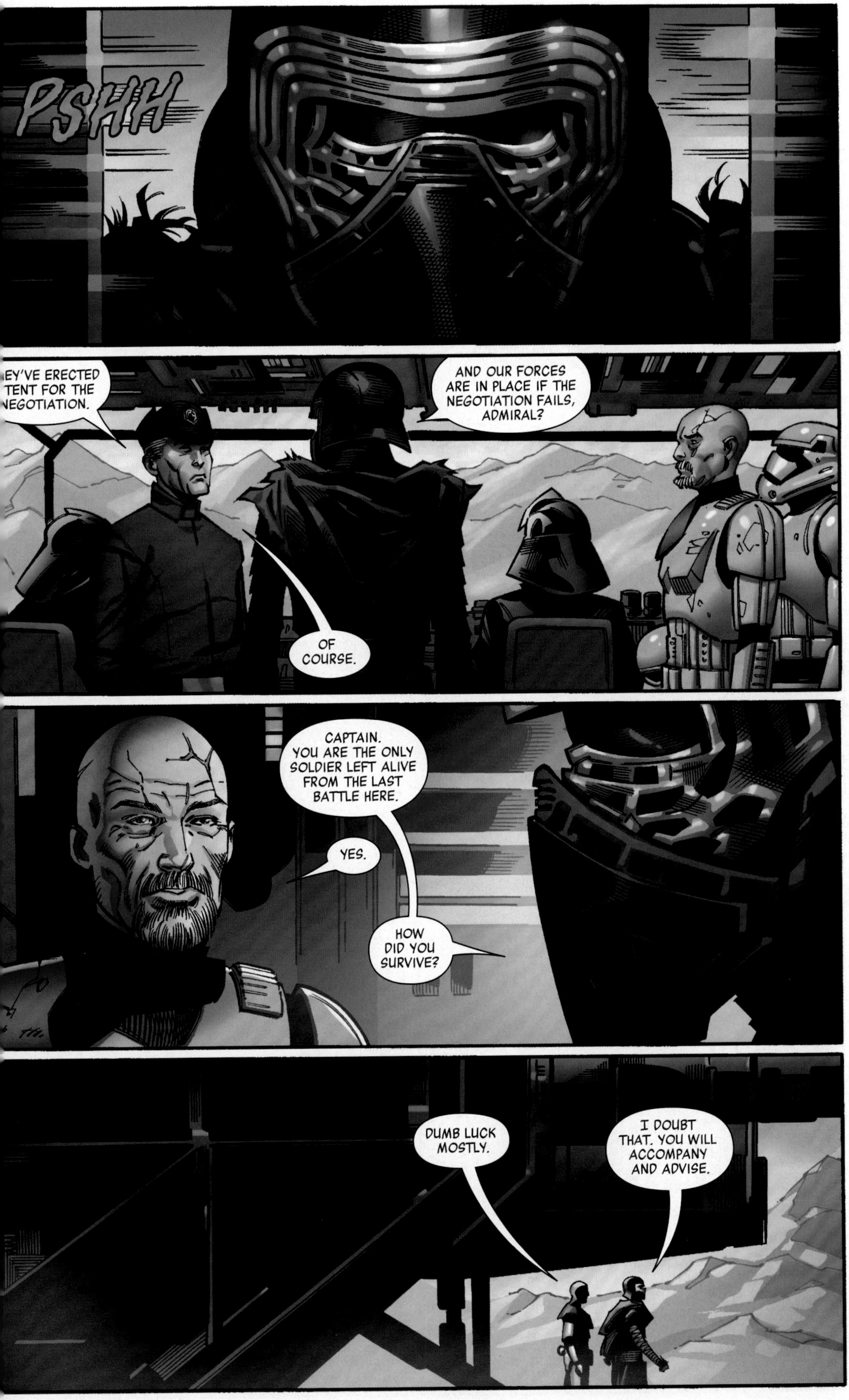
PSHH
EY'VE ERECTED TENT FOR THE NEGOTIATION.
AND OUR FORCES ARE IN PLACE IF THE NEGOTIATION FAILS, ADMIRAL?
OF COURSE.
CAPTAIN. YOU ARE THE ONLY SOLDIER LEFT ALIVE FROM THE LAST BATTLE HERE.
YES.
HOW DID YOU SURVIVE?
DUMB LUCK MOSTLY.
I DOUBT THAT. YOU WILL ACCOMPANY AND ADVISE.

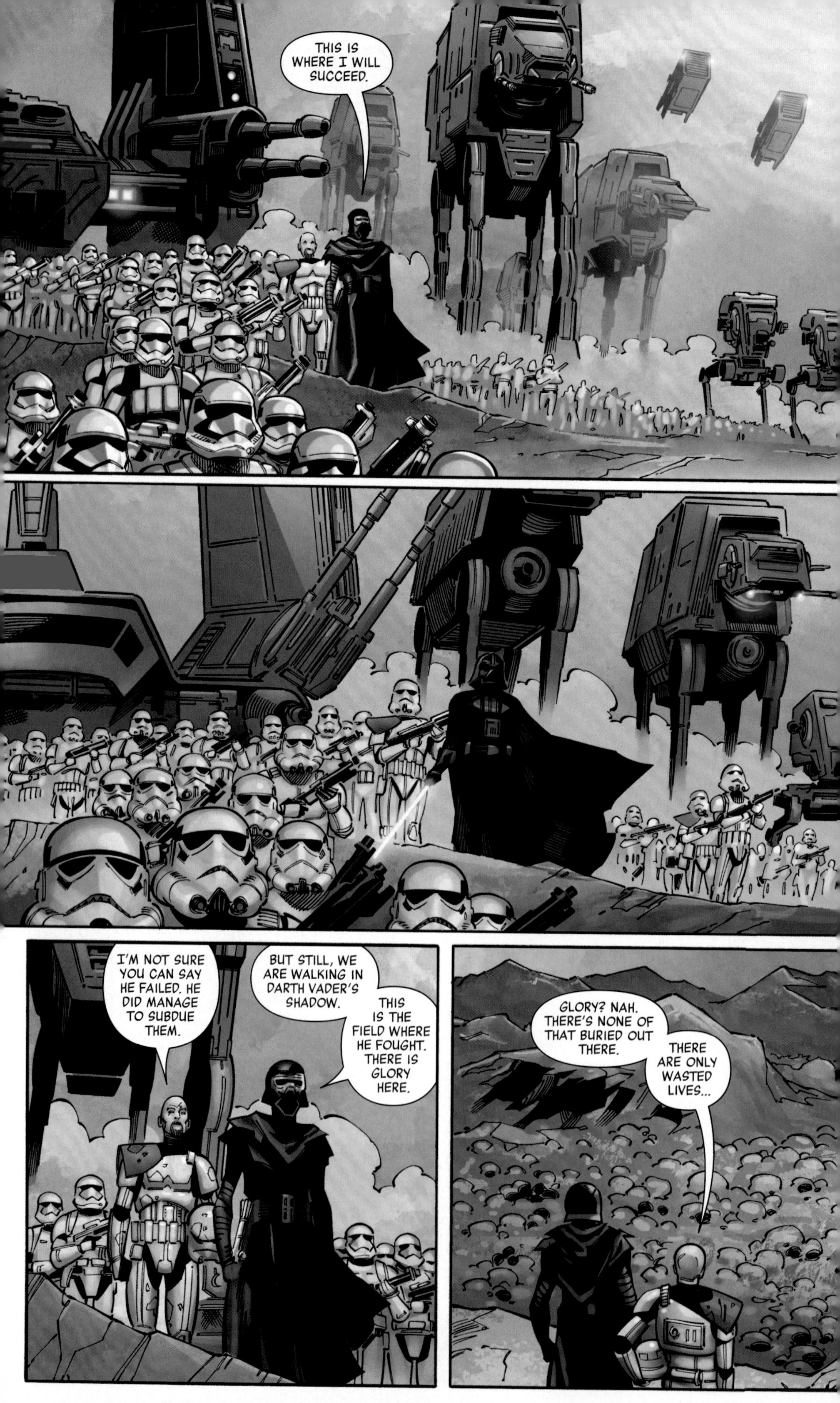
THIS IS WHERE I WILL SUCCEED.
I'M NOT SURE YOU CAN SAY HE FAILED. HE DID MANAGE TO SUBDUE THEM.
BUT STILL, WE ARE WALKING IN DARTH VADER'S SHADOW.
THIS IS THE FIELD WHERE HE FOUGHT. THERE IS GLORY HERE.
GLORY? NAH. THERE'S NONE OF THAT BURIED OUT THERE.
THERE ARE ONLY WASTED LIVES...

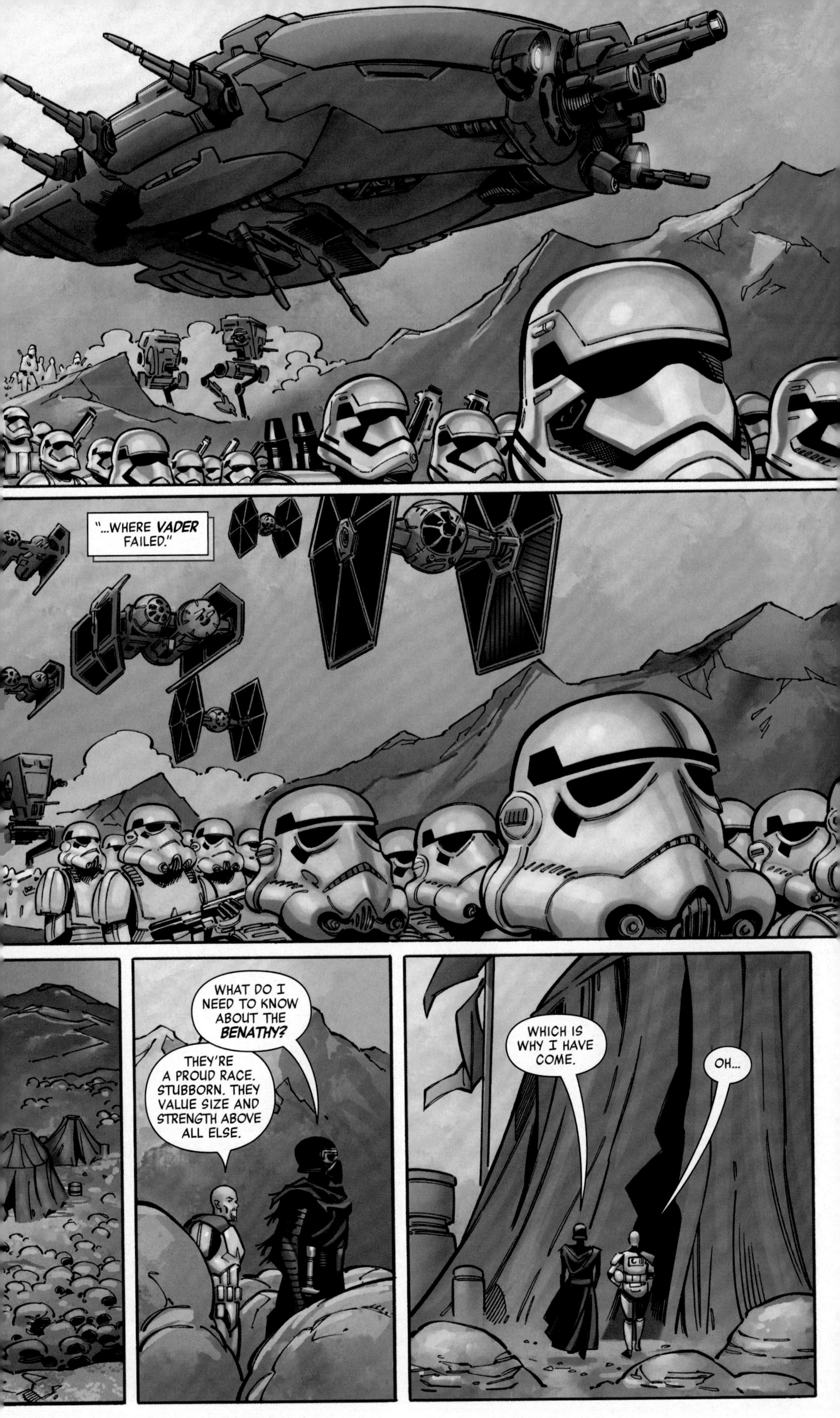
"...WHERE VADER FAILED."
WHAT DO I NEED TO KNOW ABOUT THE BENATHY?
THEY'RE A PROUD RACE. STUBBORN. THEY VALUE SIZE AND STRENGTH ABOVE ALL ELSE.
WHICH IS WHY I HAVE COME.
OH...

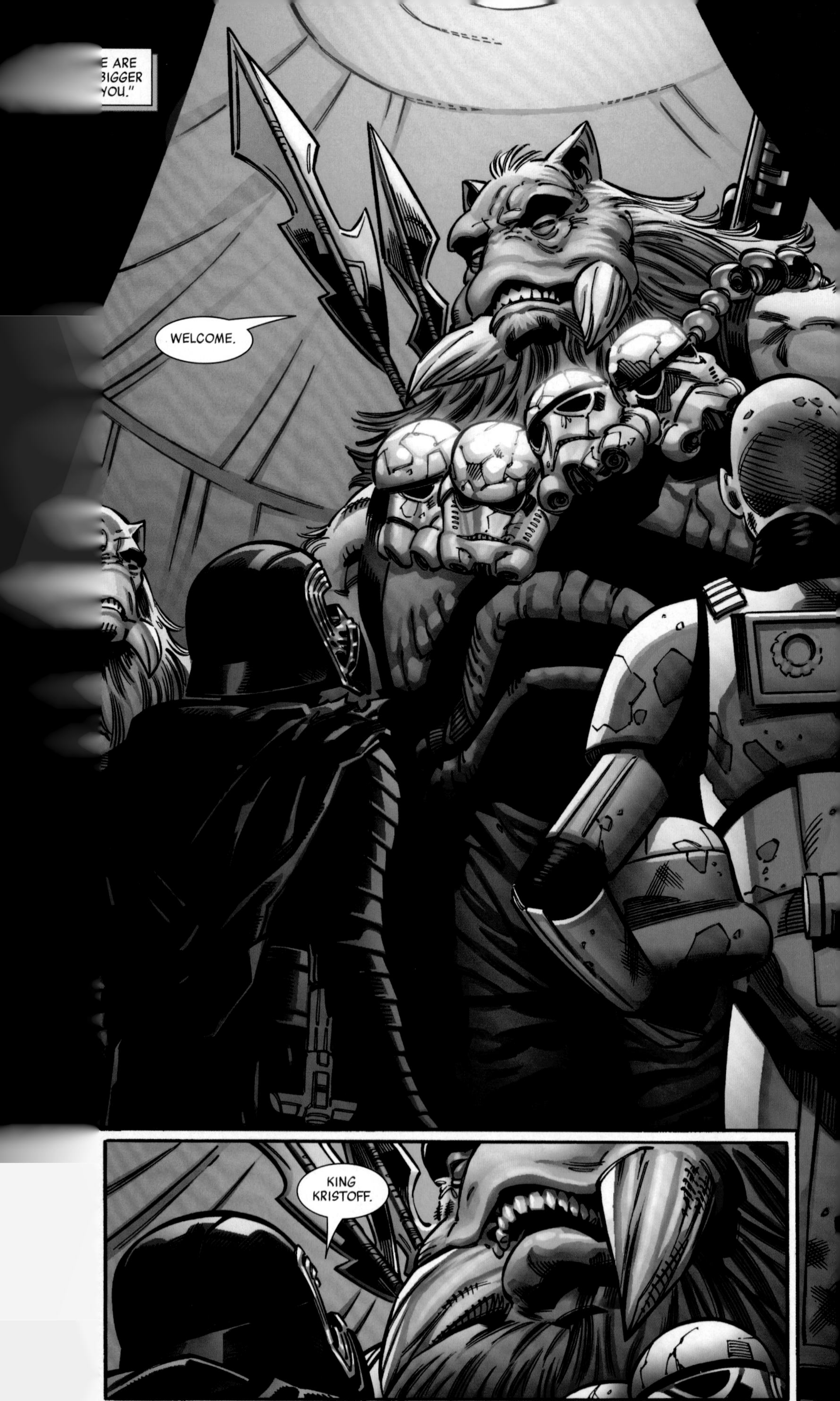
E ARE
BIGGER
YOU."
WELCOME.
KING KRISTOFF.

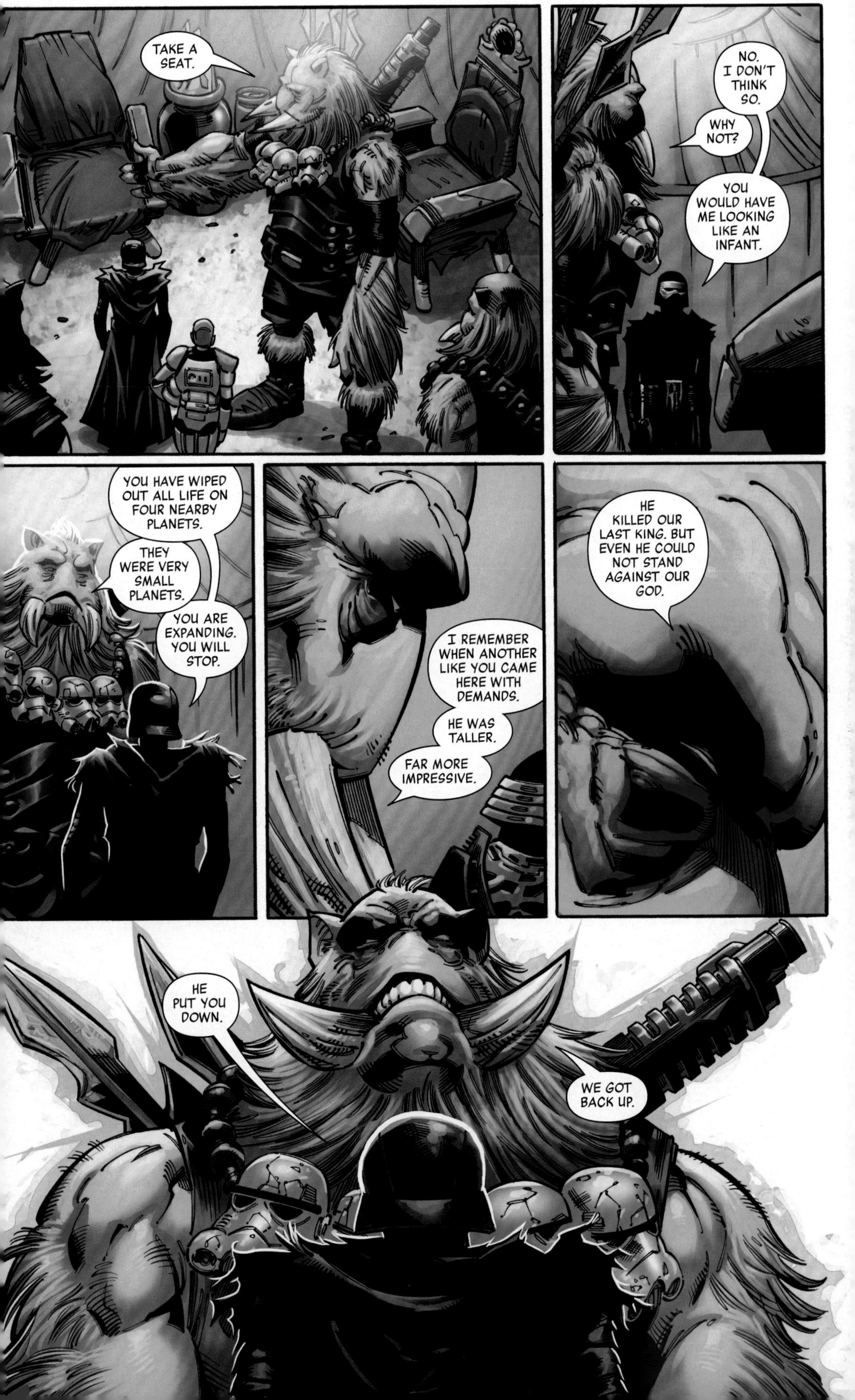
TAKE A SEAT.
NO. I DON'T THINK SO.
WHY NOT?
YOU WOULD HAVE ME LOOKING LIKE AN INFANT.
YOU HAVE WIPED OUT ALL LIFE ON FOUR NEARBY PLANETS.
THEY WERE VERY SMALL PLANETS.
YOU ARE EXPANDING. YOU WILL STOP.
I REMEMBER WHEN ANOTHER LIKE YOU CAME HERE WITH DEMANDS.
HE WAS TALLER.
FAR MORE IMPRESSIVE.
HE KILLED OUR LAST KING. BUT EVEN HE COULD NOT STAND AGAINST OUR GOD.
HE PUT YOU DOWN.
WE GOT BACK UP.

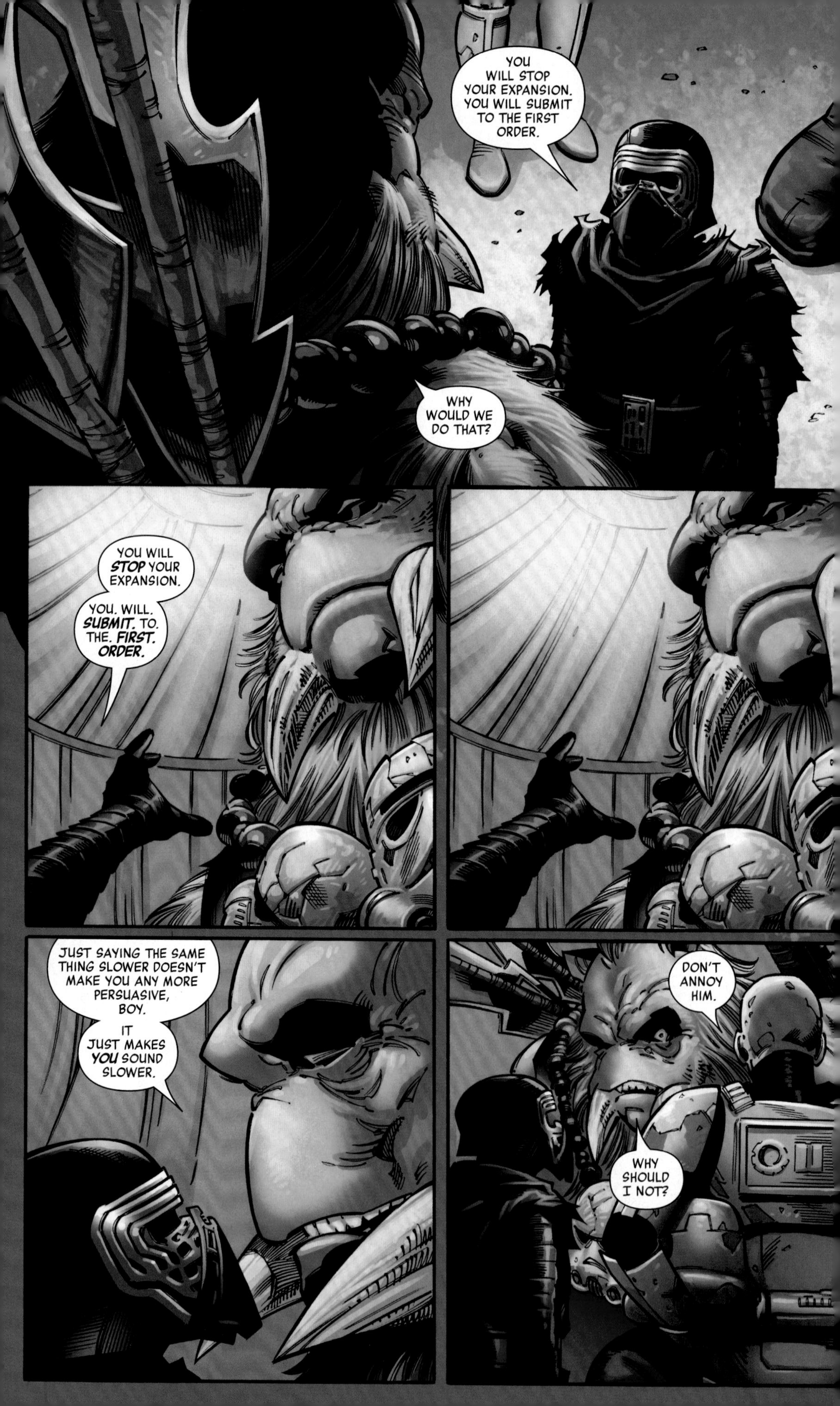
YOU WILL STOP YOUR EXPANSION. YOU WILL SUBMIT TO THE FIRST ORDER.
WHY WOULD WE DO THAT?
YOU WILL *STOP* YOUR EXPANSION.
YOU. WILL. *SUBMIT.* TO. THE. *FIRST. ORDER.*
JUST SAYING THE SAME THING SLOWER DOESN'T MAKE YOU ANY MORE PERSUASIVE, BOY.
IT JUST MAKES *YOU* SOUND SLOWER.
DON'T ANNOY HIM.
WHY SHOULD I NOT?

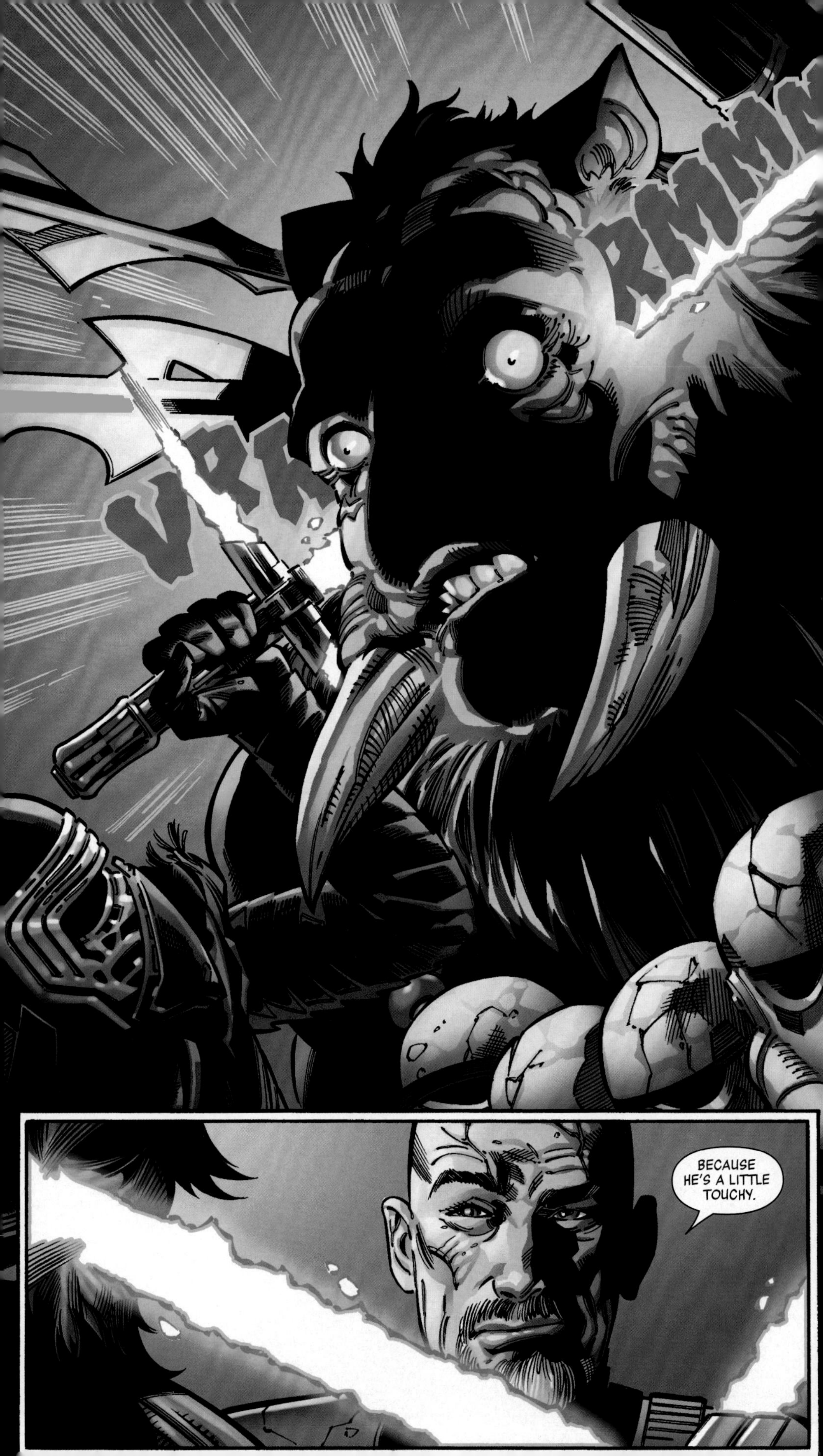
BECAUSE HE'S A LITTLE TOUCHY.

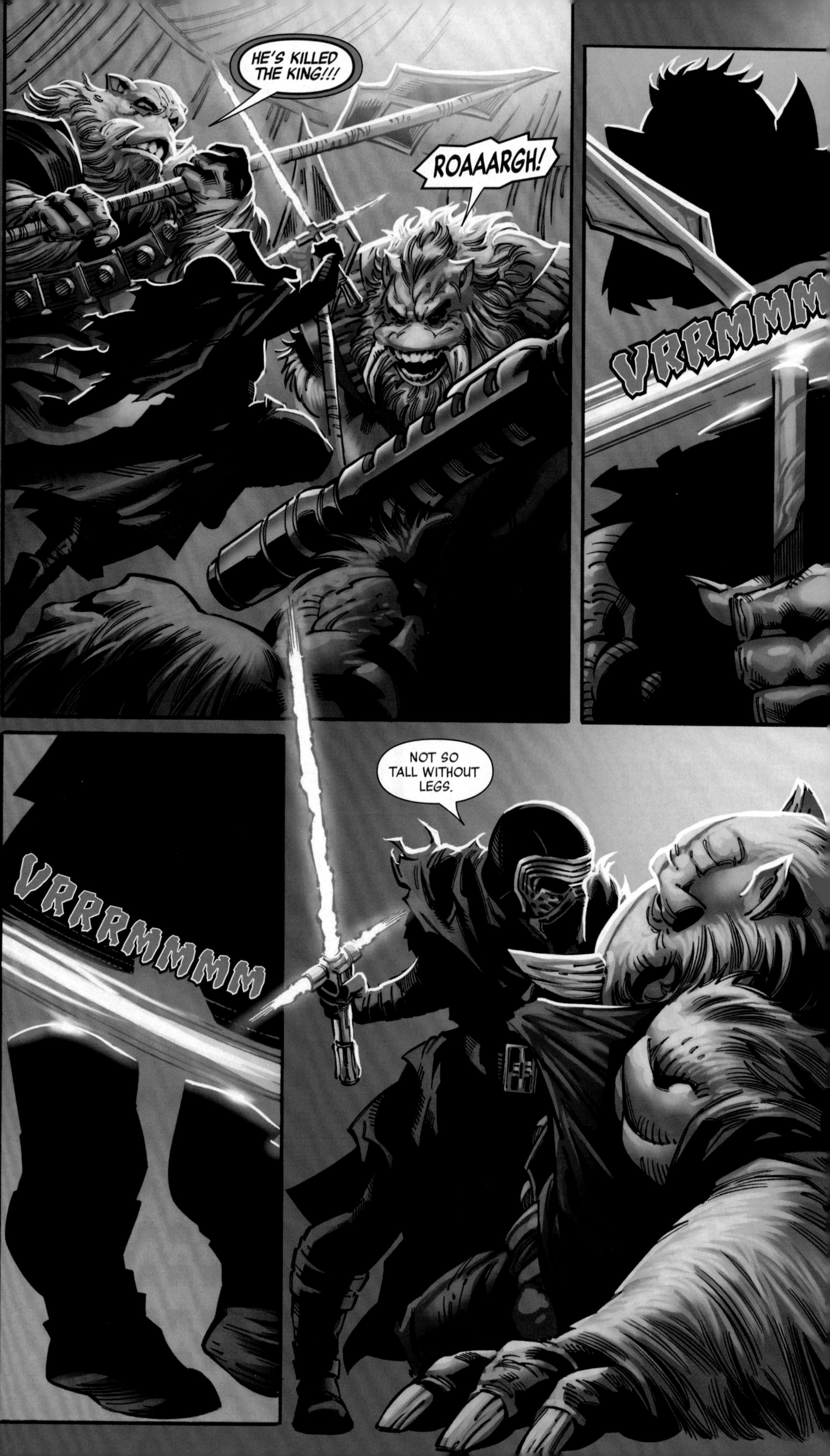

HE'S KILLED THE KING!!!
ROAAARGH!
VRRMMMM
VRRRRMMMMM
NOT SO TALL WITHOUT LEGS.

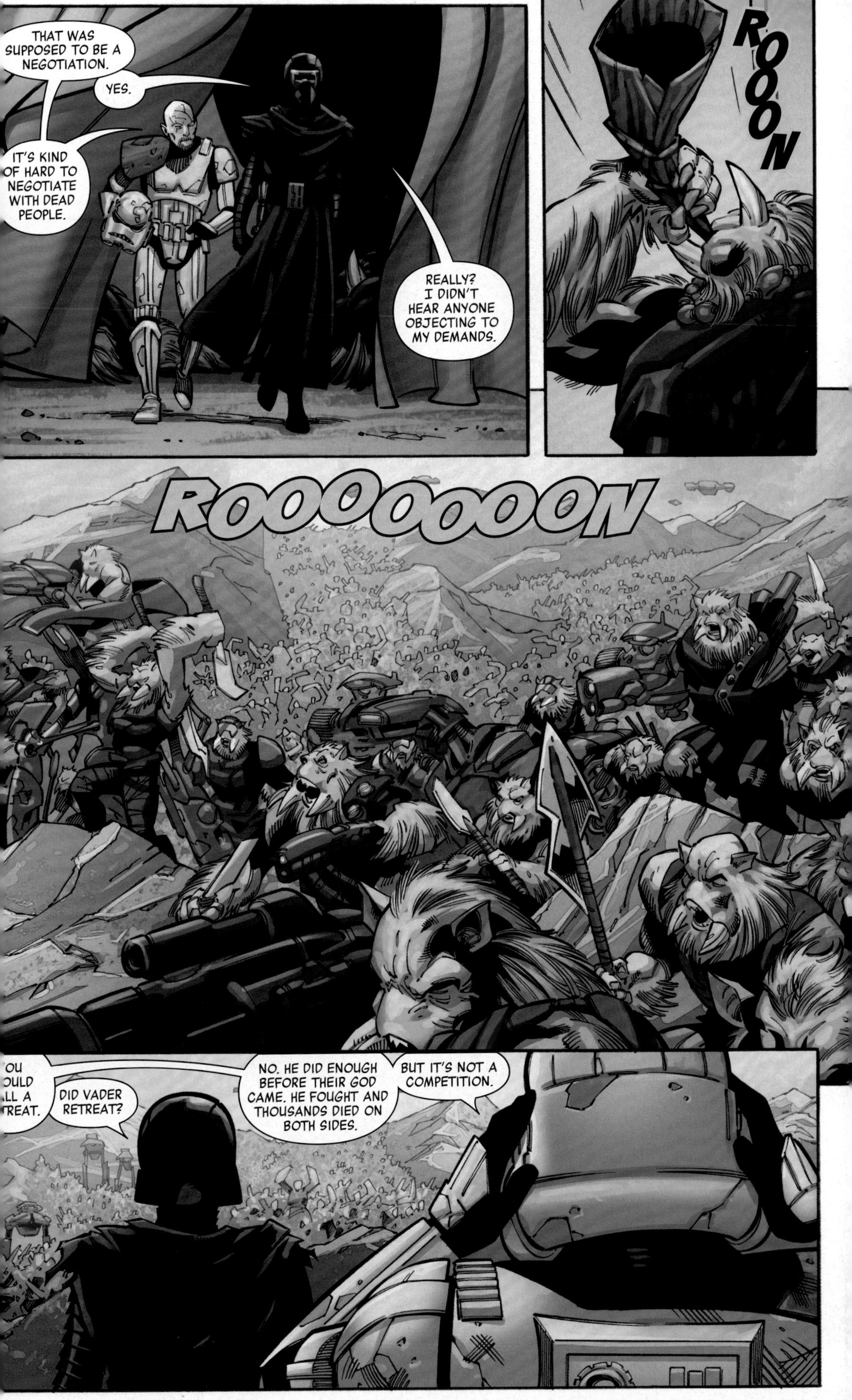
THAT WAS SUPPOSED TO BE A NEGOTIATION.
YES.
IT'S KIND OF HARD TO NEGOTIATE WITH DEAD PEOPLE.
REALLY? I DIDN'T HEAR ANYONE OBJECTING TO MY DEMANDS.
ROOON
ROOOOOOON
OU OULD LL A TREAT.
DID VADER RETREAT?
NO. HE DID ENOUGH BEFORE THEIR GOD CAME. HE FOUGHT AND THOUSANDS DIED ON BOTH SIDES.
BUT IT'S NOT A COMPETITION.

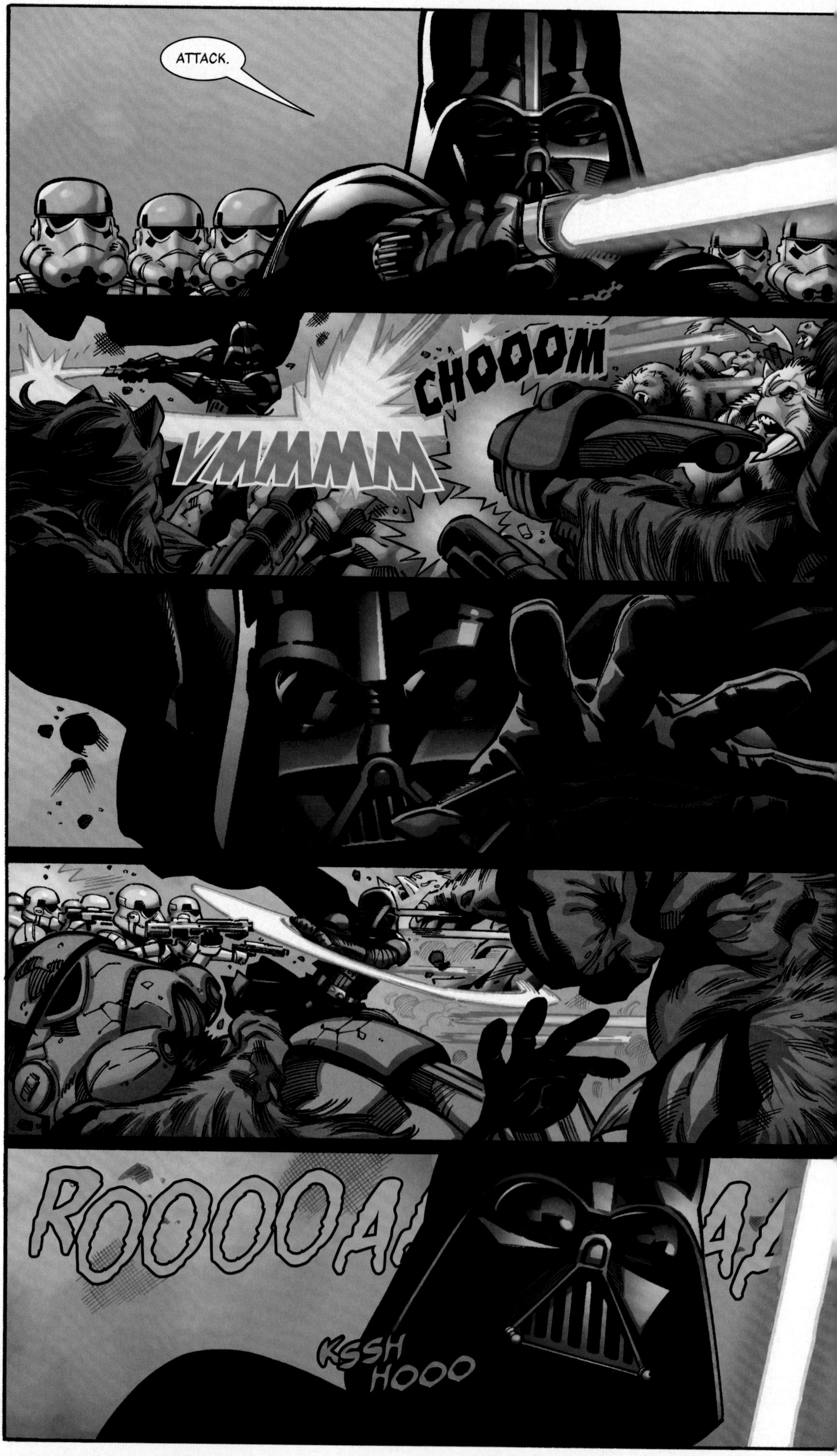
ATTACK.
CHOOOM
VMMMM
ROOOOA
KSSH
HOOO

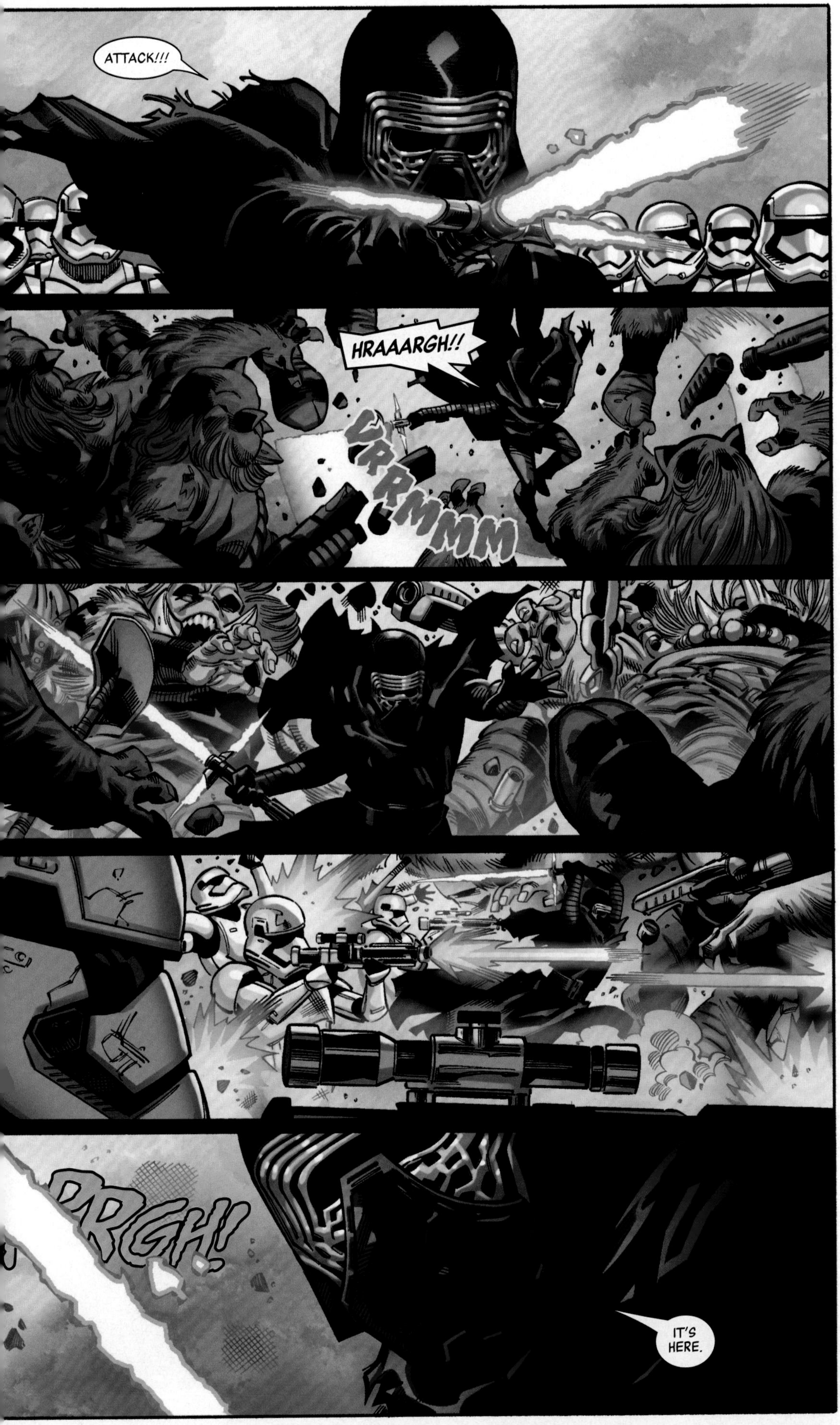
ATTACK!!!
HRAAARGH!!
VRRMMMM
RRGH!
IT'S HERE.

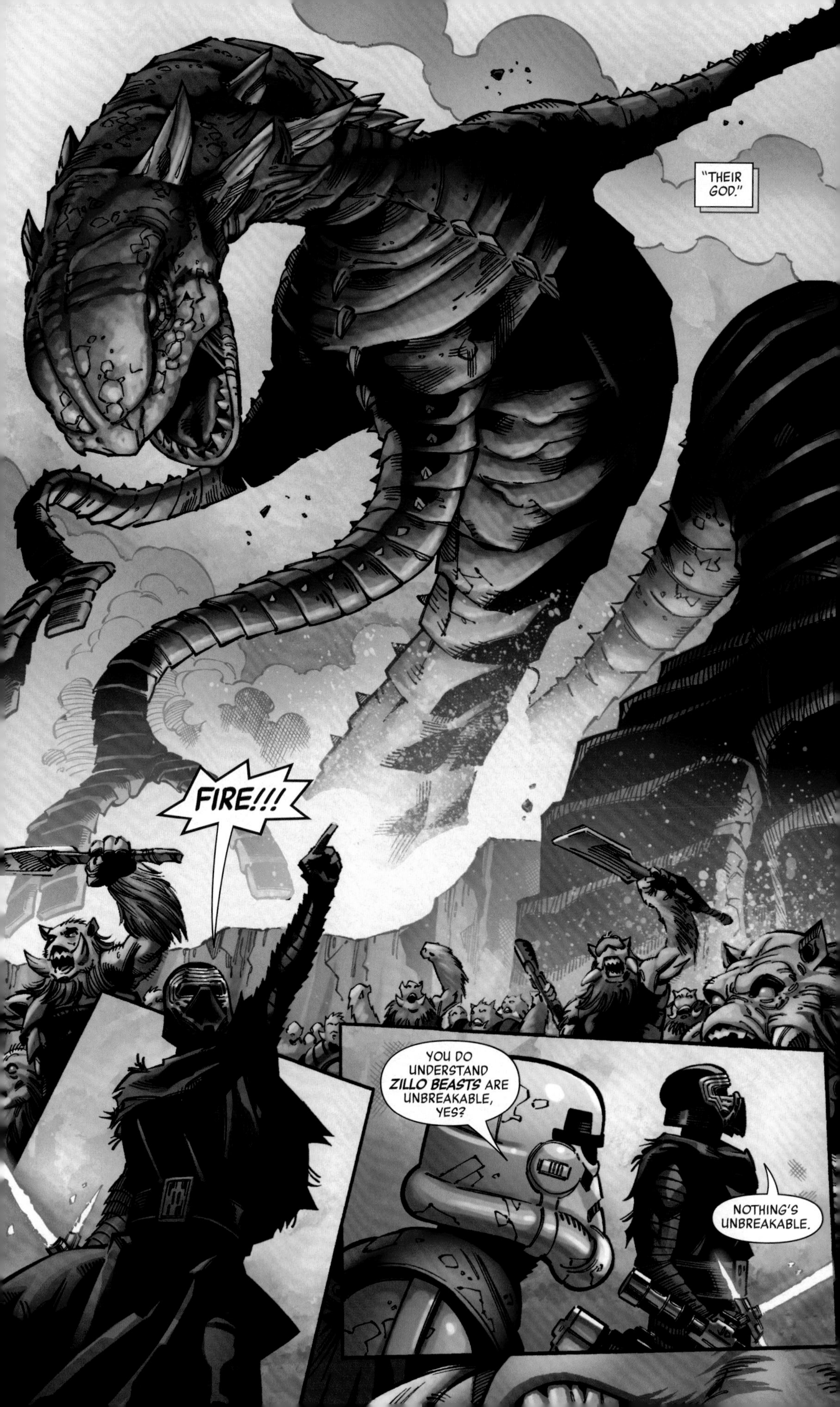
"THEIR GOD."
FIRE!!!
YOU DO UNDERSTAND ZILLO BEASTS ARE UNBREAKABLE, YES?
NOTHING'S UNBREAKABLE.

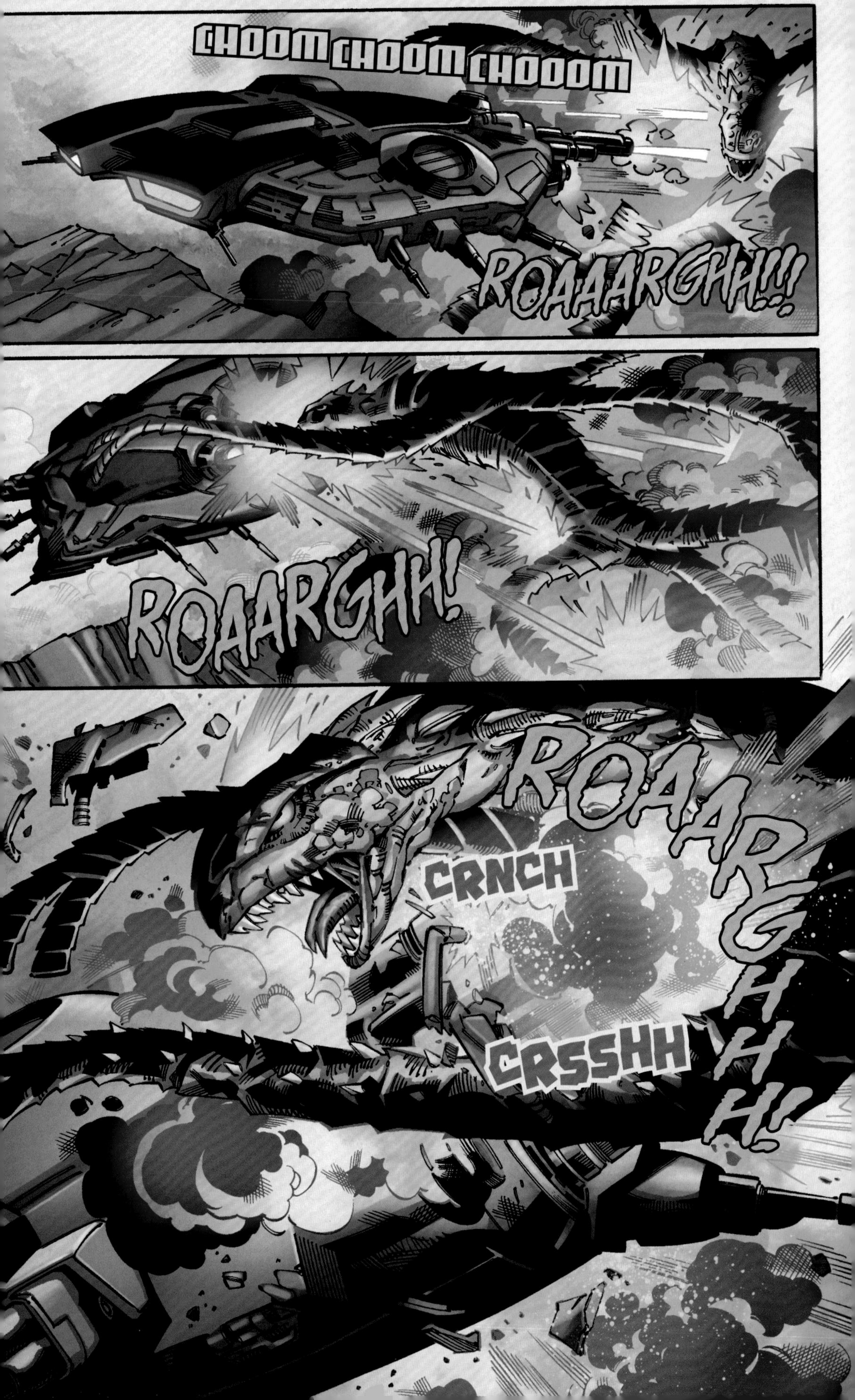
CHOOM CHOOM CHOOOM
ROAAARGHH!!!
ROAARGHH!
ROAARGHHHH!
CRNCH
CRSSHH

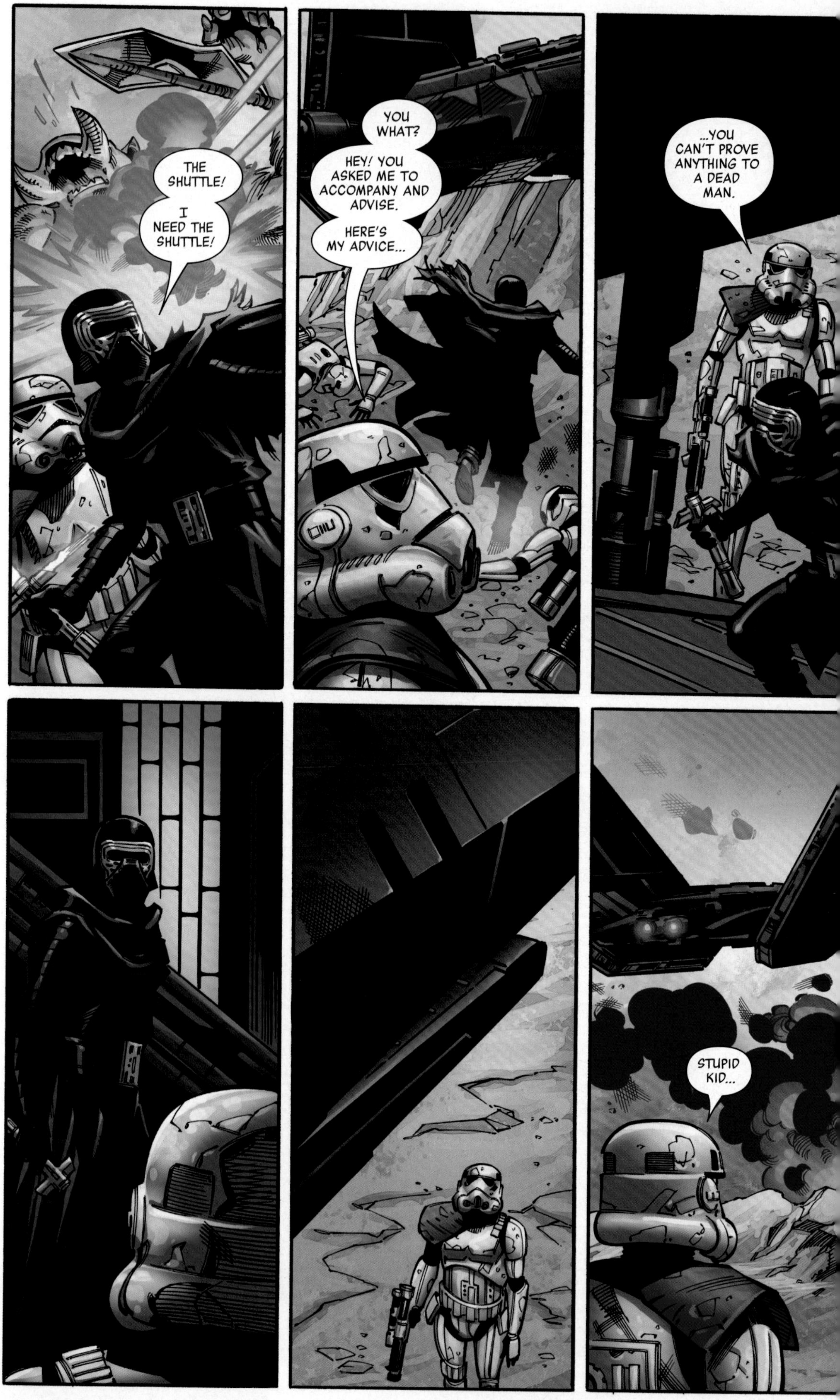
THE SHUTTLE!
I NEED THE SHUTTLE!
YOU WHAT?
HEY! YOU ASKED ME TO ACCOMPANY AND ADVISE.
HERE'S MY ADVICE...
...YOU CAN'T PROVE ANYTHING TO A DEAD MAN.
STUPID KID...

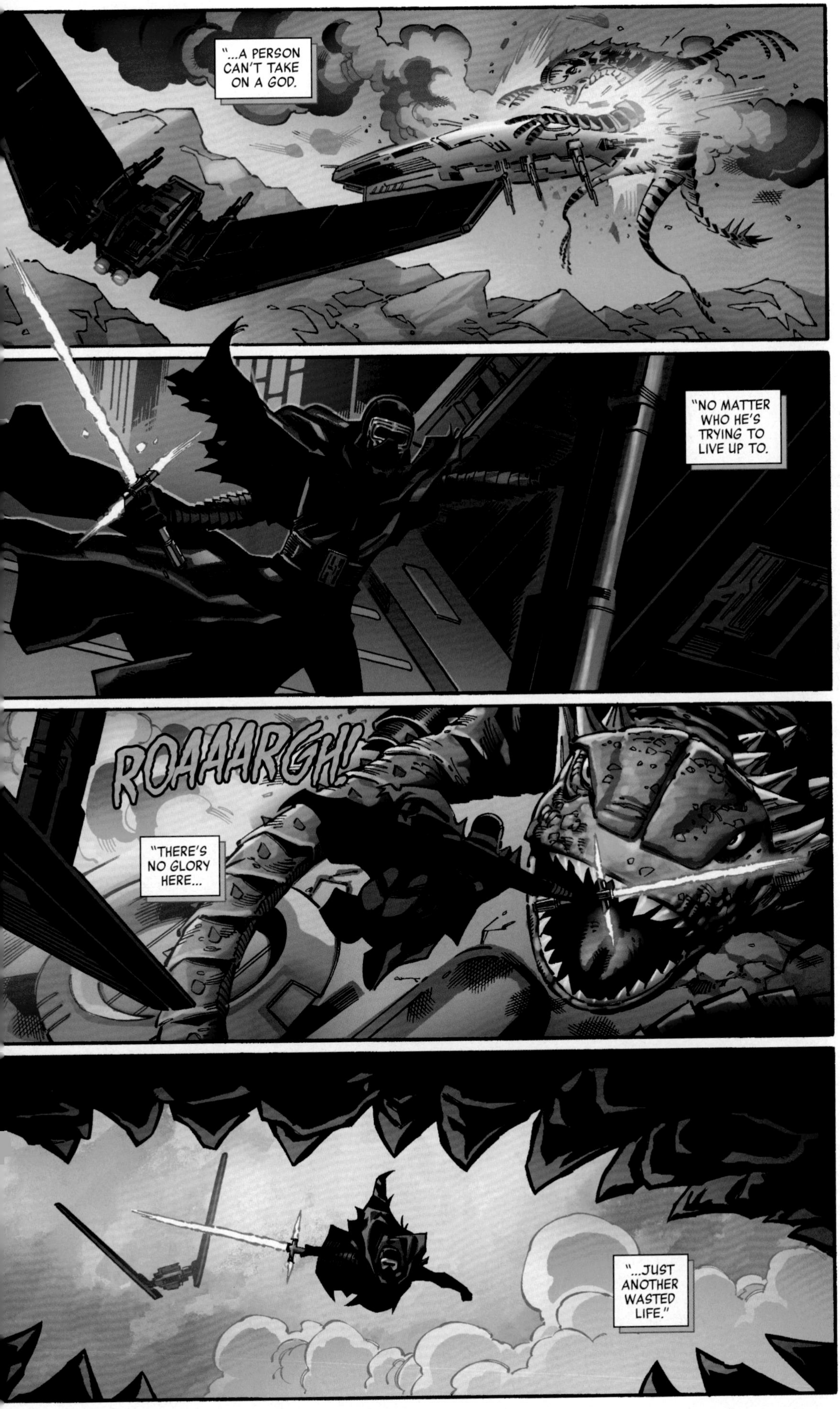
"...A PERSON CAN'T TAKE ON A GOD.
"NO MATTER WHO HE'S TRYING TO LIVE UP TO.
ROAAARGH!
"THERE'S NO GLORY HERE...
"...JUST ANOTHER WASTED LIFE."

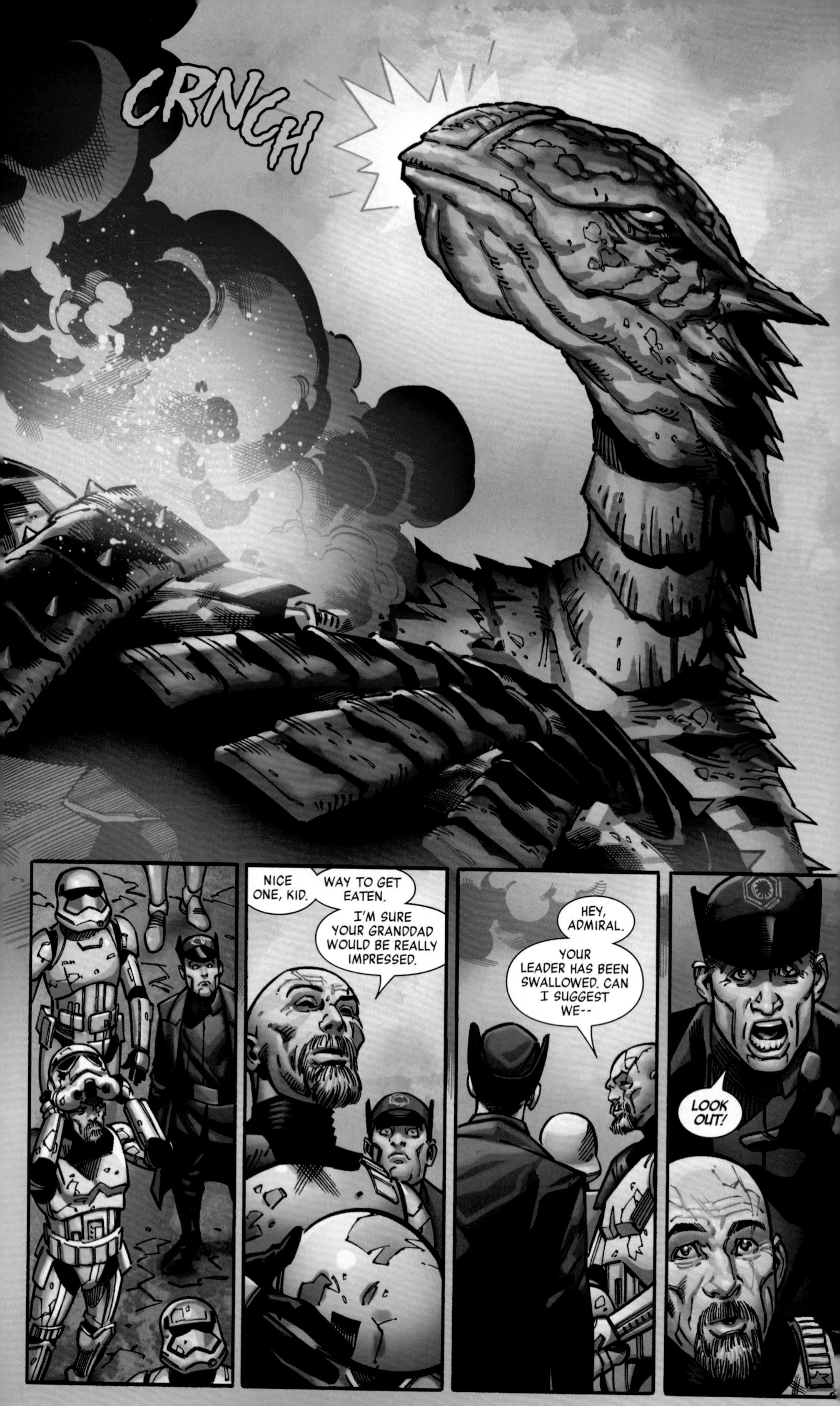
CRNCH
NICE ONE, KID.
WAY TO GET EATEN.
I'M SURE YOUR GRANDDAD WOULD BE REALLY IMPRESSED.
HEY, ADMIRAL.
YOUR LEADER HAS BEEN SWALLOWED. CAN I SUGGEST WE--
LOOK OUT!

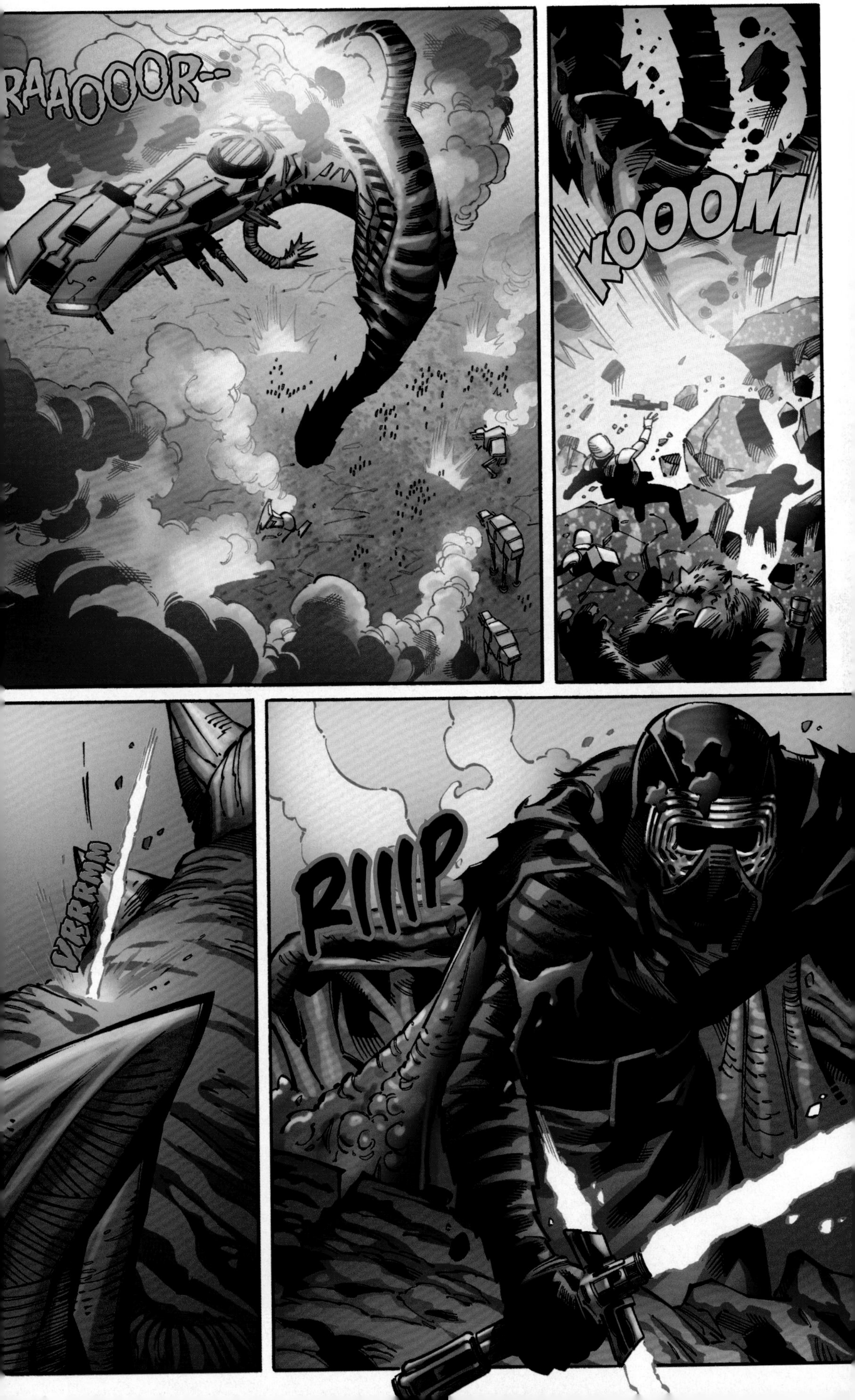
RAAOOOR--
KOOOM
VRRRMM
RIIIP

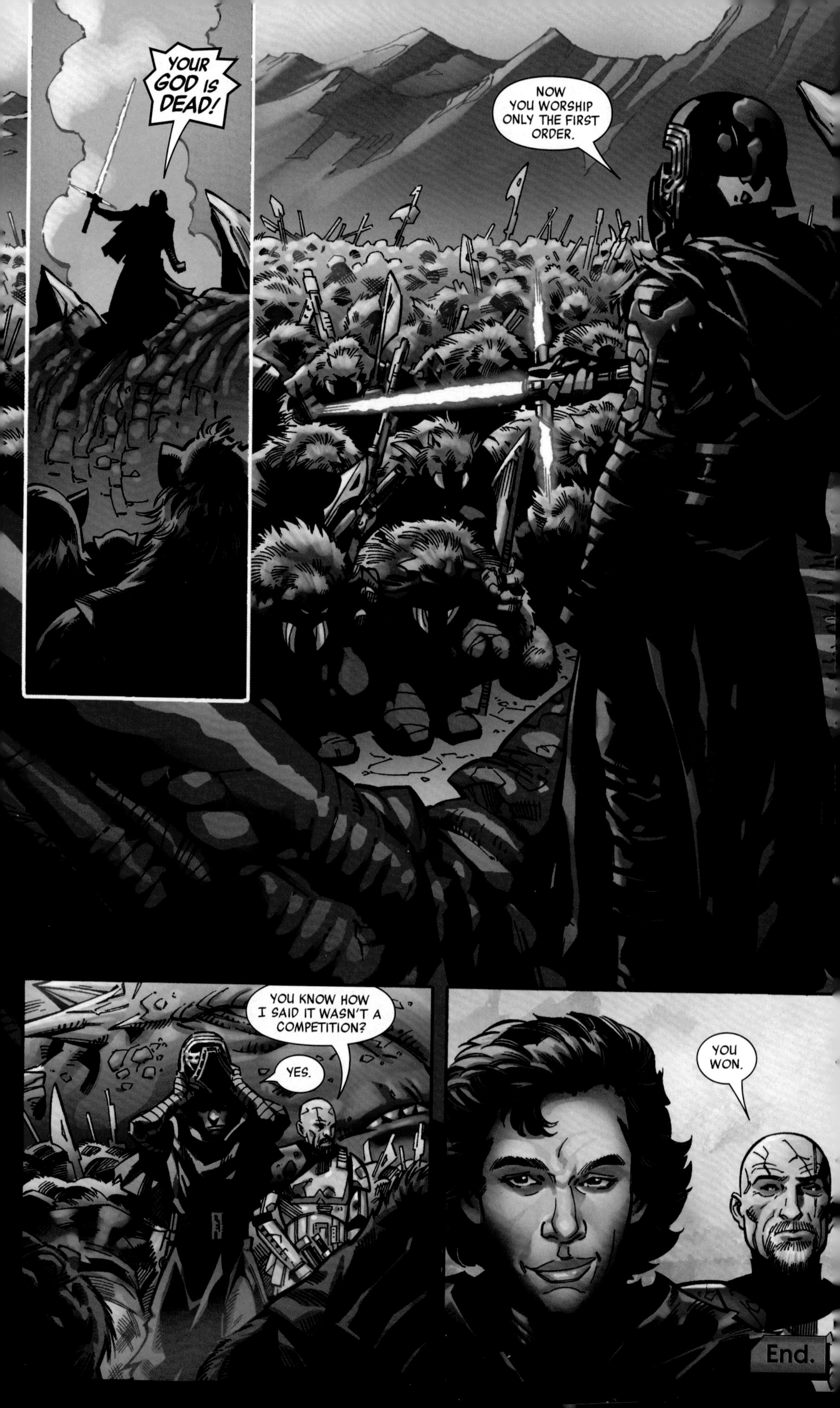
YOUR GOD IS DEAD!
NOW YOU WORSHIP ONLY THE FIRST ORDER.
YOU KNOW HOW I SAID IT WASN'T A COMPETITION?
YES.
YOU WON.
End.

AGE OF RESISTANCE

Art by Doug Chiang

AGE OF RESISTANCE
Ben Solo - Part Skywalker, Part Vader, All Solo
By Bryan Young

From the moment it was revealed that Kylo Ren was the son of Han Solo and Princess Leia, *Star Wars* fans would never be the same. Questions swirled. How could the child of two such amazing people turn so evil?

When Han Solo called out to his son across that bridge--"Ben!"--our collective hearts broke. Han still loved his son and wanted to do anything to help him, and we knew it. And then Ben did the unforgivable: He murdered his lovable scoundrel of a father, an icon beloved by many, both inside the *Star Wars* universe and in our universe as well.

Can Ben Solo come back from such a thing? Will he reconcile his feelings about Luke and Rey and his mother into something that brings him back from the brink of darkness? Or will he descend further into darkness and die the villain his parents would both be ashamed of?

Maybe his fate will be somewhere in between.

Only time will tell.

KYLO REN AT THE CROSSROADS

Whether or not you believe Kylo Ren can be redeemed for what he's done, that is the very crossroads he's at. Some view him as just a scared little boy dealing with the circumstances life gave him searching for the light; others see him

as trying to live up to the legacy of his grandfather seeking the dark; others still fall somewhere in between. Whatever your feelings about Kylo Ren and his ability to be redeemed or not are, they're completely valid and true. We all see in Kylo Ren a different aspect of his tortured persona. Since each fan views Kylo Ren through their own personal experience, the many interpretations of the available information about him means that *all* of our perspectives are valid. The answer is in the heart of the individual person bearing witness to Ben Solo's story, even if that feeling about Ben Solo is merely indifference to his plight.

For me, one of the most interesting things about Kylo Ren/Ben Solo is where he's at in his journey. He's just at the beginning of his turn, and the light rages in him as strongly as the dark.

It is inevitable to compare Kylo Ren to Darth Vader. At the beginning of Vader's journey he was still seeking out a way to bring Padmé back or be with her, battling the light until, years later, he shut out all but the tiniest spark. Luke saw that pinhole of light that no one else did and was convinced Vader could be turned back. Rey saw that same thing in Ben. Vader saw in Luke a chance to turn his son to the dark side, just as Ben sees in Rey.

Who is right?

That's what's so fascinating about Ben Solo. We all see our own image of the

swirling flow of light and dark inside of him, and it's different for all of us. He's the perfect encapsulation of the struggle between the two sides of existence for *Star Wars* fans.

THE JEDI KILLER

Kylo Ren began his life in the early treatments of *The Force Awakens* as "the Jedi Killer." The Lucasfilm art department didn't know anything about his name or his origin for years. It wasn't until much later that they learned that Kylo Ren was not only related to Han Solo, but that he would be killing his father in the course of the film. Shockwaves were felt internally, and this fact was one of the chief things protected by the extreme secrecy surrounding the first new *Star Wars* film in a decade.

Adam Driver, the actor behind Ben Solo, has known the character's eventual fate from the beginning. He told *Deadline* recently, "I had one piece of information of where it was all going, and that's where it has been in my head for a long time, and things were building toward that. It feels very theatrical, if anything."

Only one thing is for sure: As we all wait to see what Ben Solo's fate eventually is in *The Rise of Skywalker*, we'll each have our own way of understanding it.

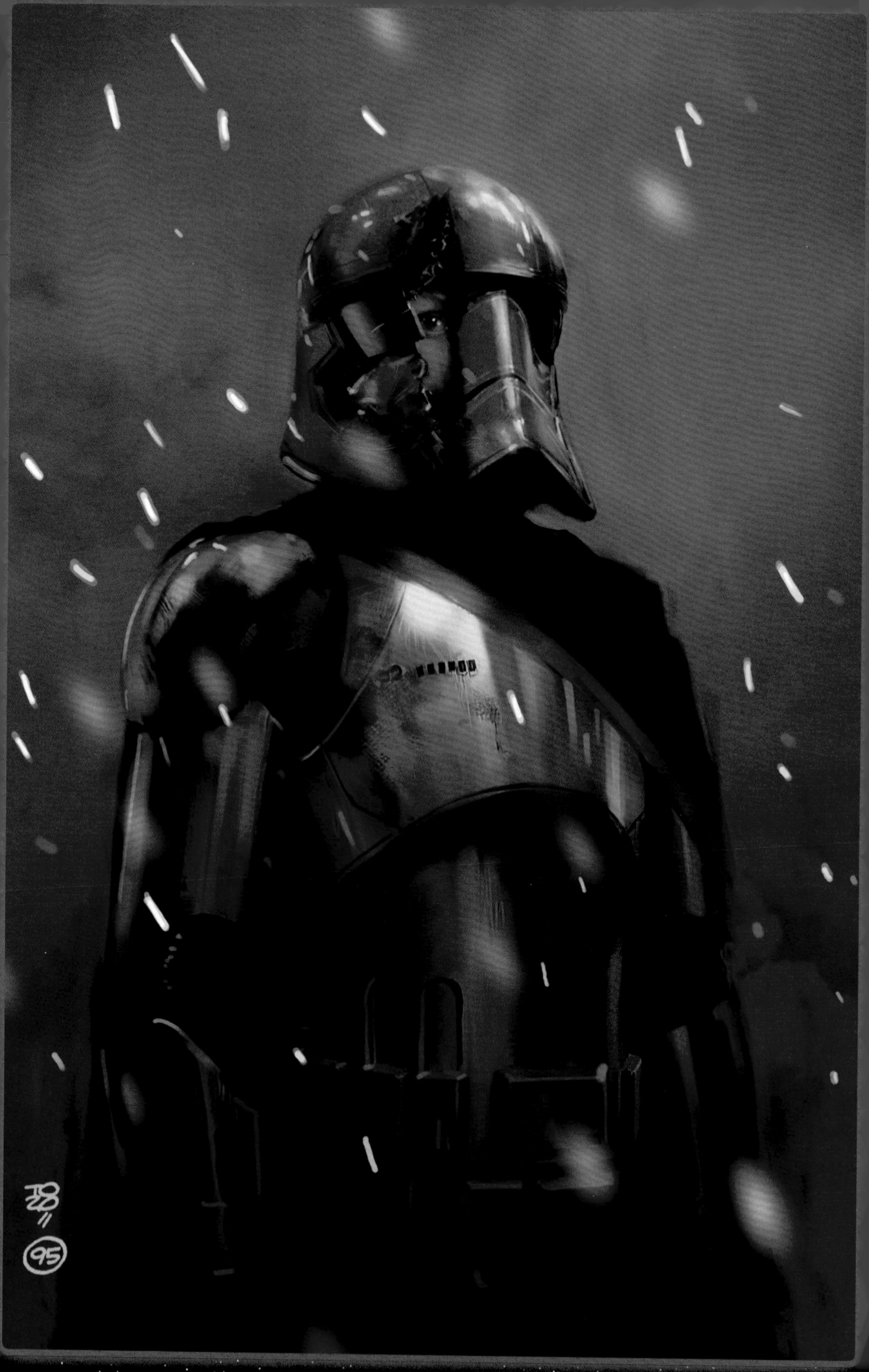

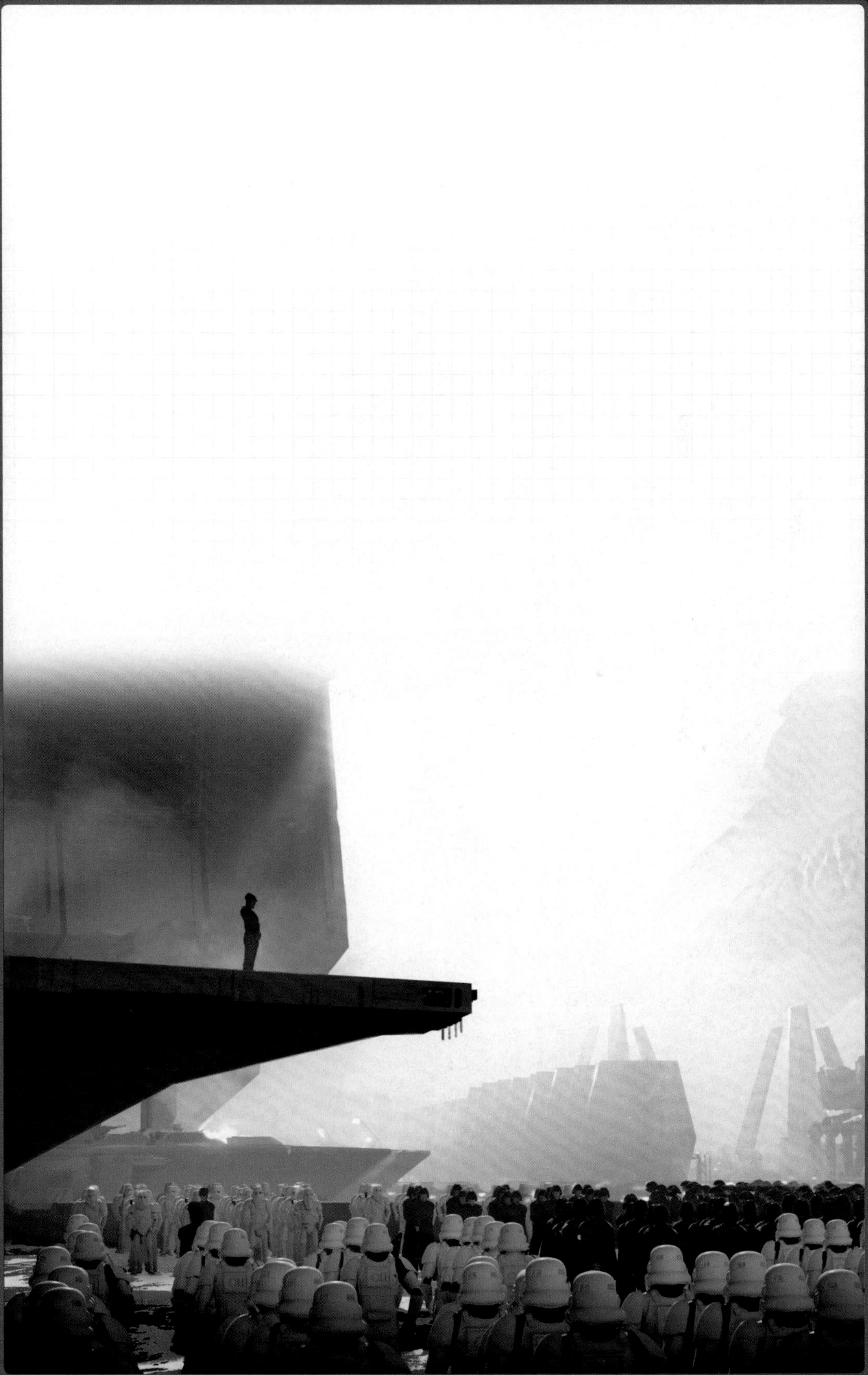

STAR WARS: AGE OF RESISTANCE — GENERAL HUX **Concept Variant by**
KEVIN JENKINS

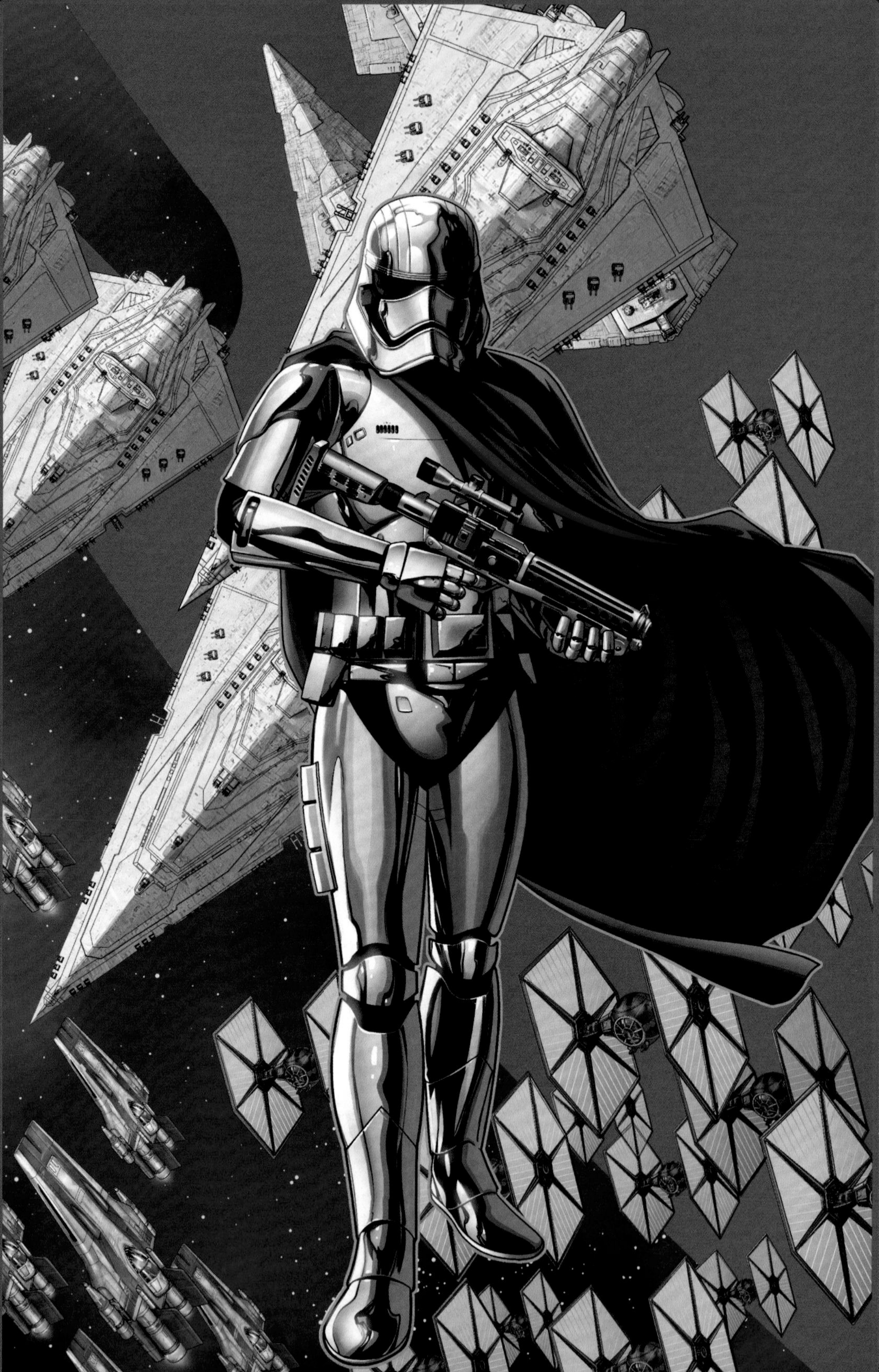

STAR WARS: AGE OF RESISTANCE — CAPTAIN PHASMA Puzzle Piece Variant by
MIKE McKONE & GURU-eFX

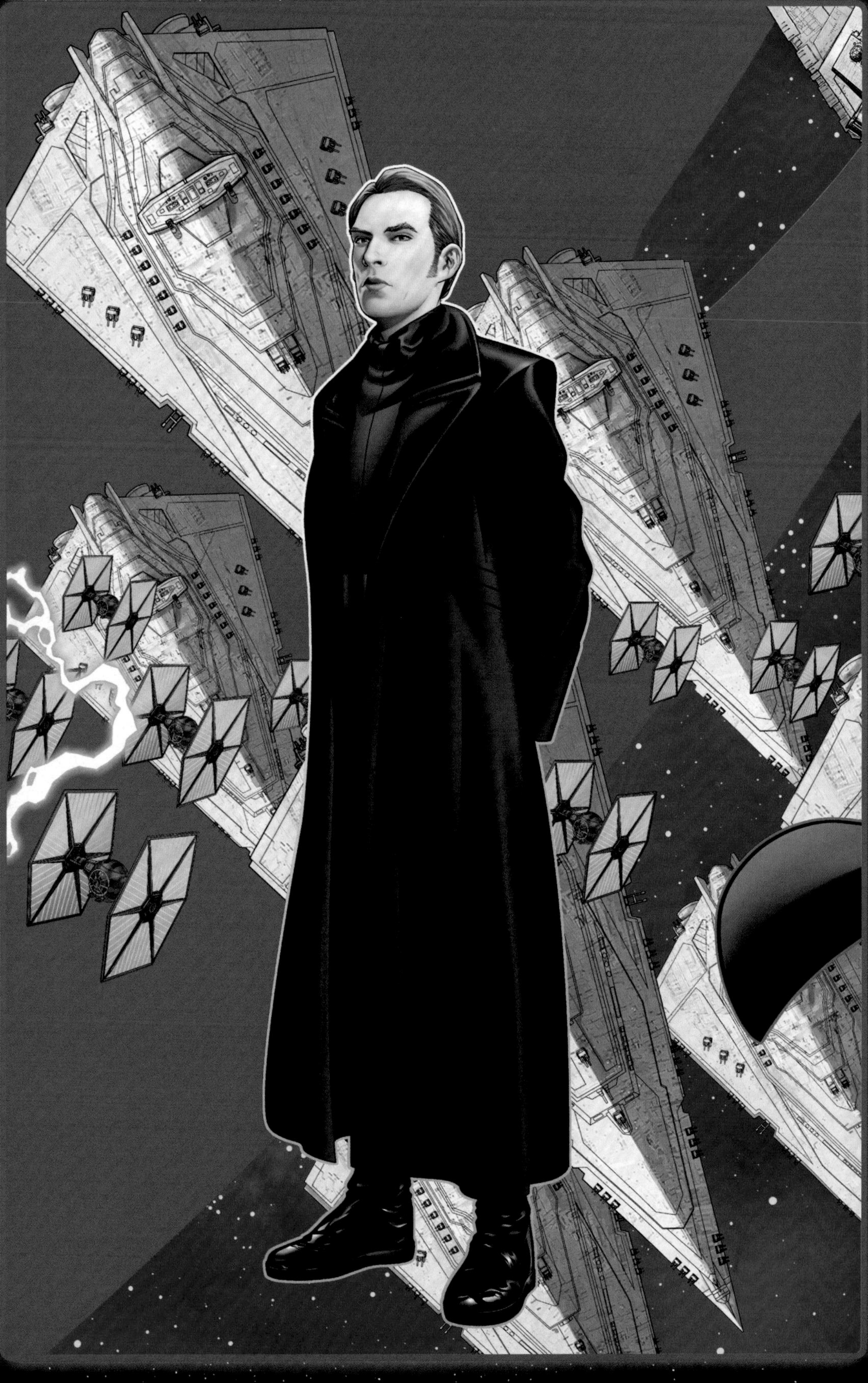

STAR WARS: AGE OF RESISTANCE — GENERAL HUX Puzzle Piece Variant by
MIKE McKONE & GURU-eFX

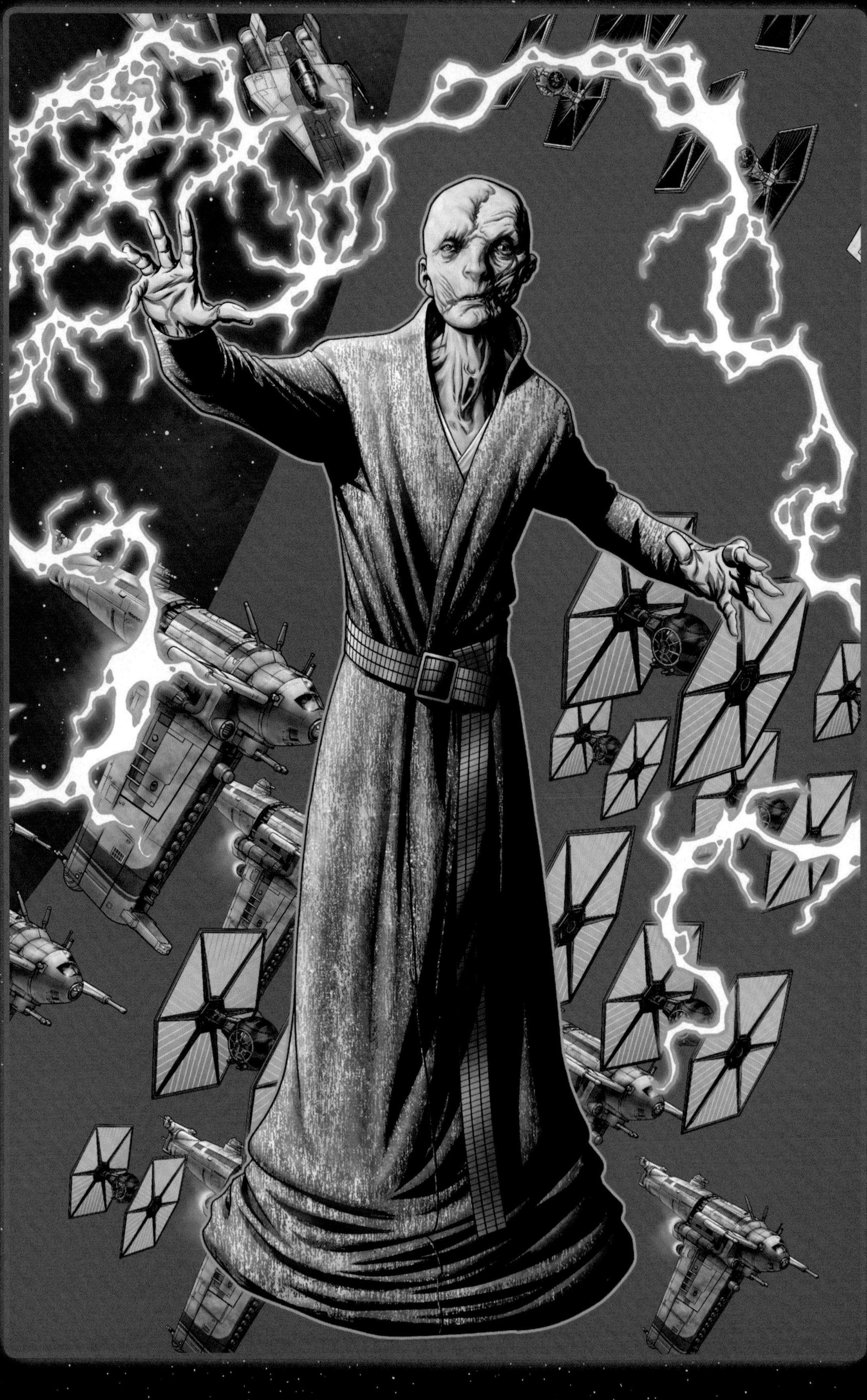

STAR WARS: AGE OF RESISTANCE — SUPREME LEADER SNOKE Puzzle Piece Variant by
MIKE McKONE & GURU-eFX

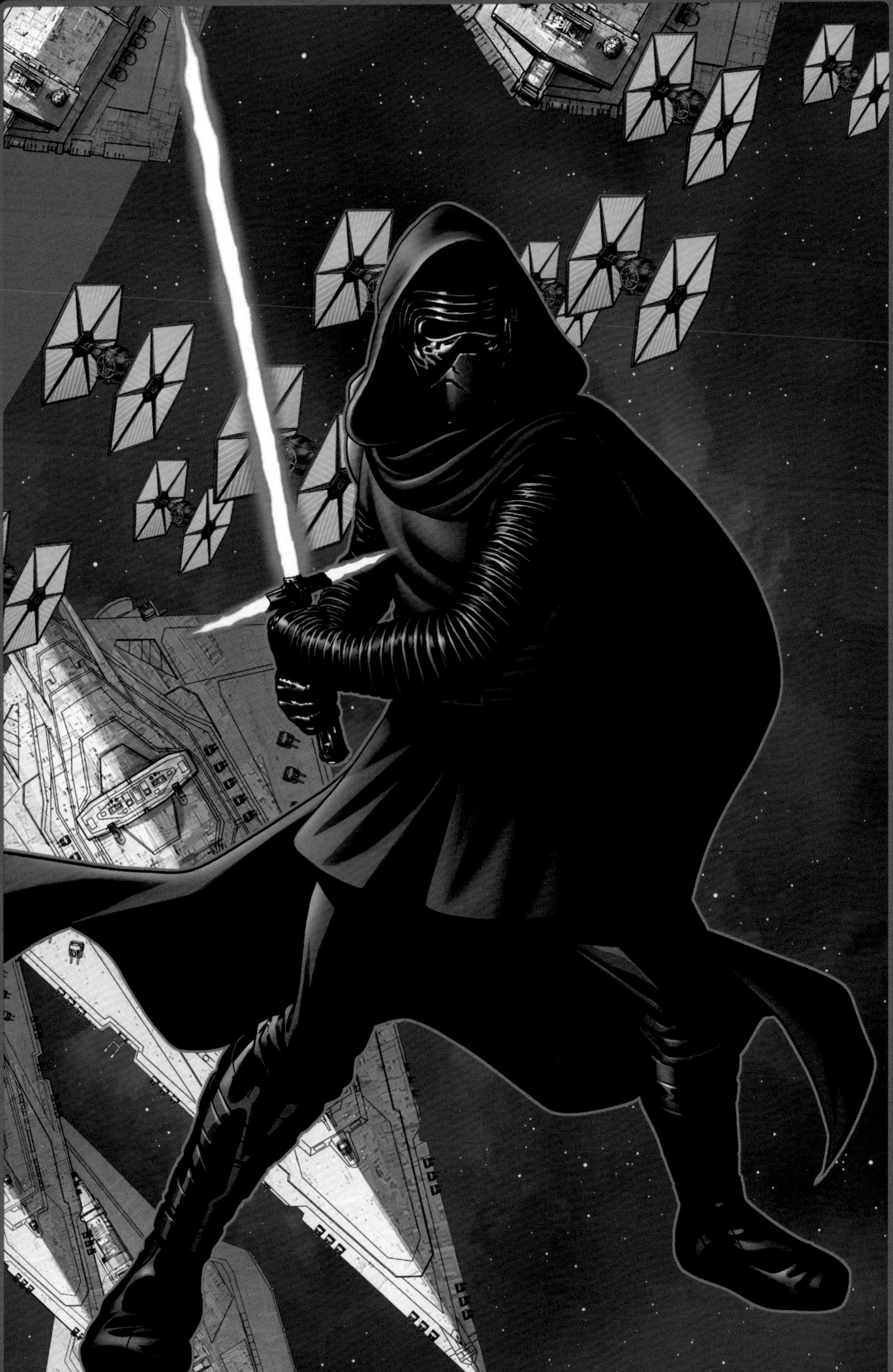

STAR WARS: AGE OF RESISTANCE — KYLO REN **Puzzle Piece Variant by**
MIKE McKONE & GURU-eFX

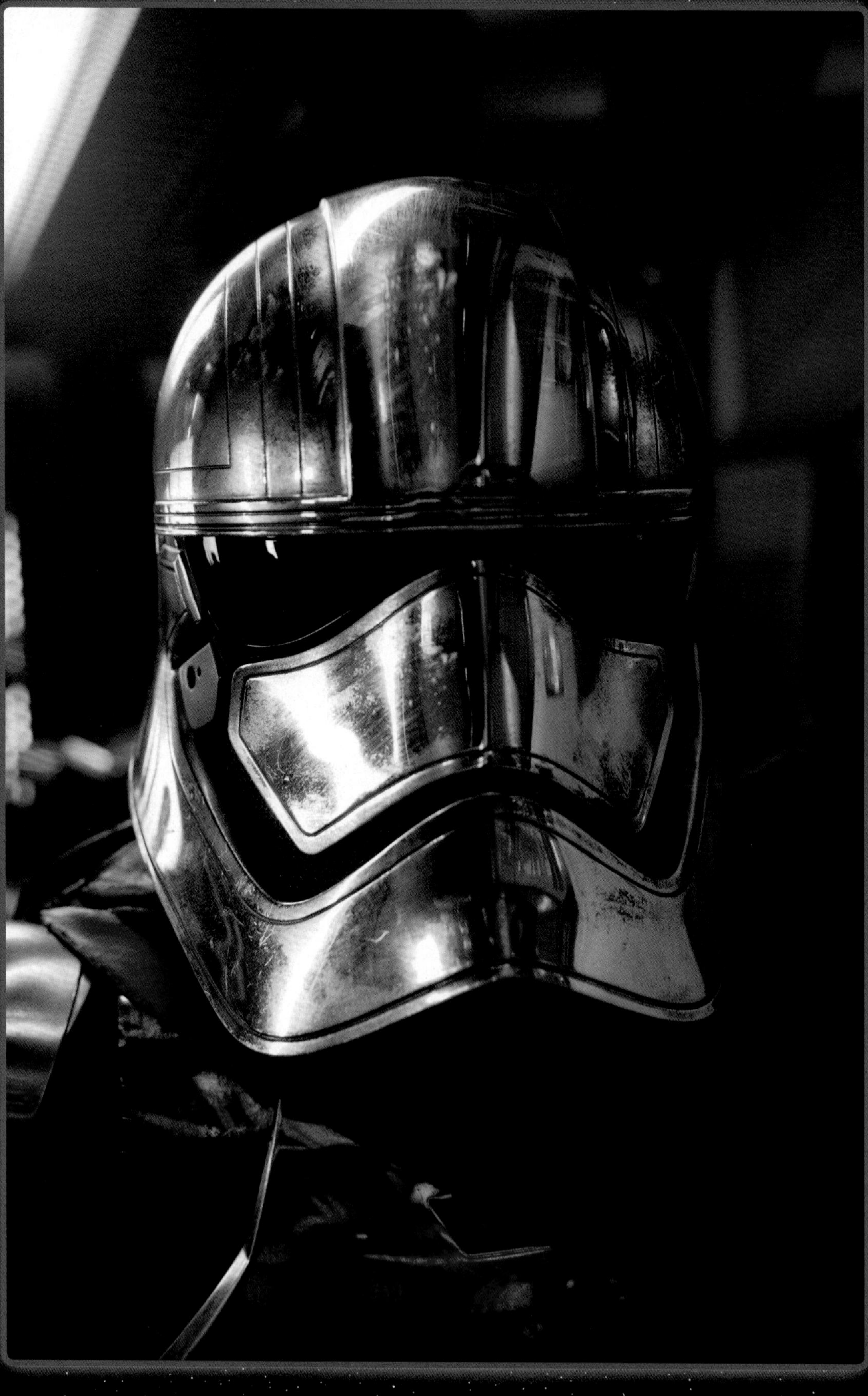

STAR WARS: AGE OF RESISTANCE — *CAPTAIN PHASMA* Movie Variant

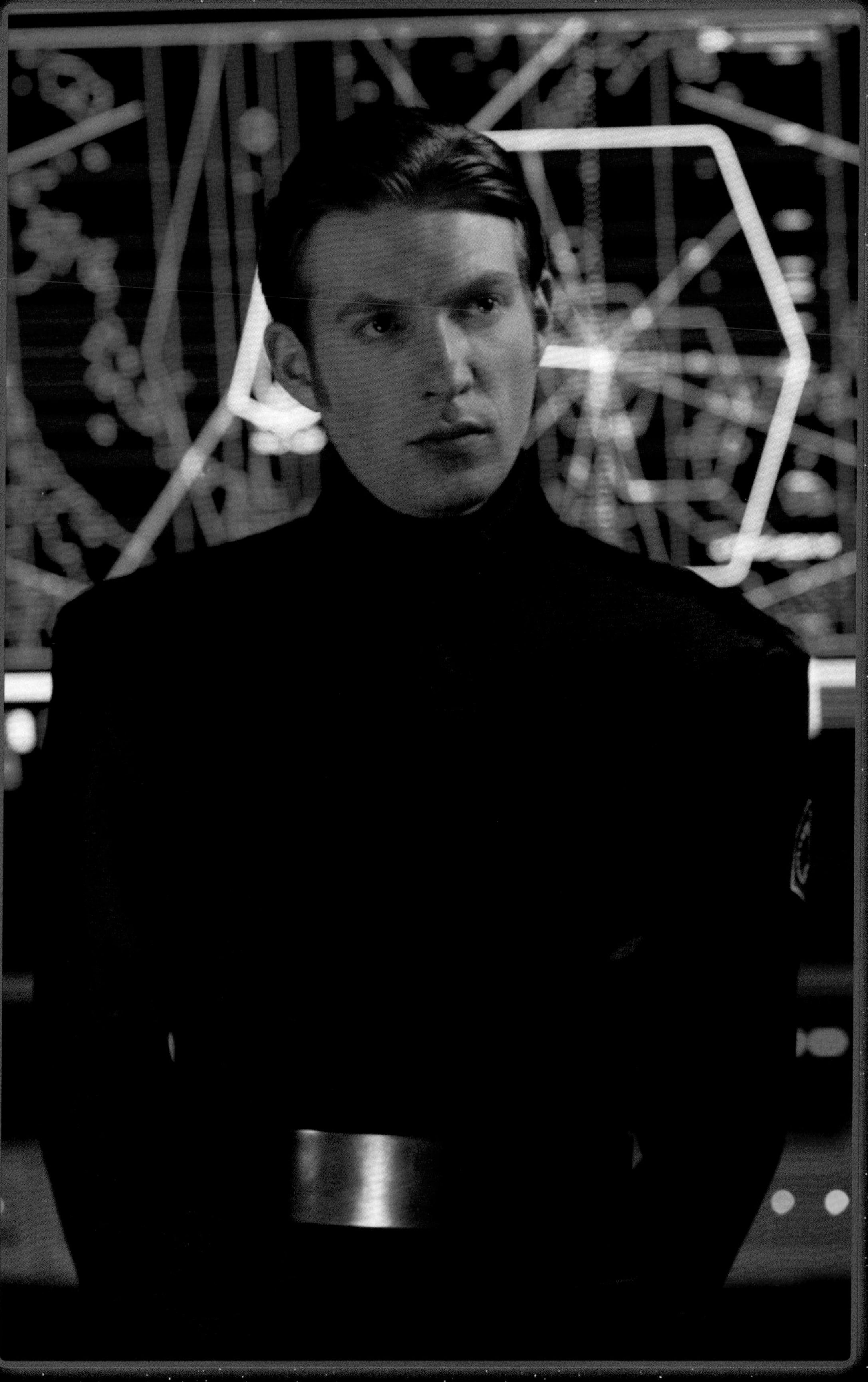

STAR WARS: AGE OF RESISTANCE — GENERAL HUX Movie Variant

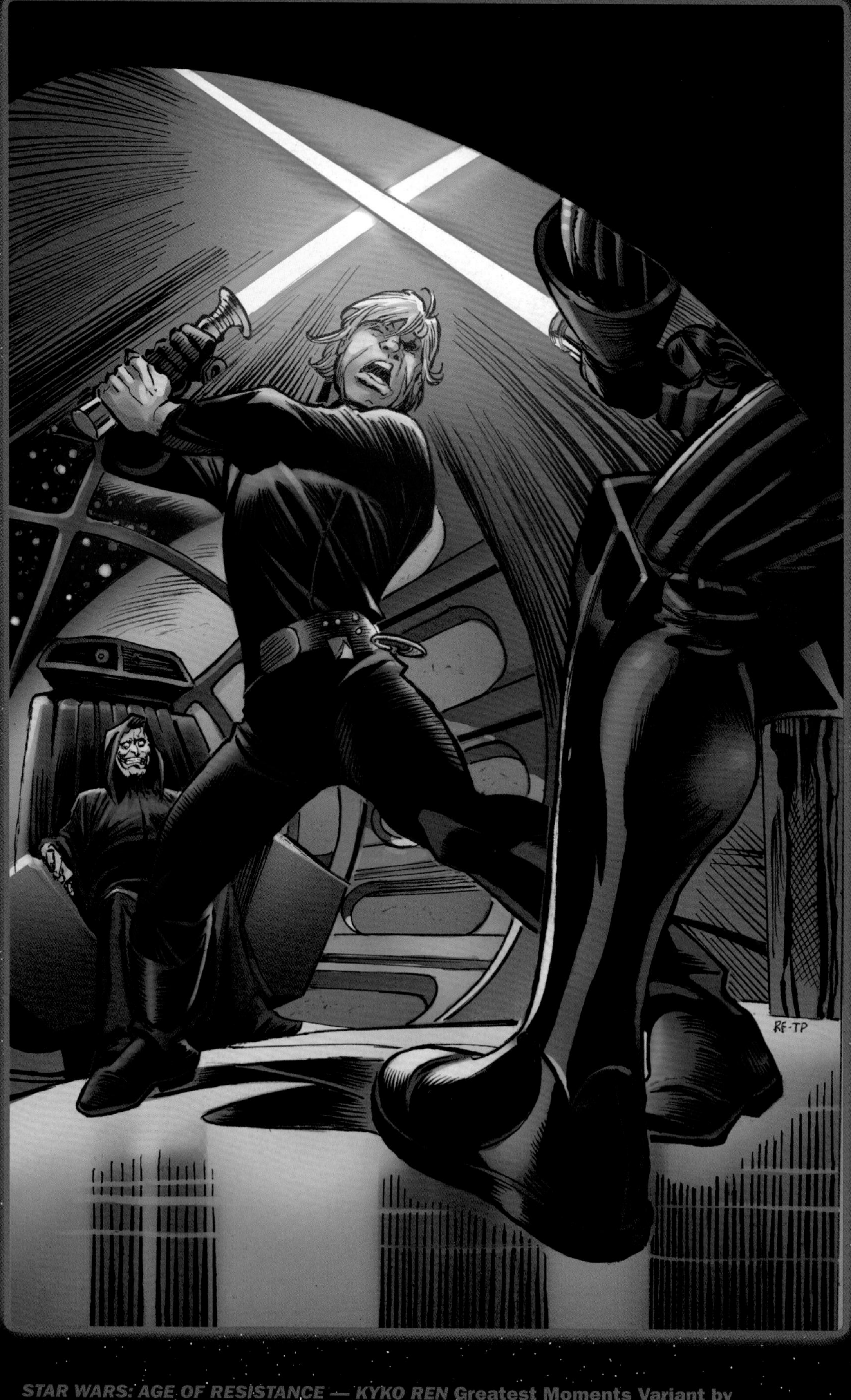
RF-TP

STAR WARS: AGE OF RESISTANCE — KYKO REN **Greatest Moments Variant by**
RON FRENZ, TOM PALMER & ANTONIO FABELA

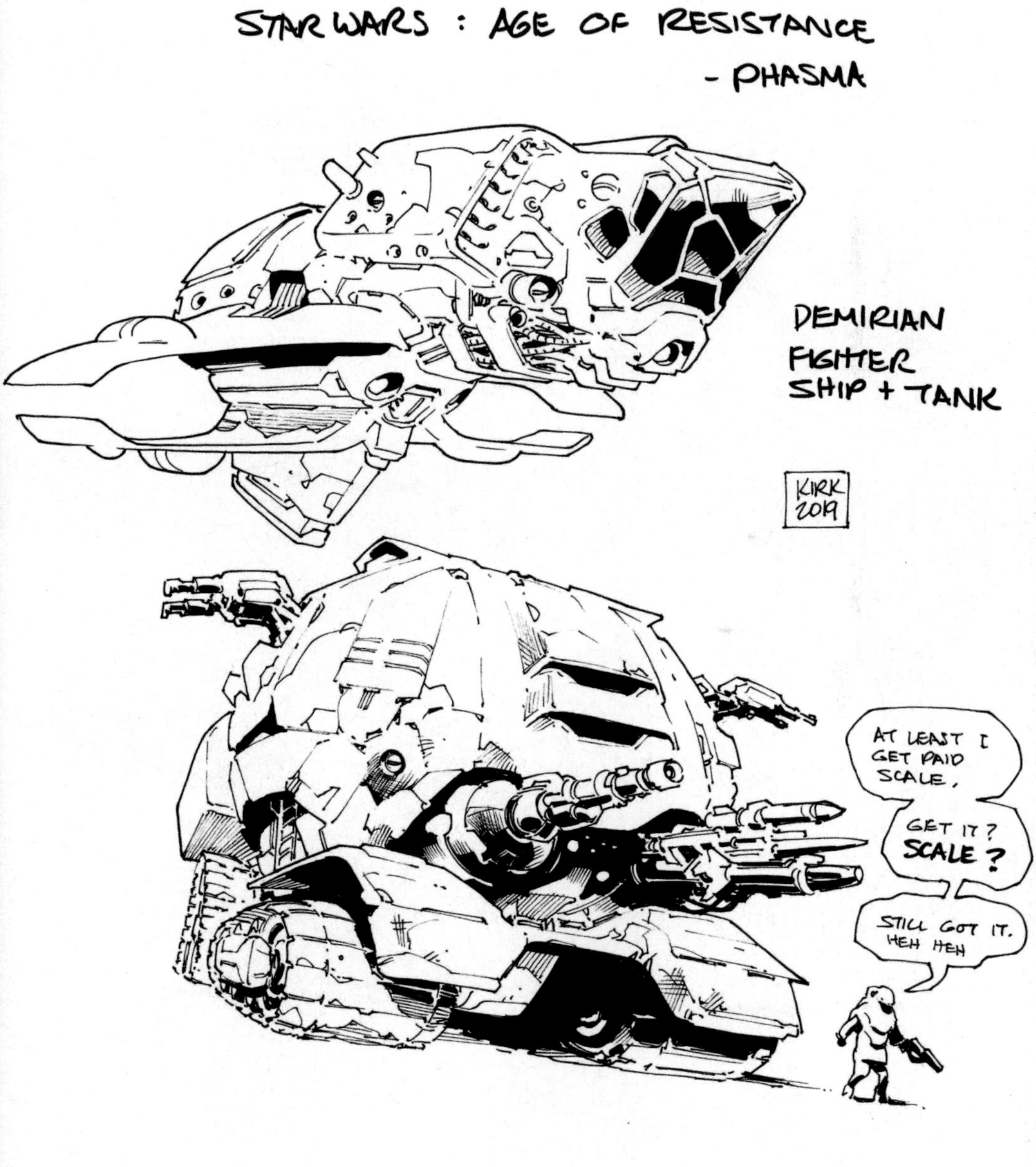
STAR WARS : AGE OF RESISTANCE
- PHASMA
DEMIRIAN FIGHTER SHIP + TANK
KIRK 2019
AT LEAST I GET PAID SCALE.
GET IT? SCALE?
STILL GOT IT. HEH HEH

STAR WARS: AGE OF RESISTANCE — CAPTAIN PHASMA **Designs by**
LEONARD KIRK

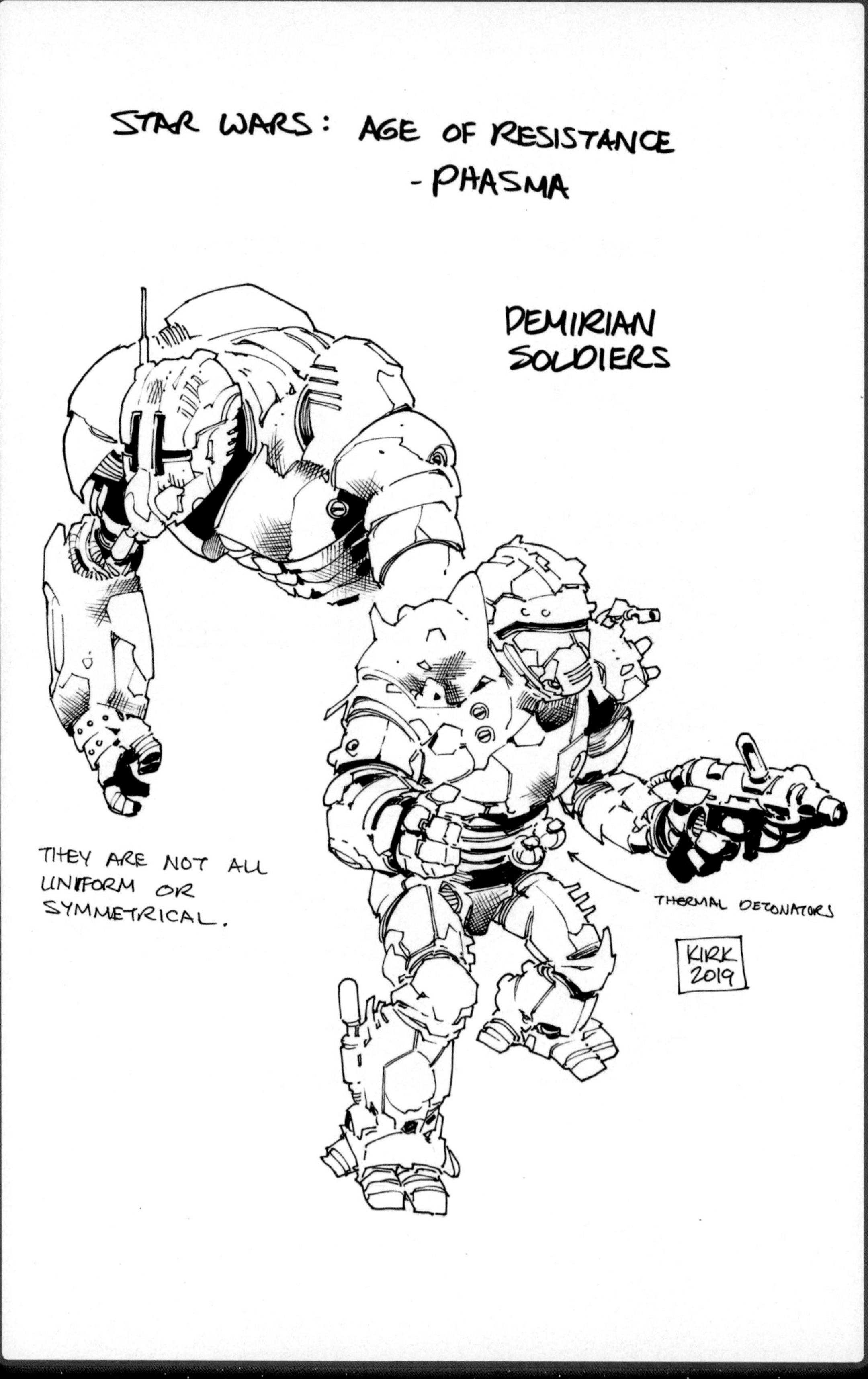
STAR WARS: AGE OF RESISTANCE
- PHASMA
DEMIRIAN SOLDIERS
THEY ARE NOT ALL UNIFORM OR SYMMETRICAL.
THERMAL DETONATORS
KIRK 2019

STAR WARS: AGE OF RESISTANCE — CAPTAIN PHASMA Designs by LEONARD KIRK

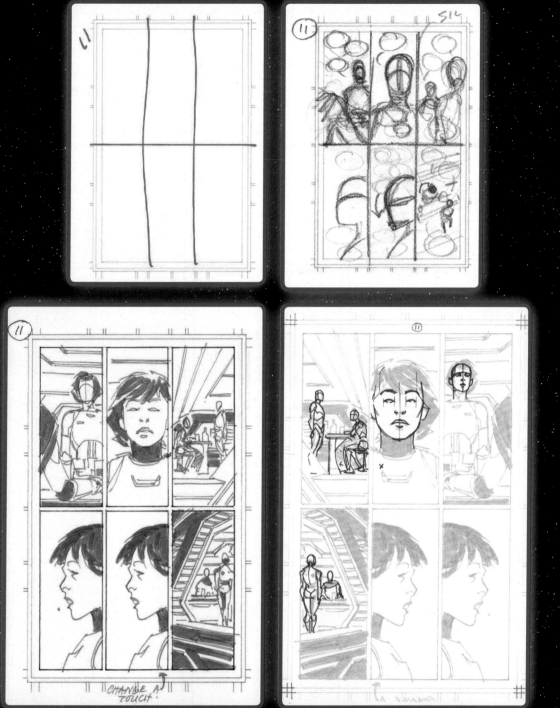

STAR WARS: AGE OF RESISTANCE — CAPTAIN PHASMA Page 11 Art Process by
LEONARD KIRK

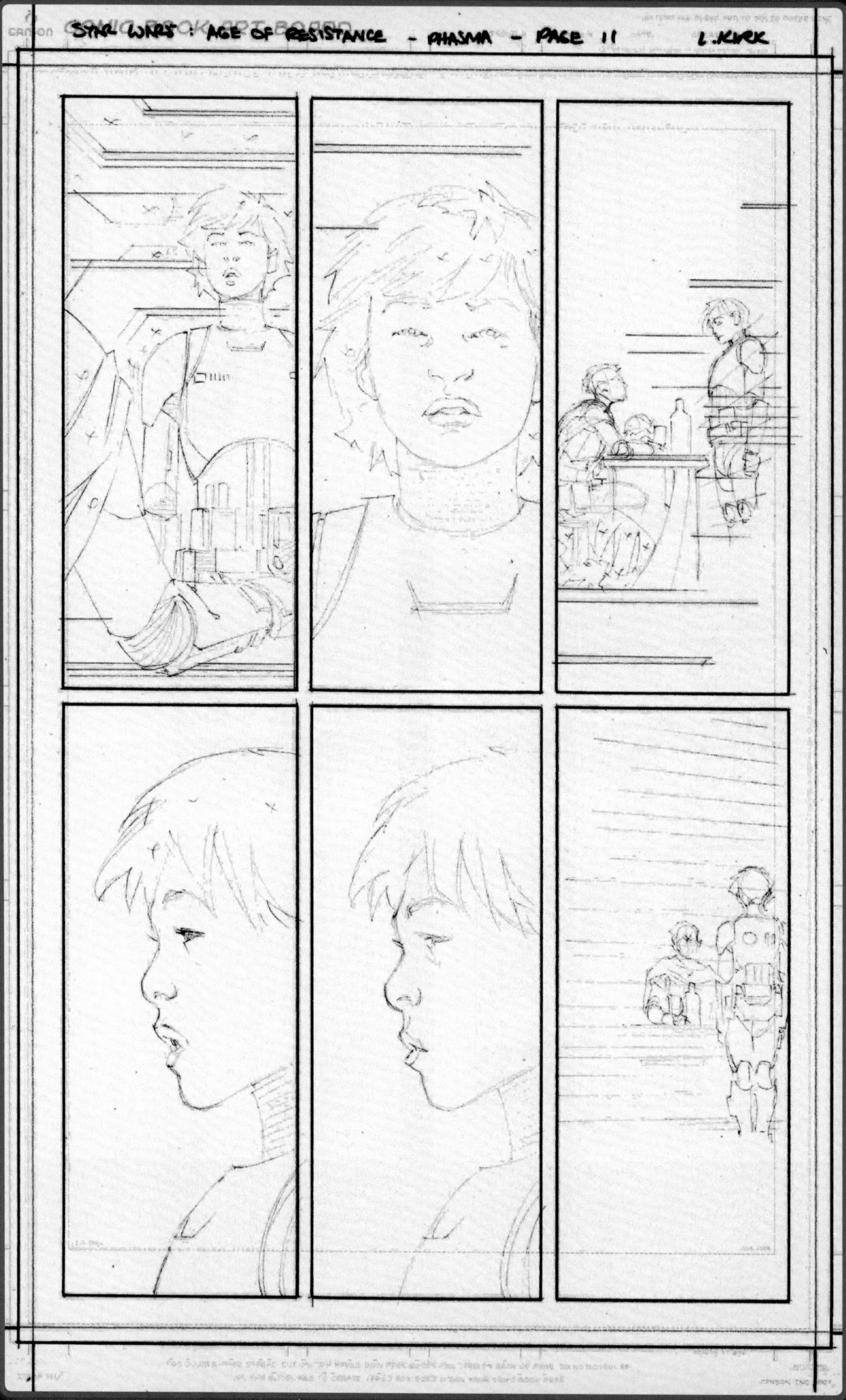
STAR WARS : AGE OF RESISTANCE - PHASMA - PAGE 11 L.KIRK

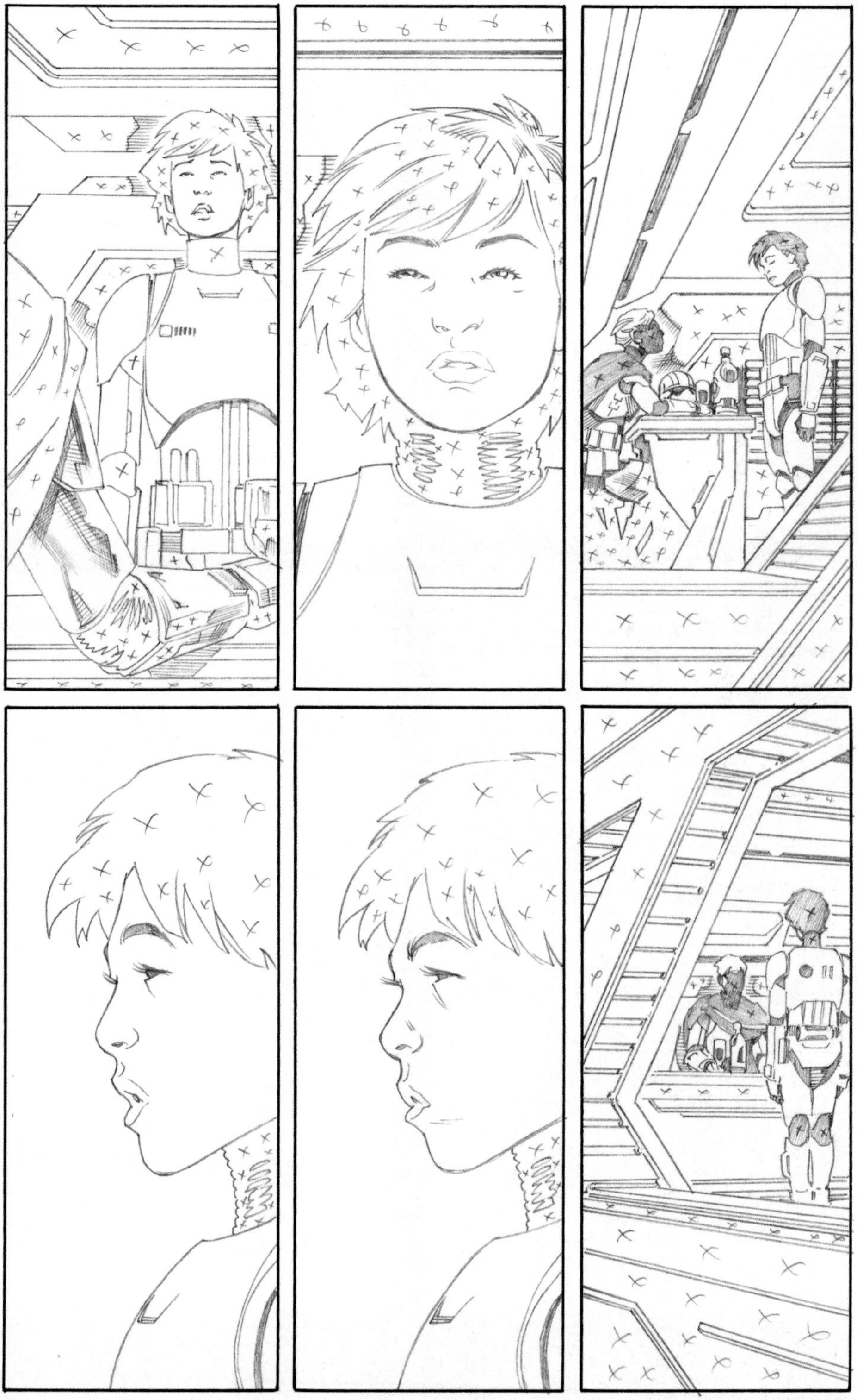

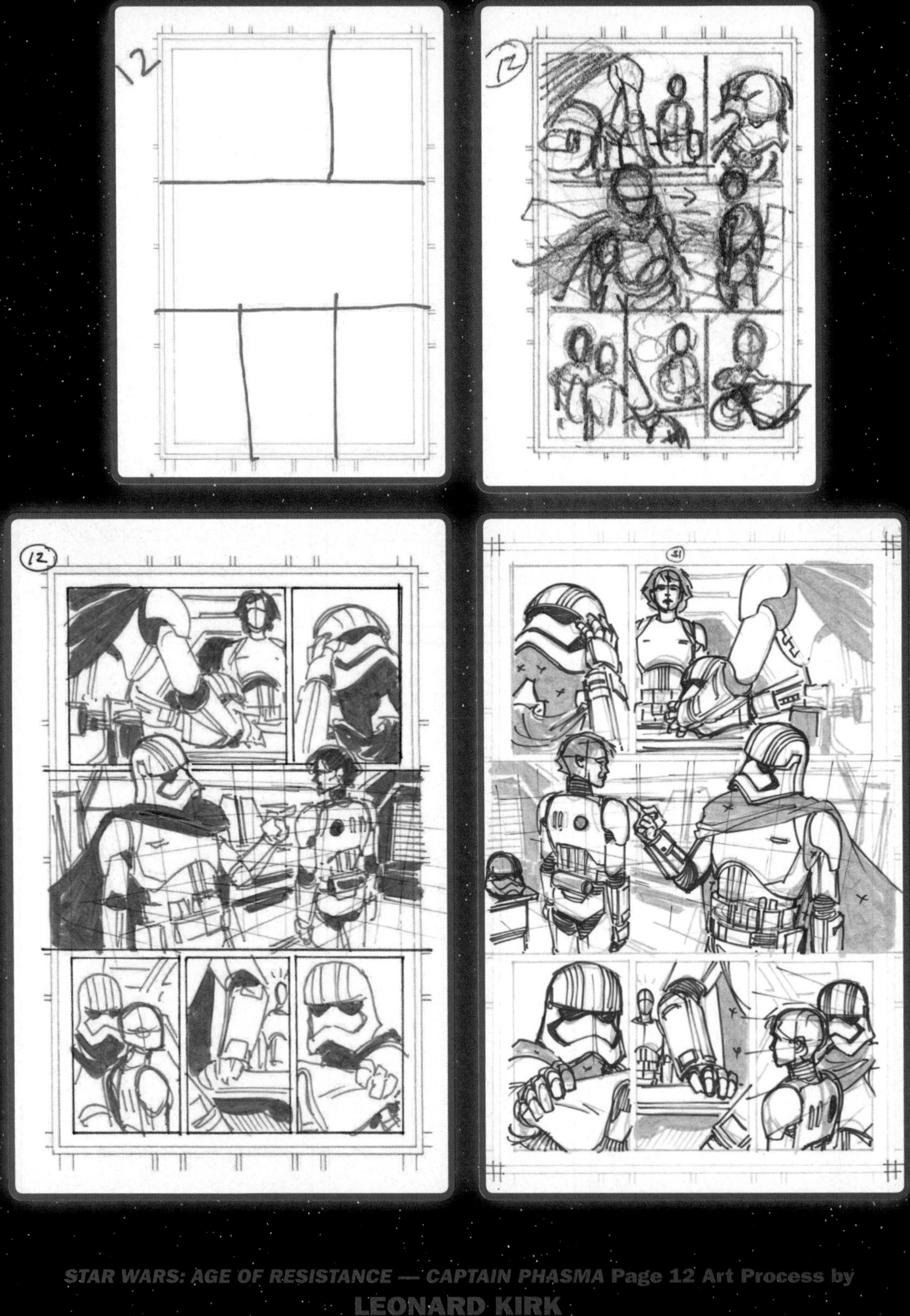

STAR WARS: AGE OF RESISTANCE — CAPTAIN PHASMA **Page 12 Art Process by**
LEONARD KIRK

STAR WARS: AGE OF RESISTANCE - PHASMA - PAGE 12 L. KIRK

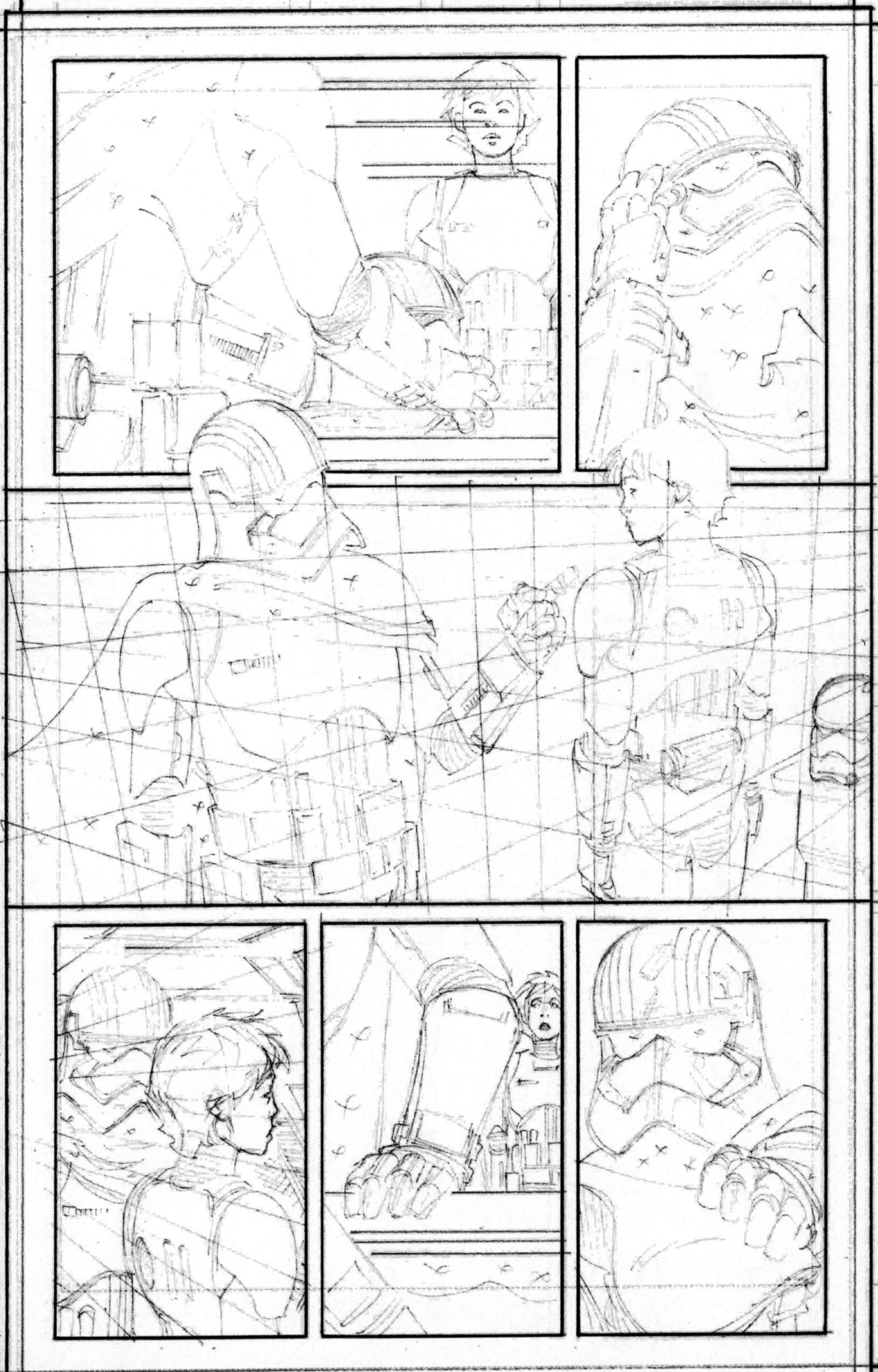

STAR WARS : AGE OF RESISTANCE - PHASMA - PAGE 12 L. KIRK

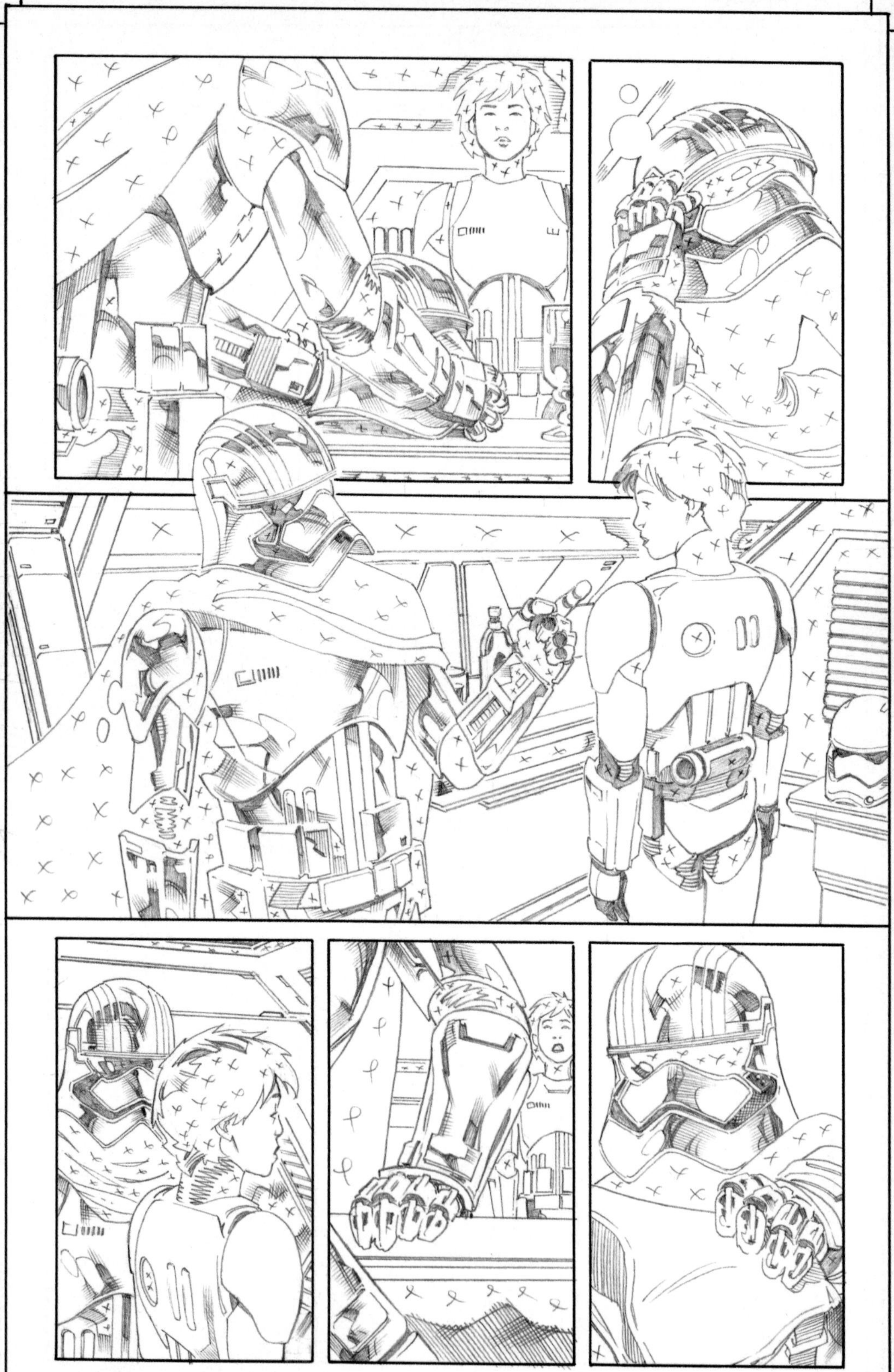

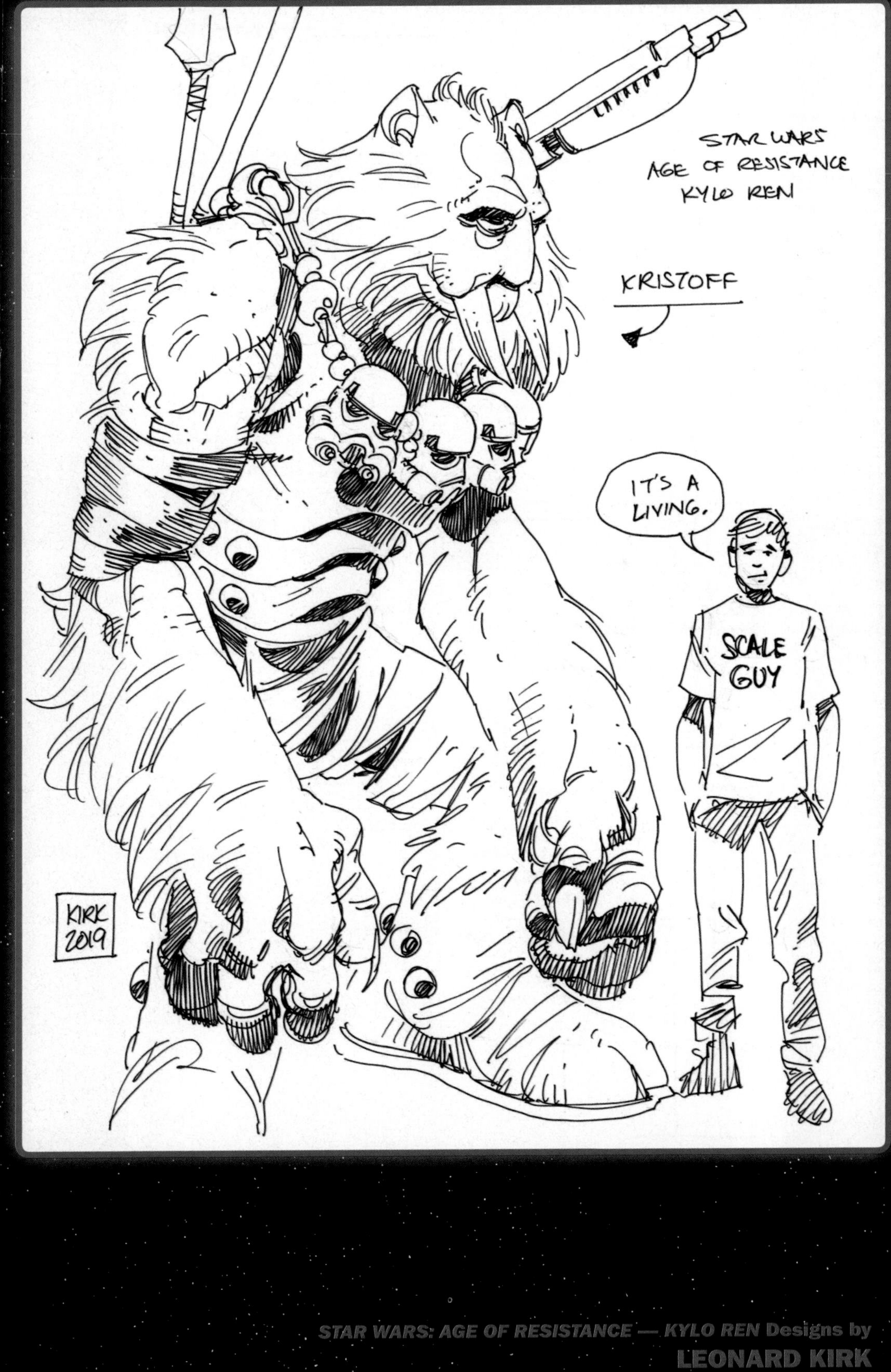
STAR WARS
AGE OF RESISTANCE
KYLO REN
KRISTOFF
IT'S A LIVING.
SCALE GUY
KIRK 2019

STAR WARS: AGE OF RESISTANCE — KYLO REN **Designs by**
LEONARD KIRK

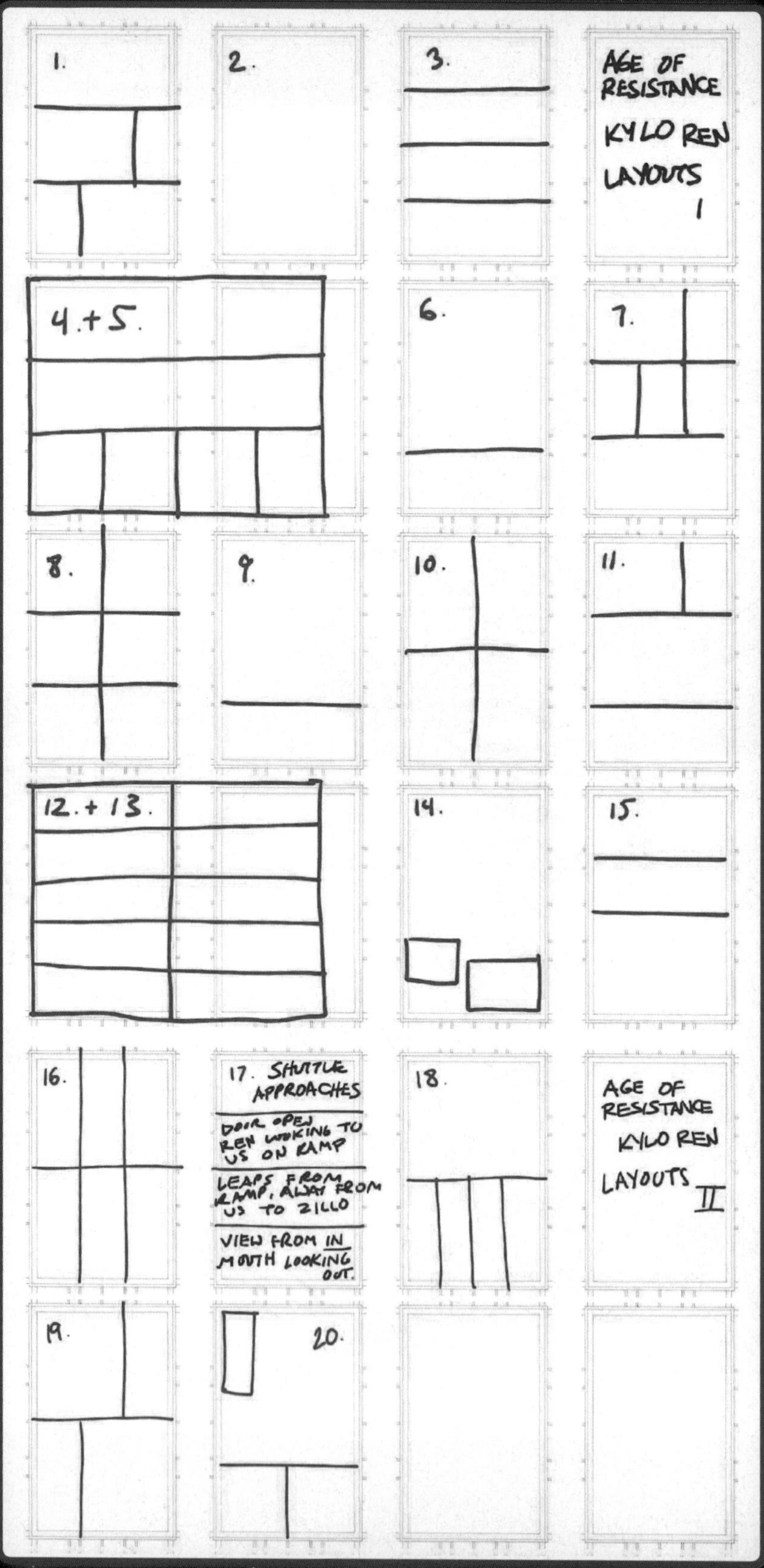
1.
2.
3.
AGE OF RESISTANCE
KYLO REN
LAYOUTS
I
4. + 5.
6.
7.
8.
9.
10.
11.
12. + 13.
14.
15.
16.
17. SHUTTLE APPROACHES
DOOR OPEN REN WALKING TO US ON RAMP
LEAPS FROM RAMP, AWAY FROM US TO ZILLO
VIEW FROM IN MOUTH LOOKING OUT.
18.
AGE OF RESISTANCE
KYLO REN
LAYOUTS
II
19.
20.

STAR WARS: AGE OF RESISTANCE — KYLO REN **Art Process by**

LEONARD KIRK

STAR WARS: AGE OF RESISTANCE - LAYOUTS
KYLO REN
L. KIRK

9

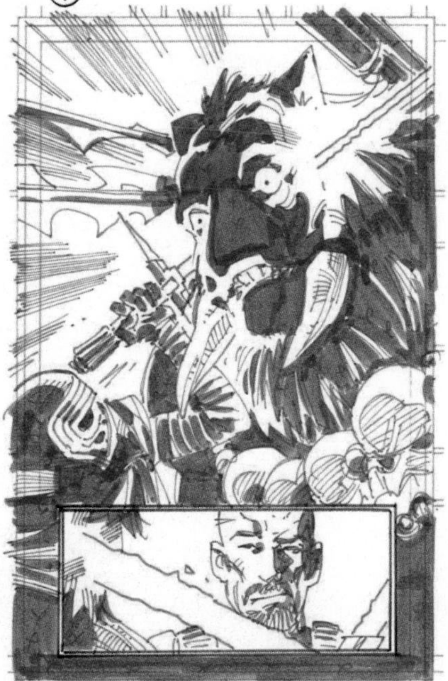

10

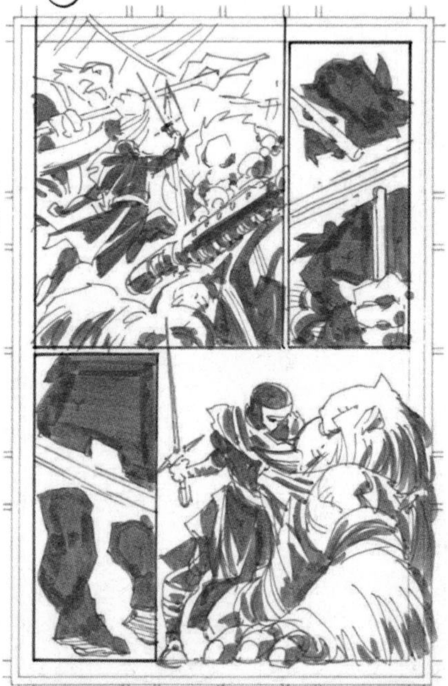

11

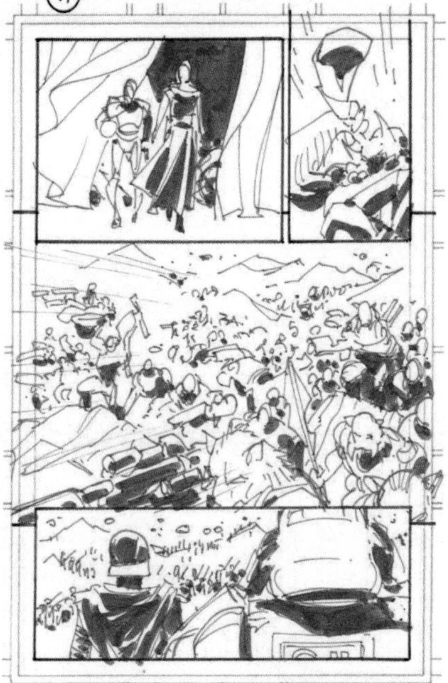

RUTHERFORD PUTS ON HELMET.

14

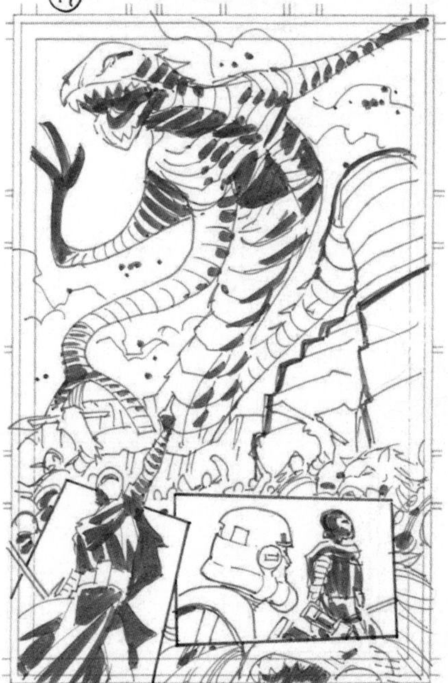

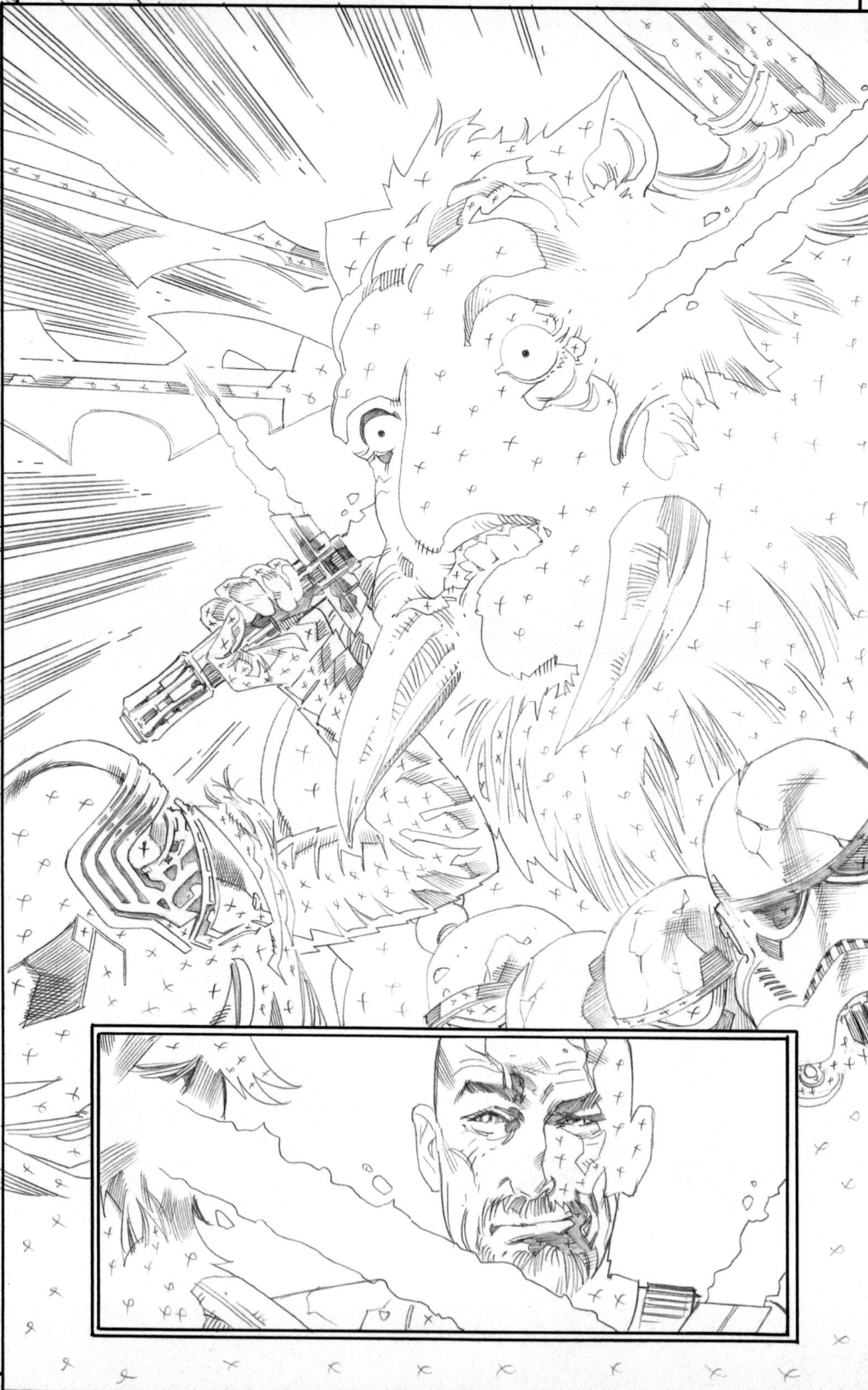

STAR WARS : AGE OF RESISTANCE - KYLO REN 010 L.KIRK

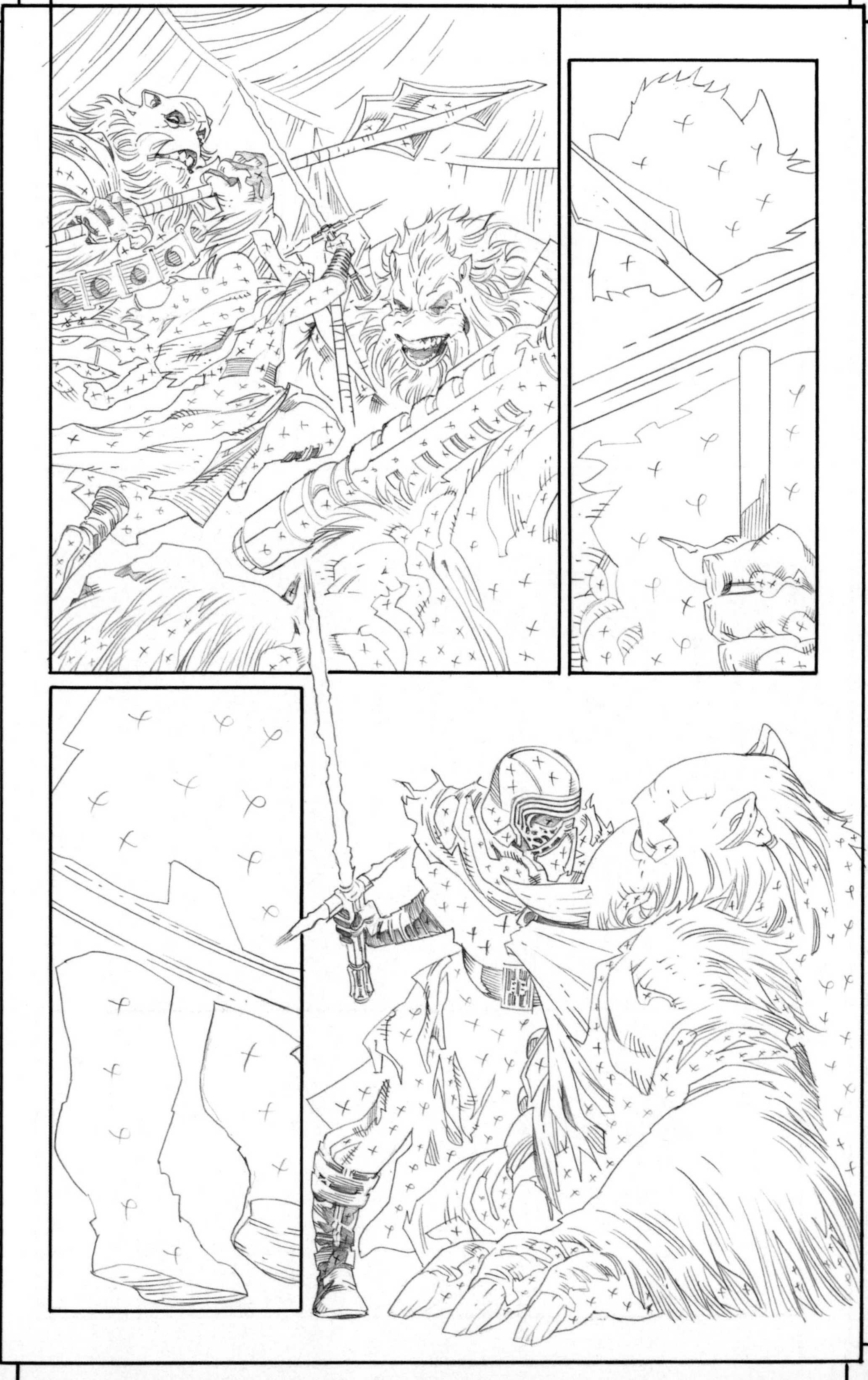

STAR WARS : AGE OF RESISTANCE KYLO REN 011 L.KIRK

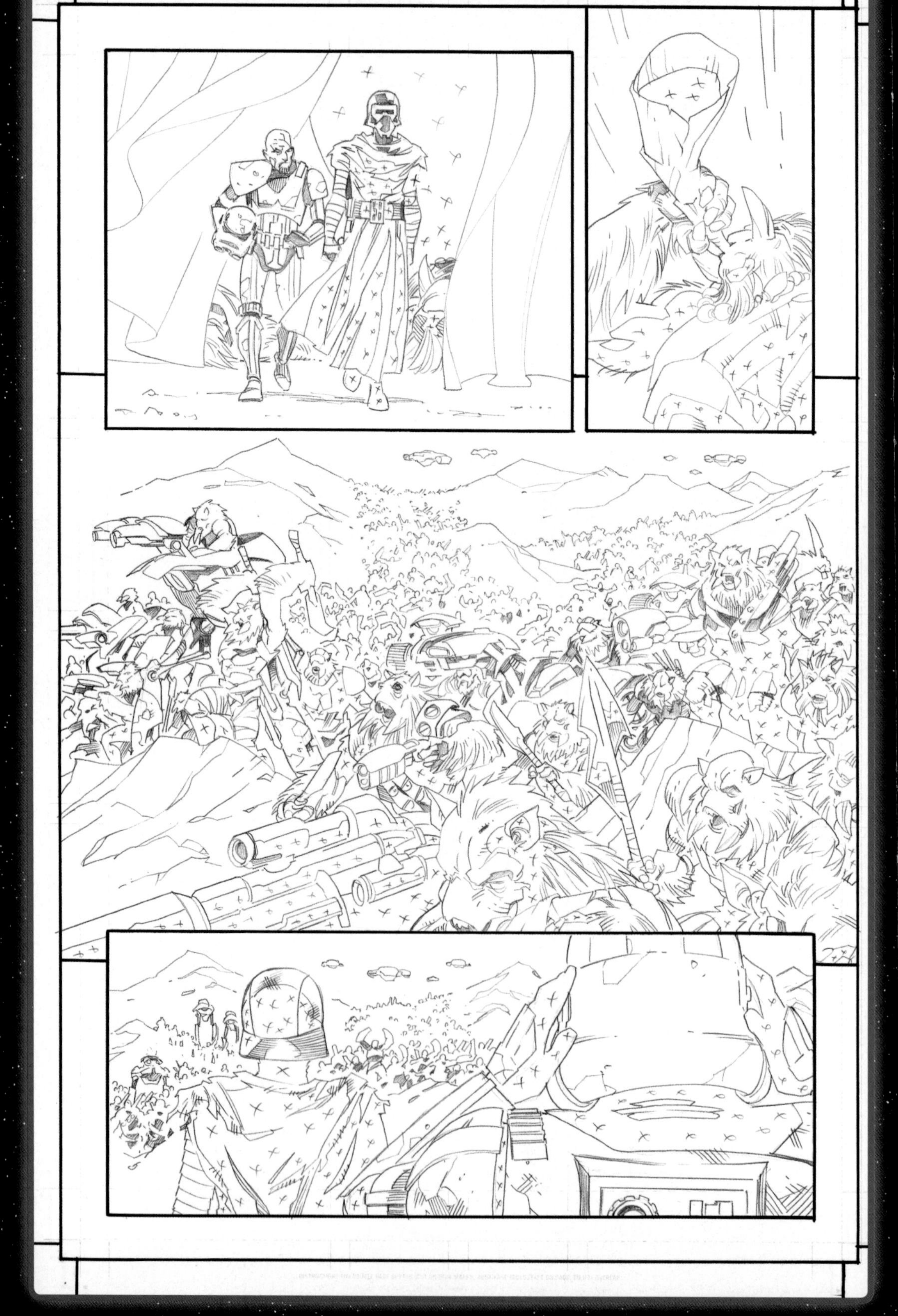

STAR WARS: AGE OF RESISTANCE KYLO REN 014 L. KIRK

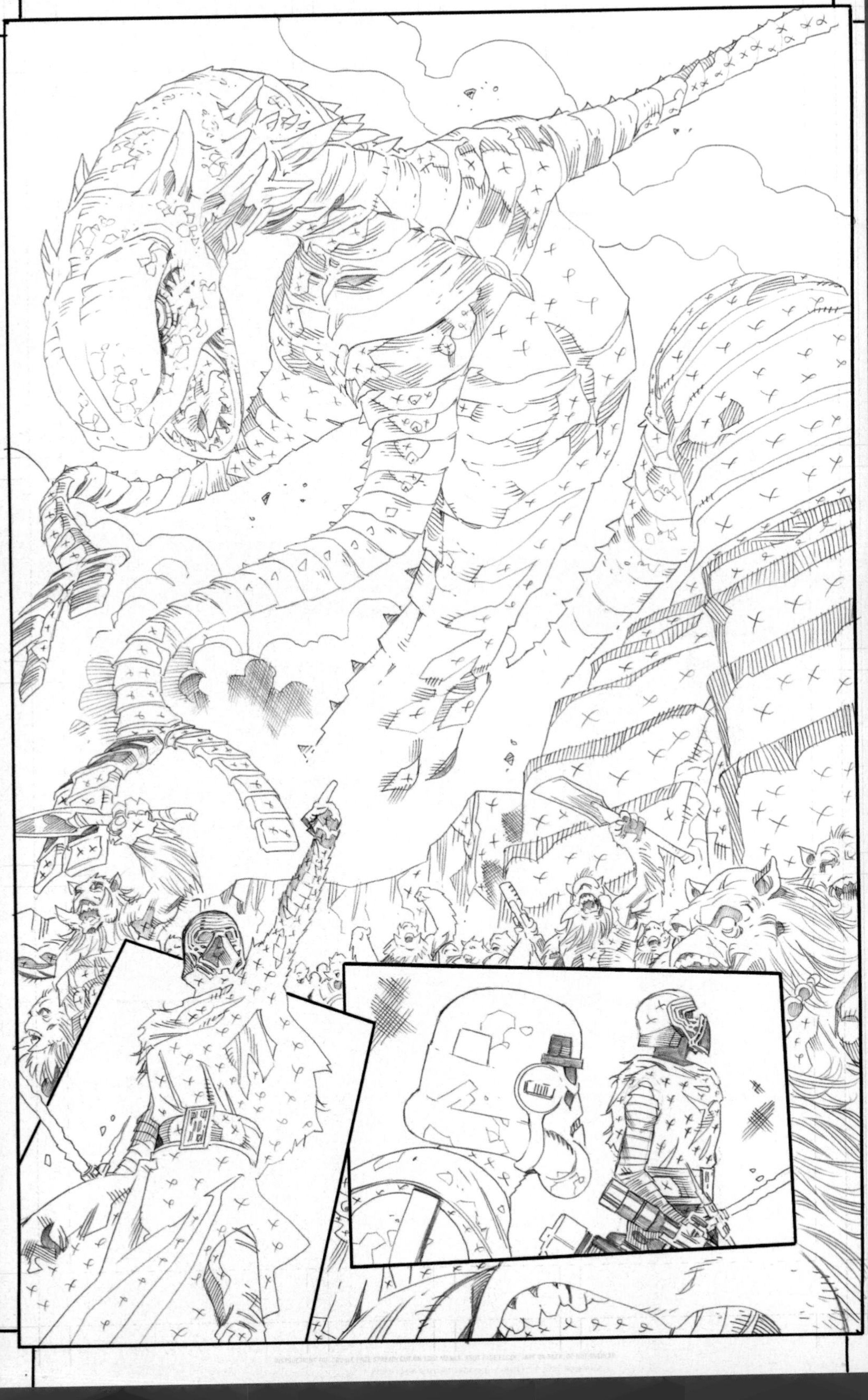

STAR WARS™

THERE ARE HEROES — AND VILLAINS — ON BOTH SIDES

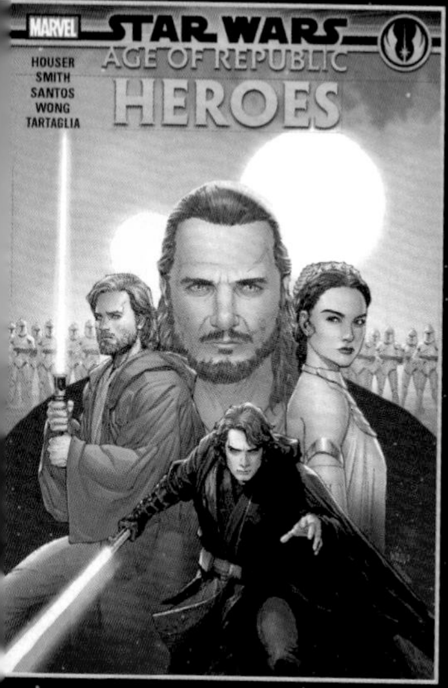
MARVEL
STAR WARS
AGE OF REPUBLIC
HEROES
HOUSER
SMITH
SANTOS
WONG
TARTAGLIA

STAR WARS: AGE OF REPUBLIC – HEROES TPB
ISBN: 978-1302917104
ON SALE NOW!

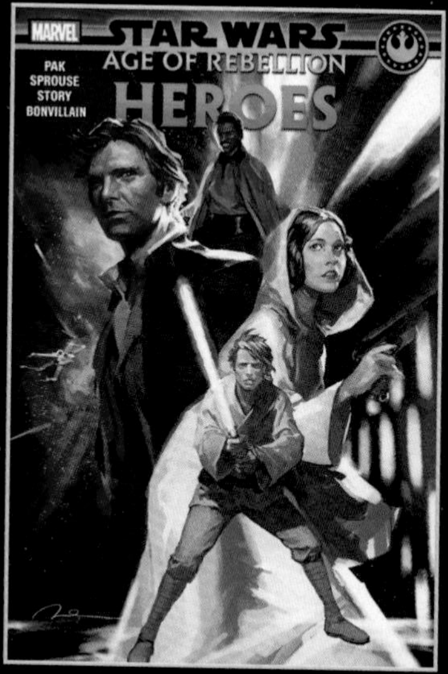
MARVEL
STAR WARS
AGE OF REBELLION
HEROES
PAK
SPROUSE
STORY
BONVILLAIN

STAR WARS: AGE OF REBELLION – HEROES TPB
ISBN: 978-1302917081
ON SALE NOW!

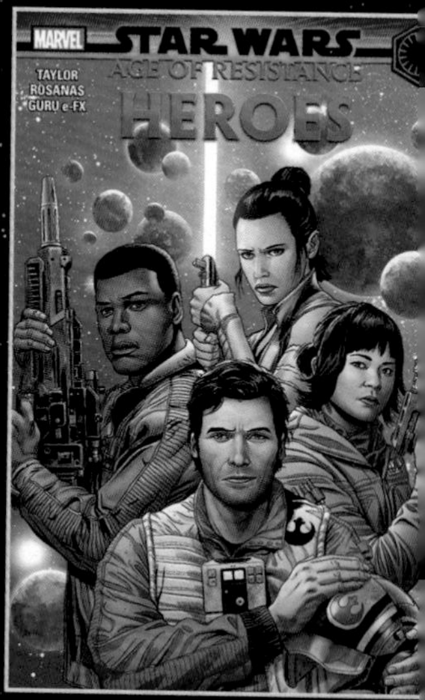
MARVEL
STAR WARS
AGE OF RESISTANCE
HEROES
TAYLOR
ROSANAS
GURU e-FX

STAR WARS: AGE OF RESISTANCE – HEROES TP
ISBN: 978-1302917128
NOVEMBER 2019

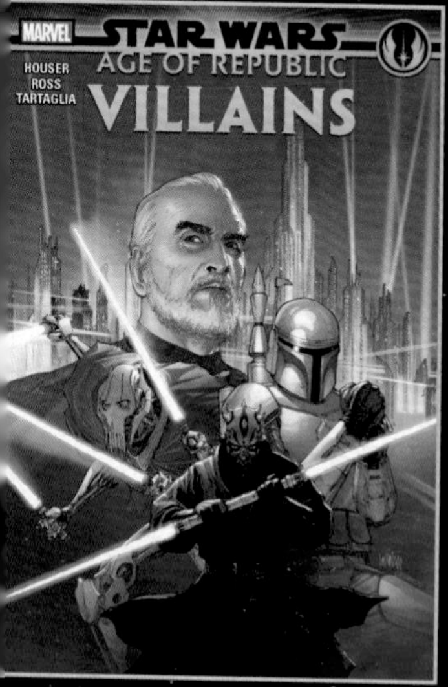
MARVEL
STAR WARS
AGE OF REPUBLIC
VILLAINS
HOUSER
ROSS
TARTAGLIA

STAR WARS: AGE OF REPUBLIC – VILLAINS TPB
ISBN: 978-1302917296
ON SALE NOW!

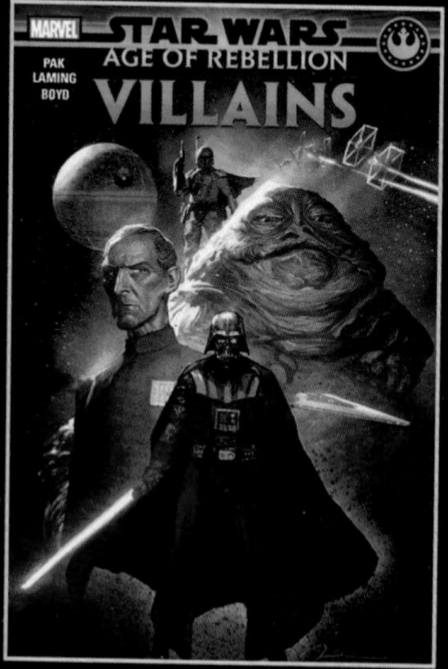
MARVEL
STAR WARS
AGE OF REBELLION
VILLAINS
PAK
LAMING
BOYD

STAR WARS: AGE OF REBELLION – VILLAINS TPB
ISBN: 978-1302917296
ON SALE NOW!

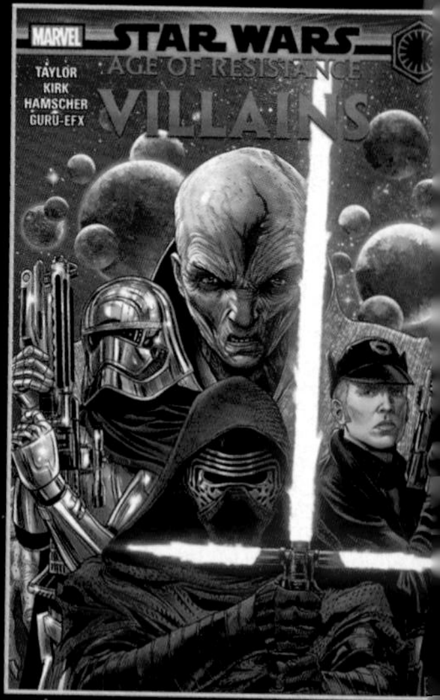
MARVEL
STAR WARS
AGE OF RESISTANCE
VILLAINS
TAYLOR
KIRK
HAMSCHER
GURU-EFX

STAR WARS: AGE OF RESISTANCE – VILLAINS TP
ISBN: 978-1302917302
NOVEMBER 2019

IN PRINT AND DIGITAL WHEREVER BOOKS ARE SOLD.
TO FIND A COMIC SHOP NEAR YOU, VISIT COMICSHOPLOCATOR.COM